D0202945

THE CARE AND FEEDING OF THE OFFSHORE CREW

By the same authors

CRUISING IN *SERAFFYN*

SERAFFYN'S EUROPEAN ADVENTURE

THE CARE AND FEEDING OF THE OFFSHORE CREW

Lin Pardey with Larry Pardey
Illustrated by Tadami Takahashi

W. W. NORTON & COMPANY
New York London

Printed in the United States of America.

W. W. Norton & Company, Inc., 500 Fifth Avenue, New York, N. Y. 10110
W. W. Norton & Company Ltd., 10 Coptic Street, London WC1A 1PU

Library of Congress Cataloging in Publication Data

Pardey, Lin.
The care and feeding of the offshore crew.

1. Cookery, Marine. 2. Sailboat living.
I. Pardey, Larry. II. Title.
TX840.M7P35 1980 641.5'573 79-29661
ISBN 0-393-03249-3

5 6 7 8 9 0

To
Annabelle Yates
who makes spoiling her crew an art

Contents

Acknowledgments

MUCH OF THIS BOOK was written while we were at sea during our North Pacific crossing. Each evening after Larry climbed into the bunk, I'd write down what we'd eaten, what the weather had been like, and some of my thoughts on being cook. Then I'd try to outline and write a chapter on one of the subjects that required more than a few paragraphs of explanation. The next morning, after Larry's first sight, I'd read what I'd written to him, and he'd add his comments and suggestions. Larry made the list of liquors and suggested several new chapters. When we arrived in Victoria, we had filled three notebooks of 100 pages each.

Three months later we left *Seraffyn* in Vancouver and flew down to spend the winter in Southern California at the home of Gingerlee Field, who loaned us her delightful garage studio apartment and made us feel like part of her family. As I began typing up the handwritten pages, I was vastly encouraged by Gingerlee and Larry to expand the information wherever I could. So several new chapters were added. Every person I asked for help readily came through. Tom Berry of Vic Berry's sheet-metal shop spent time with me both on the phone and in person describing tanks and water systems. The Orange County Health Department sent me information and ideas; racing sailors and cruising sailors answered each questionnaire I sent out. Several wrote back giving me names of other people they thought I'd like to contact. Dr. Charles Morrison checked over the chapter on vitamins and added his suggestions. Two special friends, Mary Baldwin, who has spent a year cruising the South Pacific, and Celia Vanderpool, who is off next month on a cruise to the Marquesas, read this manuscript and gave me encouragement plus some excellent suggestions and information. Fred Brodie, bound south from Vancouver in his Westsail 32, read this and gave a man's opinions. I'd like to give my special thanks to all of them and to those people whose names appear in the sections on shopping overseas and cooking on raceboats.

I'd like to add a small word of thanks to Marion Zatkin, my mother, who taught me from the first that cooking is an adventure and that nothing receives more immediate response than a good meal when all hell breaks loose.

Parts of this manuscript have appeared in *SAIL* magazine, *Pacific Yachting, Cruising World, Boating, Yachting Monthly, Yachting, Practical Boatowner* and *SeaCraft.* Their editors and staffs have all been willing and available to add their ideas when I needed them.

Cathy Everrett was the young, dynamic cook on board the seventy-one-foot English charter ketch *Happy Captain V.* She started it all by saying, "Why don't you write a book about cooking at sea?" We wrote two other books first, but this one was definitely inspired by her.

Though Larry didn't actually write down much of what appears in this book, more than 50 percent of the ideas were his, along with all the technical sketches. He also knew just when I needed that bit of encouragement after a bad day with the typewriter or a case of spring fever.

It's almost May now. Next week we rejoin *Seraffyn* for a summer of cruising in the beautiful Pacific Northwest. This book project filled the hours of a voyage that would otherwise have been tedious. I'd like to thank you readers who have responded to our other books and encouraged us to keep on writing.

THE CARE AND FEEDING OF THE OFFSHORE CREW

Introduction

THE THREE OF US were lounging comfortably on the wind-cooled veranda of the Manila Yacht Club, drinking iced calamancy and rum. One hundred yards away our cruising homes bobbed at their moorings. Lois Farrington had just completed her first ocean passage, five days from Hong Kong on board *Chai Hai,* the forty-foot cutter owned by an old cruising friend of ours, Ron Amy. Together they were bound for Hawaii. Larry and I had arrived on board *Seraffyn* four days before from Brunei, and we were stocking up for our voyage first to Japan, then to Victoria, British Columbia. Linda Balser, who'd cruised the South Pacific for three years on her own thirty-footer, had just arrived from Hawaii on board forty-nine-foot Styx, with its owner Don Johnson. They were bound for Hong Kong.

All three men were off on various errands, and for half an hour Lois had been asking questions: "How long can I keep cabbages? Should I buy vitamin pills? How do I know if I've got enough food? What meal plans do you use? What happens if you get seasick?"

Linda and I tried to remember every vegetable-preserving idea we could. We answered each question Lois asked while she wrote hint after hint down in a notebook. By the time Ron arrived and took Lois off to catch the club launch, we could see we'd made her head spin. "She doesn't believe it's really nothing to worry about," Linda said.

And at first I agreed. But as our conversation continued, we both changed our minds. "I remember running out of flour on one passage," Linda commented. "Then there was the time all of my cans went puffy on the same day," I countered. As we thought back over sixteen years of combined cruising experience, we realized that both of us had learned from trial and error. We'd made mistakes. We'd worried. We'd read what books we could find, but not one told us what it's really like to be cook on a long-distance voyage.

Lots of books dealt with the problems of cooking in a small galley. Several told good ways of using native foods, of seafood catching, preparing, and cooking. A dozen books told how to pour two, three, or five cans together and spice them up. Some books gave recommended stores lists for the cruising sailor on his first voyage away from home. But all these books had some basic ommissions as far as people like Lois were concerned. All assumed the voyage was from home to somewhere else. The stores recommended were easy to find in the United States or England, not so easy in Manila, Sri Lanka, Papeete, or the Azores. Each of these books devoted themselves to recipes and tips for galleys, but not one told what it's really like when there's motion, fatigue, and sometimes seasickness to contend with. Not one book gave an actual account of what people ate and how they prepared food while under way, where the weather, sea conditions, and the cooks' mood often decide each day's menu.

As we sailed north from Manila toward Japan, Larry and I talked about this gap. Somehow the idea came up, "Why not write a log of all your thoughts and activities as we cross the Pacific from Yokohama to Victoria? That will be a good long voyage. You'll be buying stores in a strange land, the weather conditions are bound to be changeable. You'll have at least forty to forty-five days to think about it all."

And so the idea for this book was born. Keeping a log would serve a twofold purpose. I'd be able to share the experience we'd gained in eleven years of voyaging, deliver-

Food on a cruising boat can be as exciting as you like in port or during short cruises, because ingredients that you had to search for at home are readily available in the new ports you'll visit. Here we dine on mussels steamed in garlic, onions, and tomatoes; prawns with cocktail sauce, and local Spanish wine.

ing yachts, racing, and chatting with other voyagers, and I'd have something to occupy my thoughts during what finally turned out to be a 4,500-mile, forty-nine-day-long passage.

Cordon Bleu cookery is just as possible in a boat as it is in a home, if your boat is on a peaceful short passage or moored in a calm anchorage. In fact, as you voyage worldwide it is possible to cook even better than at home because those exotic ingredients you search for in the United States or England will be at your fingertips as you visit new ports in the Orient or South America. So if you enjoy cookbooks, bring along *The Joy of Cooking* or James Beard's manuals. Bring a good book on seafood, and try to find a guide to exotic vegetable cooking. But if you are bound for a world cruise, taking a year off to explore the Pacific, planning a race to Honolulu, or delivering a boat to the Mediterranean, this book has as much information as we can give you on what it's like to buy stores for a voyage to or from a foreign land, to cook in a seaway, to have one's moods affected by wind strength, to take care of health problems at sea, and what the cook does besides cooking. Each day's menu for our forty-nine-day passage is included. This is not a cookbook, but recipes for any dishes that are not obvious are explained.

With the help of various cruising friends we've made a list of what stores are available in different countries and their relative cost. There's information on wines and duty-free stores. We've interviewed both the crews and cooks on various ocean racing yachts ranging in size from *Windward Passage,* a seventy-two-footer with up to sixteen crew on board, down to *Aquarius,* which carries an average of six as crew. Their hints are included, too.

The food we eat on board *Seraffyn* may be quite different from what you'd choose. Our stores buying is governed by a cruising budget of $350 to $400 a month (1978). We enjoy wine with most dinners, in harbor or at sea. We're also willing to spend more money for our meals during ocean passages than we might on food ashore, because good eating is our main form of entertainment when we are 1,000 miles from the nearest land. When we are feeding a delivery crew, we spend more money on snack foods than we do for a passage with the two of us alone. Keeping a racing crew happy, requires carrying more food than we might for cruising or deliveries and spending more money, because easy-to-eat, quick-to-prepare meals are a must between sail changes.

I won't say the stores and food we used on this voyage are typical or standard. Every voyage we've been on has started from a new port; there have been completely different foods and stores available to choose from and a different schedule for buying stores. In Malta I had the whole winter to find new ideas; in Japan we had only three weeks to get to know the local foods. Sometimes the different galleys in boats we were delivering affected stores buying and preserving. Different climates affected the way stores were preserved and protected. For these reasons each voyage on a small yacht is an adventure to me. Each offshore cook has to learn to feed and care for his or her crew through trial and error. But I'll ultimately agree with Linda: after two or three voyages the cook has nothing to worry about.

It has been brought to our attention by one of our kind editors that we seem to use excessively large amounts of garlic in some of our recipes. The garlic we use is a delightful, very mild Oriental spring variety. I would recommend using half or third of the amount of the more common Italian-style cloves to achieve the same flavor. When garlic is measured in teaspoons, we are referring to garlic powder.

The Day Before

Tied at Yokohama Shimin Yacht haven

sunny, warm weather

EXCEPT FOR THE UNUSUALLY DELIGHTFUL farewell party that ended it all, today was a normal last day in port. I started out worrying. Had I forgotten to order something? Would the chandlers remember to bring things today? Would they bring the right things? Had I bought enough canned goods in Singapore and Manila, or should I try to find more?

Larry stayed at the yacht club to finish putting water on board, receive stores, and generally get *Seraffyn* ready for sea. I took the bus into Yokohama city to get our port-clearance papers and pick up some more yen. Unfortunately for us, during our four-week stay in Japan the American dollar had dropped drastically, so instead of needing to change $280 to pay for the stores we'd ordered, we had to change $350. This was an unusual situation; rarely did the value of the dollar fluctuate more than 3 or 4 percent during our stay in any country. But we've found it's wise to set aside extra money for stores whenever we are preparing for an offshore voyage. Something always seems to foul up the budget.

By the time I got back to *Seraffyn,* the first of our stores had arrived from the chandler who carried duty-free wine and liquor. Usually duty-free stores have to be delivered in the presence of a customs officer. They are then put on board into a sealed locker, which the customs officer plasters with paper seals you aren't supposed to break until you are at sea. But the Japanese officials waived the sealed-locker requirement because of our small order (only two cases of wine, one of rum, and one of Coca-Cola). So the dock in front of *Seraffyn* was loaded with those four crates plus two more of vegetables.

Before we could eat a quick lunch, the second chandler arrived with twelve steaming kilos of dry ice, twenty kilos of regular ice, two kilos of frozen shrimp, five kilos of cheddar cheese, and three cases of special canned goods (mostly peanut butter and jam). Because there is at least a 100 percent duty on all food imports in Japan, we saved a tremendous amount by buying what we could through the chandlers. A pound of Australian cheese in the local stores was six dollars; we paid two dollars. Shrimps ran nine to twelve dollars; we paid $1.80. The only problem with buying through chandlers is that they are set up to deal with big ships, so most items are in tins or sizes too large for us to handle. If we could have used a twenty-five-pound piece of beef (the minimum order), we could have bought Australian first-grade sirloin steak for

$1.50 a pound duty-free. In the local stores any beef started at seventeen dollars.

I left Larry to finish his preparations and walked one mile to the local public market. Three days before I'd inspected each stall until I found that number 196 carried most of the vegetables I needed. No one there spoke English, but as soon as they saw I was trying to ask something important, one of the men ran off and returned minutes later with a tall, carefully dressed young man in tow. After apologizing for his poor English, he explained that he had a photographic shop deeper in the market and that he'd like to know what my problem was.

"My husband and I are setting sail for Canada on board a small sailing boat this Saturday, and we need lots of produce specially chosen so that it will last at least a month." His astonishment was matched by that of all four people in the vegetable stall. I was glad I'd carried some wallet photographs of *Seraffyn,* Larry, and the two of us out sailing. "Ah so, ah so" murmured each of my new acquaintances, bowing and looking at each other. The "ah so's" traveled from stall to stall along with the photos, and fifteen minutes and as many questions later, our translator started making a meticulous list of what I needed, first in English and then in Japanese symbols. When I left, polite bows followed me all the way through the market.

Now when I walked into the covered market area, the news spread before me, and the photographer *cum* translator walked out to meet me. "All you ordered has arrived, a man is waiting to deliver it."

I was delighted with the beautiful produce stall 196 had found. But as usual Japanese prices shocked me, and I was caught short of yen. The two of us went through my order, but there was nothing I was willing to delete. I had U.S. cash with me, but no bank except the central ones eight miles away would change foreign currency. "No problem," the photographer said, "I'll drive you to the bank." As we rode to the bank and back, the photographer fired question after question. Everywhere we've cruised we've had the same results. With patience, lots of smiles, and some photos in our wallet, we've always found someone with enough knowledge of English or Spanish who's willing to help out. I've tried reciprocating by offering a cup of coffee, lunch, or a glass of wine. But a gift photograph of the boat always seems to be the best thank-you of all.

Our produce was loaded onto a specially designed Japanese motorcycle:

100 farm-fresh eggs
25 tomatoes
2 large heads of lettuce
25 carrots
30 small green peppers
15 pieces of ginger
2 large pumpkin squash
30 garlics
10 cucumbers
6 giant apples
3 bunches of bananas
3 cantaloupe-type melons

The chandler had already brought us:

9 kilos of hard cabbage
9 kilos of onions
5 kilos of potatoes

I used up the last of our yen buying fresh meat. The extremely high price of non-duty-free meat in Japan affected what we took for that one passage. I only bought:

½ pound beef steak
¼ pound sliced ham
1½ pounds ground beef
½ pound chipped pork
¾ pound boned chicken breasts

This came to thirty dollars. Normally I'd have bought three times as much fresh meat to put in the ice chest.

This time when I got back to *Seraffyn,* utter chaos reigned. The dock in front of *Seraffyn* was full of crates and boxes; Larry was upside down in the cockpit locker rearranging boat gear so he could store away a few more spare water jugs; the inside of the cabin was littered with fruit and vegetables. One look at the clock gave me the jitters—our Japanese friends would be down in an hour and a half for last farewells.

As usual Larry's calm logic saved my day. "Forget about storing anything away today. We'll set it on the side deck, cover it with a canvas for tonight, then set it all on the cabin sole tomorrow before we sail. We can store it once we're under way. Right now let's have a drink, then one last hot shower." Larry helped me spruce up *Seraffyn* for our guests; we showered and shared a drink, then our guests began to arrive.

Eleven Japanese sailors, including both the female and male Lazer dinghy champions, showed up accompanied by two translators. Each new friend presented us with a beautiful souvenir of our three-week stay in Yokohama. We set up a display of the lovely gifts in our quarter berth: a hand-painted porcelain ceremonial tea set, a pair of happy coats, bottles of Suntory Whiskey, sake, a lacquered musical jewelry box, a hand-painted umbrella, and half a dozen beautiful ears of fresh corn.

I was glad I'd prepared a really American dish to serve

because our friends had brought their guitars, a violin, and a banjo. Our open-house cocktail party turned into an evening of song and laughter. Bluegrass music rang across the Yokohama Shimin Yacht Haven until ten minutes before midnight. We danced on the dock, sang, laughed, and promised we'd return some day. By the time the final farewell bows had been exchanged, our friends had to run to catch the last train to Tokyo and central Yokohama.

We climbed into our bunk still humming, completely undaunted by the pile of stores waiting to be put away when we set off to sea.

SLOPPY JOES FOR A FAREWELL PARTY

Sauté 1 large chopped onion, 1 pound of ground beef in 2 tbs. of cooking oil until browned.

Add 1 can peeled whole tomatoes
1 can tomato paste
1 can tomato sauce
¼ cup of sugar
1 tsp. oregano
2 tsp. chili powder
1 tsp. garlic powder
1 green pepper cut into small chunks

Simmer forty minutes, stirring occasionally, until the sauce thickens. Then pour a big portion of the sauce into a hamburger bun, top with a slice of cheese, and serve with lots of napkins.

Day 1

heavy rain, clear toward evening, eight-knot breeze, fog

Breakfast for us and farewell wishers—banana nut cake
coffee and tea

Lunch for us and two guests—egg salad sandwiches
fresh whole tomatoes
tossed salad with mayonnaise and lemon dressing
gift cake

Snack—hot buttered rum and apple slices

Dinner at anchor—fried beef steak with wine sauce
fresh corn on the cob
broiled tomatoes (grilled)

camembert cheese (Dufo brand
Danish canned camembert—best
we've ever tasted)
biscuits
red Bulgarian wine

STORING FRESH FOOD

When the rain started hitting our faces about 0400, we woke up and Larry closed the forehatch over our double bunk. I was almost asleep again when I remembered the pile of stores sitting on deck. Both of us scrambled out of the bunk, tossed the crates, boxes, and baskets on the cabin sole, onto the quarter berth, and on top of the stove, then climbed back into the bunk.

The 0730 alarm came much too early. In the gray, damp daylight the mess in the main cabin looked formidable. I cleared a path, set coffee to perk, and got out the baskets we use for storing fruit and vegetables. Since we almost never use the double bunk forward to sleep on when we are at sea, it becomes the extra storage area we need for long passages. We cover the cushion with old charts, then line the bunk with the baskets. Although handwoven natural baskets are more handsome and allow a better flow of air around your produce, we've found they create a storage problem between passages. Cardboard boxes harbor insects and their eggs and don't allow enough air circulation; wooden crates scratch the boat, hanging hammock nets require too much room since they must be free to swing without hitting anything. So for long-distance voyages when we need food to last more than a week, we've finally settled for stacking plastic baskets rather like the hand-carried shopping baskets some small markets use. These are lightweight, easy to wash, cheap to buy (in Singapore we paid one dollar each), and since they

We found that plastic baskets keep vegetables and fruit best for long voyages and can be easily stored away when we aren't using them.

stack, we can stash them in a stern locker between voyages.

Potatoes and onions went together into one large basket. Cabbages and carrots filled two others. Softer fruits went into individual baskets—melons in the chain locker with rags under them to keep them from moving. We've found the chain locker is a good place for watermelons, too. The ventilator scoop keeps them well aired. Soon the forepeak and bunk looked almost like stall 196. I put up the lee cloth and wedged some books between the mast and baskets so they couldn't shift. Our guitar and gifts from the night before filled the rest of the bunk.

Before we could drink our coffee and tea, the commodore of the New Yokohama Yacht Club came to present us with a crate of fresh tomatoes as a parting gift. There were twenty three-quarter-pound tomatoes in the cardboard crate, each the same shape and the same glossy red. The tomatoes looked too ripe to last, and I already had a basketful. But because of the extremely careful handling given Japanese produce, with careful storage and the cool weather we found, they lasted twenty-three days.

As we were bowing our thanks to the commodore, Jim Parker arrived with a banana nut cake his Japanese wife, Sanae, had sent. Jim is an English language instructor who has lived in Japan fourteen years and loves sailing. We'd met on the dock at the club, and he and his wife had spent most of their spare time introducing us to Japan. We'd invited them to join us for the sail to the mouth of Tokyo Bay. Sanae was working, but in spite of the rain, Jim was eager to go.

By 0900 the dock was full of umbrella-covered Japanese friends. Jim was busy helping pile cases of duty-free liquor and cola between the forward bunk and linen locker. A box of unstored cans nestled next to the stove. To get into the forepeak was next to impossible. "We'll put it all away when we get out to sea," Larry reminded me. "Right now forget about it and enjoy saying good-bye. These people want to get out of the rain." So we finished lashing the six five-gallon spare water jugs in place, topped up our gravity-feed deck tank, and unbagged our sails. Just about this time the only other American we'd come to know during our three-week stay in Yokohama arrived. Don Harrington, professor of English, dreamed of cruising off some day. When we said, "Join us for the reach down the bay," he hesitated only momentarily, jumped on board, and helped Larry set our sweep in place to row 200 yards away from the dock to where a breeze was blowing. Eager hands helped us cast off. "Sayonora" rang across the water. Our two guests helped set the main and jib. *Seraffyn* heeled lightly and slowly gained speed as if she were half-reluctant, half-eager to challenge the Pacific. *Rinky Dink* trailed docily behind.

I shed my wet gear and climbed below to hide from the wet and to try to make some order out of the chaos. By the time I was ready to make lunch, most of the canned goods were in their proper lockers. That's when I discovered I needed a fresh jar of mayonnaise. Of course, the spare mayonnaise is stored under the forward bunk, which was now covered with all the fresh stores. I could have dreamed up something else to serve for lunch. But my stubborn streak made me climb over all the boxes and stores, move the guitar, six boxes of gifts, and the cushion to get one of the six jars from its locker.

The three men seemed to love the rain and wolfed lunch down as we approached the narrow mouth of Tokyo Bay. We planned to row Jim and Don ashore near the entrance to the bay. But the closer we came to the congested area at the narrows, the foggier the air became. After talking it over, we decided against sailing into the heavy shipping lanes until the fog cleared. So we reached into a small fishing port eleven miles from where we'd started, set our anchor, and warmed our damp crew with hot buttered rums.

After we'd rowed Jim and Don ashore, we spent the afternoon putting away our duty-free stores. We used the area under the floors for the two cases of wine and case of cola. This area sometimes gets wet, but that doesn't bother bottles. Moreover, wine and cola stay cooler in the bilges, and the weight is centered and low, where it should be, and the chance of breakage nil. We have no engine, thus no oil, so every bit of the bilge can be used for clean storage.

This is not the first time we'd set sail on a voyage only to anchor in a harbor just down the line, then really sort ourselves out. Between farewell parties, last-minute showers, and the dozen distractions of sailing day, it's usually impossible to get everything stowed away properly. I'd recommend that everyone setting out on a first voyage have their farewell parties, sail away from their home dock, and find a quiet anchorage for the night, even if it is only the other side of the bay. Then you can really set the boat to rights, have a quiet evening, get a good night's sleep, and set off on your voyage in a refreshed frame of mind.

We did. By the time we went to bed together in our double bunk for the last time in forty-nine days, every bottle, can, and jar, every gift, and each vegetable had its place. The rain had stopped, and we'd taken one last row around *Seraffyn* to see if she was sitting level in the water. We had hoisted the dinghy on board, lashed it down, rigged the spare water jugs more securely, put up our off shore, shoulder-height lifelines, and turned in for the night.

Day two That final pause before setting sail keeps the cook from feeling buried under an avalanche of stores.

Day 2

beating-in light winds through heavy shipping
sunny and clear

Breakfast—whole fresh tomatoes with salt
bread and jam
coffee and tea
Lunch—mackerel salad sandwiches with sliced sweet pickles and tomatoes

MACKEREL SALAD

Drain 1 small can mackerel in brine
Chop 1 small green pepper
1 small onion
Mix together with
3 tbs. mayonnaise

½ tbs. sugar
1 tsp. lemon juice

Let stand for one hour in a cool place before spreading.

Dinner—broiled pork chops
steamed carrots
tossed salad—lettuce, tomatoes, onions with Thousand Island dressing

THOUSAND ISLAND DRESSING

2 parts mayonnaise
1 part catsup
1 tsp. lemon juice
pinch of MSG and garlic

I MUST SAY IT IS NICE to start out fresh. We both feel relaxed and ready to go. Now that all the stores are organized, I can see we've got enough. But I do know that *Seraffyn* is too small to carry the stores I'd like if three people were making this passage instead of only two.

We figure on making good an average speed of 100 nautical miles a day for ocean passages. We've got 4,500 miles to go. For safety I plan on having stores to last the number of days we should be at sea plus 50 percent extra to cover the possibility of a slow passage. Then we carry survival rations for twenty days more. The survival rations consist of rice, grain, pasta or cereals (three-fourths a cup of dried per person per day), plus one can of fruit or fruit juice per day and vitamin pills.

This is the longest single passage we've ever planned on board *Seraffyn.* In addition to all of our worldly possessions, she is carrying canned and packaged stores for sixty to seventy days, the survival rations, plus:

70 gallons of water
100 eggs
120 pounds of fresh vegetables
60 pounds of ice
2 cases of wine
2 cases of rum
1 case of whiskey
1 case of Coca-Cola
2 shopping bags full of paperback books
gifts for our families
gifts from our Japanese friends

That totals almost 1,100 pounds more than we normally carry, and, to prove it, *Seraffyn* is two inches below her load waterline.

CARGO CAPACITY FOR CRUISING

When we were rowing around *Seraffyn* for our one last look yesterday, we got into quite a discussion of light-displacement versus heavy-displacement boats for cruising. Larry commented, "Almost every one we know averages 100 to 120 miles a day year in year out if they have a boat from twenty-four to forty-five feet on deck. So they have to carry just as many stores as we do when they are making an ocean passage, and if their boat is bigger they'll have heavier boat gear to carry besides. If you load 1,100 pounds of extra stores into a twenty-four-footer that is designed to sail her best at 5,000 pounds of displacement, she's going to be affected a lot more than if you loaded the same 1,100 pounds on a twenty-four-footer that is designed to sail well at 11,000 pounds displacement."

If you are looking at offshore cruising boats, consider the ones that float three or four inches high when they are launched. Then look at their displacement in proportion to the 1,000 pounds of stores minimum each person requires for passage making and cruising. It will be easy to fill any boat with enough cargo to get it down to its waterline marks. But it is almost impossible to put an overweight boat on a diet, and boats that are down on their lines just don't perform as well.

Someone asked Larry why he chose *Seraffyn* for cruising. Larry answered, "She is the only twenty-four-footer I know that can carry 3,000 pounds of cargo and still sail well." *Seraffyn* is twenty-four feet on deck and stripped weighs about 8,000 pounds. With all her cruising gear, our possessions, and basic local cruising stores on board, she is right on her waterline and displaces 10,800 pounds. So the extra pounds we've put on for this voyage will make her a bit slower in light winds.

PLANNING A STORES LIST

Buying sufficient stores for any voyage takes planning and can make the difference between pleasant living on board or just getting there. I refrain from saying "pleasant eating" because "stores" includes much more than just food. Toilet paper, flashlight batteries, bicarbonate of soda, Band-Aids, dish soap, all are stores, and on most voyages I've been on they've been the responsibility of the cook or whomever is assigned the job of buying food.

When it became clear that we were really going to set off on our first long voyage, I went to the library and got out all the cruising books I could and read their stores lists. Not one seemed fully suited to our plans. Either they had different tastes, more money to spend, or less; more galley space, or less.

So for the six months before we actually bought stores for

our first long voyage, I kept a list of every thing we bought for our house that wasn't main-course food. I kept track of the amount of salt, Worcestershire sauce, flour, and dish soap we used. I found items on my list such as toothbrushes, Scotch tape, toothpicks, black mending thread, erasers, and flashlight bulbs. This six-month survey revealed the shocking amount of peanut butter we consumed.

At the same time we started a custom we call "can Night." At least one night a week we ate a meal prepared from canned or packaged goods such as we would have left after a week or two at sea. This gave us a chance to see which canned goods we liked and which we didn't. It helped us avoid the problem of buying a case of canned stew that we hated but couldn't afford to throw away. "Can Night" also gave me a chance to come up with some good at-sea meals before we were actually at sea. We've continued this practice as we've cruised. Soon after we arrived in each new country, I buy some of the local canned or packaged products and try them out. If the goods aren't labeled in English, I open them for snacks or lunch so that I don't ruin a main meal if the contents aren't to our liking. I'd say our success rate on foreign canned goods is fifty-fifty.

It is well worth taking the time to look at prices, sizes, and contents of different packages in different stores. I've found that supermarkets often have lower prices than cash-and-carry firms, especially if they package their own brand-name products. Supermarkets also tend to carry more individual-serving-sized cans than cash and carry, chandlers, or wholesalers do. But try store brands before you stock up. Larry loves Safeway tomato soup but won't eat Sainsbury's.

Look at the ingredients and weights on different packages. On all American and English packages, ingredients are listed in the order of their volume. One beef stew might have its ingredients listed as beef, potatoes, carrots, starch. The other

It's worth taking the time to read the labels. The American label, above, lists this product as pork and beans, whereas Canadian labeling laws require a more carefully descriptive name. Both contain only one or two small hunks of pork.

The low cost jam, above, had very little actual fruit in it; the flavor and texture were a disappointment. The Empress brand jam was an excellent product but cost 30% more.

might list potatoes, beef, starch. The first can will have more meat in it. A whole canned chicken is usually no bargain. You are paying for bone, water, and skin. Three small tins of chicken meat cost about the same. They contain solid meat and take half the space and preparation time. Condensed soup gives you twice the soup for only 10 percent extra cost.

Some freeze-dried products provide excellent results, take up little space, and are light. But there is a catch: they take extra water, fuel, and time to prepare. Try any you think you'd like before you invest too heavily. Several times in our foreign cruising, people from other boats have offered to trade leftover freeze-dried products in five-pound cans. Their crews had simply grown tired of them.

Try some of the canned goods sold in the refrigeration section of the market. Most of them keep extremely well when stored low in the boat. Canned brie and camembert cheeses keep for two or three months if stored at about seventy degrees. Since the lockers below your waterline will stay at about water temperature, you can be sure that many of these items will last well except in the deep tropics or Red Sea where water temperatures exceed seventy-eight degrees. The same goes for sausages such as salami or pepperoni and hard cheeses packed in wax. They'll keep up to four weeks in a cool place.

Economy sizes have no place on a boat with a crew of fewer than five. A small container of dish soap is easier to handle and easier to store. If it breaks open, it makes a smaller mess. Noodles in meal-sized packages are the only way to go—unused noodles attract weevils and mold. Leftovers are difficult to keep on board at sea. A can just large enough for one meal means you can clear up the galley without trying to find a way to preserve half a can of corn. This is especially important in the tropics where food that isn't refrigerated rarely lasts two days.

Check the different types of packaging. Cans are heavy and take more space than flexible foil packages but do last longer. I buy coffee that comes in well-sealed foil bags, but if I plan to keep it longer than two months, I purchase canned coffee instead. Sugar, flour, and rice I buy in three- or five-pound bags, then I seal each one in two plastic bags, one inside the other. This way if one package of rice or sugar goes bad or breaks, I haven't lost my whole supply. (See bread-baking section for hints on buying and keeping flour.)

Avoid large, flexible plastic containers for things like cooking oil, syrup, or mayonnaise. If you can press with your finger and cause an indentation in the container, it might break under the conditions in a storage locker during a gale at sea. I speak from experience. I had to clean out a whole can locker, Larry's tool locker and the bilge when a plastic pint container of cooking oil split and spilled. Larry had an even worse job when a quart of boiled linseed oil in a plastic container developed a leak. Glass is much safer. To date I have never broken a glass container either while it was stored or when I was using it on board. And glass containers are easily reusable for canning, storage, or painting. If you get too many empties to keep during a long passage, they are easy to sink.

Once the initial product-and-price research is over, how do you do your actual list planning? Few long-distance cruising or racing cooks depend on a menu plan for voyages of more than a week. It just doesn't work. After the first time, few of these people make a detailed shopping list. Instead most seem to use a similar method to ours. I go to the shops I've found to be the best value and buy main-course items for the length of our voyage plus 50 percent. In other words, during this passage we figure an average speed of 100 miles a day for 45 days plus 22 for unforeseeable holdups. So I bought about sixty-five cans of dinner-meat products plus the same number of lunch items. I figure on four eggs equaling one can. I stock up more on corned beef than I do on ham because I know of more uses for corned beef. I buy at least twenty-four cans of stewing beef because it can be used several different ways.

Next I purchase fruits and vegetables (canned), rice, powdered potatoes, flour, noodles, peanut butter, jam, and non-food items for the same period. I take this all back to the boat and store it. This way I can see how much space I have left over. I then go back to the shops and buy luxury items to fill the empty spaces—tins of nuts, canned paté, brie, candy, dried fruits, what we call fun foods. These add variety to our menu as we cruise.

My final purchase is twelve complete, very easy-to-prepare meals which I store in the most accessible place possible. Meals such as hot dogs and baked beans, chicken in cream sauce, or beef and mushroom stew that can be simply opened and heated in one pan are for those times when it's too rough for anything else. When I am too seasick to cook, Larry knows exactly where to look for something to stave off his starvation. I then feel a bit better about being seasick because I've done my bit when I stopped for stores.

Fresh fruit, vegetables, and meat are the last things we buy. I waited until the last possible day to pick them out. Other than potatoes and onions, I consider these to be in excess of the amount of food planned for the voyage.

New potatoes last forever, so we buy thirty pounds for the two of us whenever our stocks get low, even if we're not bound on a voyage. With onions it's the same. Tomatoes purchased green ripen slowly and can be good three or four weeks later. Lemons wrapped in aluminum foil and stored in a sealed container are good for two months. Other fresh produce can be a gamble but is nice to have, so we always carry some. It's rarely wasted, but there have been times when we had apple fritters, applesauce, and apple fruit salad all in one day to use up apples before they turned. (See list of produce and how to keep it.)

When the boat is full to the brim and I can't think of anything I've forgotten, I take a stroll through one or two markets and drugstores looking at each item they sell. This often jolts my memory or else reassures me that we haven't forgotten anything. If the voyage is going to be a long one, I use this chance to buy a few surprise gifts for any birthdays on board or just jokes that might perk up an otherwise depressing day. I also spend the rest of the local currency that is lying around the bottom of my change purse.

If you are stocking up in a foreign country, making a stores list is more difficult. A good cookbook that describes vegetables and foods from all parts of the world and ways to use them is invaluable. But no book tells you what is inside foreign cans, so be extra careful about trying canned goods before buying by the case. I found this out the hard way in Antigua, British West Indies, when I bought six cans of cooking butter from Australia. It turned out to be colored bright orange. It tasted great, but the crew wouldn't spread it on their toast, and cookies made with it came out yellow. In 50 percent of the countries around the world, labels are in English, but where they aren't it pays to find some local person to shop along with you and describe the contents. Japan was a special problem. All labels were in Kanji (Japanese symbols), and the pictures on the labels didn't resemble anything I knew. An English-speaking Japanese friend tried to help as much as she could, but beyond the language barrier there was a culture barrier, she couldn't imagine why I was disappointed when a can of what was described as fruit cocktail contained one-quarter fruit, three-quarters unflavored-gelatine cubes. If all else fails in a foreign country, look for Chinatown. Almost all goods shipped from Red China have labels in English.

One thing will soon become obvious as you cruise abroad. You won't be able to afford to eat the same as you do at home. Your stores list for offshore passages will change if you are stocking up in an island economy, where all imports are expensive, or if you are in a primitive economy like Costa Rica, where canned peaches cost five times what a pound of beefsteak does.

And finally some advice that Larry often repeats—overbuy. Fill the boat to the brim. When you see stores you like, buy them. They might not be available in the next country you visit. Keep the boat full and refill it every chance you get. Full lockers in port mean freedom from that endless round of shop, cook, wash the dishes and clothes, shop, cook . . . that turns many wives away from cruising. When you are making passages, extra food on board means you are free to change your plans, extend your stay at a deserted island, and avoid civilization for just that extra bit of time that will make your cruise a joy.

Day three One of the most frustrating parts of any long-distance voyage involves having to shop where no one understands a word you say.

Day 3

95 miles noon to noon

Calm and sunny, moving about three knots on a beam reach. Wind freshened in the afternoon

Breakfast—canteloupe
canned Danish concentrate of orange juice
coffee and tea
Lunch—grilled cheese and tomato sandwiches, soft drinks
Dinner—breast of chicken sautéed in butter, then
simmered with fresh tomatoes, garlic, onions,
and sage
corn on the cob
red wine

LATE LAST NIGHT WE SAW the last of Japan's shore lights. Today we are really "at sea." We plotted our first *X* on the large-scale chart of the western North Pacific. We've got 2,400 miles to go until we reach the eastern North Pacific chart, which shows Victoria and the United States, including Hawaii. But with the weather like this, lockers overflowing with cans, a forepeak full of fresh food, and eighty paperback books to read, the distance is only a myth, a seventy-inch-wide white space on two big sheets of paper.

SHOPPING FOR STORES IN A FOREIGN COUNTRY

One of the most exciting, intriguing, unexpected, and frustrating events of your first cruise to a foreign country will happen after your anchor or mooring lines are fully secured, after you've cleared customs, and after you have enjoyed that long-anticipated hot shower. You'll row ashore looking for those fresh foods you have been hungering for. You'll locate the shopping district. And you'll find that almost all the people in the world shop for food completely differently than we North Americans do. They often use a different language. They all use metrics, counting weight in kilos, liquids in liters. They use unfamiliar currencies. And few places have corner supermarkets. Nowhere else will you be able to buy everything you need to last for the coming week in one hour-and-a-half stop. Ninety percent of the people in the world still shop daily in public marketplaces. They buy their food from small shops or stalls that specialize in meat, vegetables, dry goods, or fruit. To most of the people of the world, shopping is not a chore but an important part of daily social life. It is a time for gossip, ribald jokes, and news exchanging.

When you arrive fresh from an ocean passage, anxious to fill the gaps in your depleted stores lockers, the vastness and confusion of your first public market can be overwhelming. The shopkeepers may be shy or even frightened because you don't speak their language. They won't understand your confusion, since the marketplace is part of their way of life. Few foreign merchants will be prepared for the vast amounts of food you as a cruising person wish to buy. No shopkeeper will understand the impatience of the average North American who is used to checkout stands, bag carriers, and cash registers.

If you are on a leisurely cruise and regard shopping as one of the adventures you've come for, you might learn to prefer the marketplace way. But if you are on a delivery or making a pit stop for three days to buy provisions, then pushing on because the seasons are pressing, shopping in foreign ports can make provisioning for your sailing life a drag. Either way, there are lots of steps you can take to make provisioning more pleasant.

I've learned from repeated and sometimes expensive mistakes not to buy anything except food for dinner and the next morning's breakfast on the first day in port. Even if you've only got two days to buy your provisions, it pays to spend a day looking around first. By pricing food in several places, you'll get an idea of what is available and what prices are standard. I often remember when we were rushing through the Kiel Canal trying to leave the Baltic before a November snowstorm caught us. As soon as we docked in Cuxhaven we rushed into the first butcher's shop we saw, pointed at three lamb chops, and almost gasped when we realized we'd spent seven dollars for less than a pound of meat. We walked back toward the boat along a different route and saw other, slightly less elegant shops where nice-looking pork chops could have made us a meal for only three dollars a pound.

By spending this first afternoon window shopping around the streets of the town you'll get some idea of how to organize provisioning day, and you'll probably see some items to add to your list. You'll know what to bring with you when you are ready to shop and where the banks or money exchangers are.

If you are buying provisions for a long voyage from a foreign port, check out not only the public market and local

Day 3 The cheese vendor in a Mexican market

PHOTO BY LIN PARDEY

shops but also the wholesalers and ship chandlers. It will pay to talk to any other cruising sailor who has been in the port longer than you have. If there is a yacht club nearby, try to meet some of the members and their wives. Pleasant conversations around many yacht club lounges have turned into wonderful outings when local women realized how little I knew about the shopping facilities of their hometown. In Port Said, Egypt, Marja, the wife of the port health officer, took me along as she did her daily shopping. Without her guidance I'd have never found the only shop in the city that sold cheese; it was tucked away on a side street in the basement of an office building four blocks away from the shopping street. Not only did I learn where to shop but Marja told me what to bargain for. Her hints on her country and its customs couldn't have been culled from a book.

Other cruising people are a good guide, but most have one thing in common. Because they don't own cars and have not lived in an area for that long, their knowledge of the shopping places beyond walking distance is definitely limited. If you are buying food to last for the next four or five days, take your new cruising friends' advice. But when you are buying for a long passage, check every possibility for yourself. Doing so will save you money and get you food of the best quality, greatest longevity, and widest variety.

The public marketplace is almost always the best place to buy fresh fruit, vegetables, and eggs. Meat bought in the market is usually fresher than that found in small shops since it is brought in daily. Prices are usually lower because of the direct competition between stalls. But canned food in public markets often stays on the shelves longer, so cans may already be rusty when you buy them. We've been in public markets in at least thirty-five countries and have found they can range from delightful to depressing. The most primitive ones we've been in in Egypt, Sri Lanka, and Tunisia—had muddy floors, beggars, crowing chickens, and animals being slaughtered on the spot. But this is not the norm. Most governments are providing clean, well-ventilated buildings where the local farmers and vendors set up their stalls. But because of the lack of laws governing packaging and meat vending, it is normal for animals to be sold with their heads on so that the local people can tell what they are getting. Cows that have been freshly slaughtered have bright, shiny eyes, just like fish. Rabbit heads are left on so cats can't be mistaken for rabbits. All of this will seem strange and possibly repulsive to the cruising sailor, after the plastic packages of the American-style supermarket. But it pays to get used to the public market, because that is where you will do most of your outfitting for offshore passages once you go foreign.

Local small shops and minimarkets have one distinct advantage over the public market. Here you are most likely to find people who speak a little English. They also appear to be more organized, and their canned goods are usually fresher. Be sure to ask for anything you don't see on the shelves. These small shops often have a back room full of hidden treasures, and if the shopkeeper can't find what you want, he'll probably direct you to the shop that has it. If you buy more than fifty dollars worth of goods in most shops in southern Europe, Africa, or the Far East, you'll probably be entitled to a 10 percent discount. Such a quantity is considered a wholesale lot when you are shopping where the average income is less than sixty dollars a week.

Throughout the Pacific and Far East you'll find Indian and Chinese shops in competition with each other. Though the Chinese shops will often appear cleaner and more tasteful to the western eye, I've found that Indian shops tend to have lower prices. On the other hand, the Chinese shops usually carry a larger variety of packaged goods, so it pays to check out both.

If you don't see what you want, ask for it. The dry-goods shop in the public market at Mazatlan, Mexico.

Wholesalers can offer you savings of up to 35 percent on some brands of canned and packaged goods. I've never found one who wasn't willing to let us use his facilities as long as our order was for more than seventy-five dollars' worth of goods. It's best to find the wholesalers who supply the goods for the corner store as they will have the largest variety available. Supermarket chains in some large ports such as Singapore and Yokohama have wholesale outlets that supply big ships. Their prices tend to be lower than general wholesalers. Look for the office numbers of these suppliers in the telephone directory for the port, or ask the local shopkeepers.

Ship chandlers will supply yachtsmen who are going foreign. They are often the only good source of those imported (American, English) brands you miss so much even though you want to use local foods. The chandler is also the source of the cruising man's delight—duty-free liquor—and, for the smoker, duty-free cigarettes. Most chandlers are listed in the telephone directory or port directory. If not, ask the port captain, customs officer, or any ship agent. Before you start any large shopping expedition, ask several chandlers for their printed price list. If you don't see an item you need, ask the chandler to find a price for you. All chandlers have someone in their office who speaks English; all their lists are available in English. Check the different price lists and use them as a guide to your survey of the local markets and wholesaler. When it is time to order from the chandler, don't be shy about ordering from two or three different ones. One chandler in Yokohama listed only hard liquor, with Black and White whiskey costing $2.25 a fifth. He also had Skippy Peanut Butter at wholesale American prices. The other chandler had both wine and hard liquor plus a wonderful selection of canned and processed cheeses at rock-bottom prices. But his Black and White whiskey cost $2.85 a fifth, and he had no peanut butter at all.

But all is not roses with chandlers. They are only found in big ports that have extensive international shipping traffic. They can only put duty-free stores on board vessels that are bound overseas, and a customs officer has to come and seal these stores, so you can't get them put on board until the day you are leaving. The stores most chandlers carry are planned for large ships; usually only case lots or huge containers are available. Some chandlers will split cases if you ask, but they can't give you five pounds of instant mashed potatoes out of a twenty-five-pound can. And finally, the prices chandlers charge for canned goods may not be as low as those you'll find in the local shops or wholesalers.

Once you've done your looking around but before you're ready for the first major assault on the marketplace, consider several ways to make the experience more pleasant.

Before you go cruising, start learning about metric weights and measures. Many of today's cans and packages have their metric equivalent listed. If you start noticing the difference between metrics and pounds now, it will be one fewer problem to overcome. Since kilos equal 1,000 grams, you'll find it easier to figure prices using metrics. Meat that costs thirty cents for 100 grams costs $3.00 for one kilo, $1.20 for 400 grams. Try figuring that for something that costs thirty cents an ounce. Since I was brought up with pounds, I convert by thinking, "400 grams is nearly one pound, 100 grams a quarter of a pound." It's close enough.

Before you go shopping, figure out what the conversion rate is for the local currency. Make a small chart and choose one of the local coins or bills that has a similar value to a coin from your own country. Then use the coin as your standard for figuring prices. In England fifty pence was equal to ninety-three cents U.S., so I equated a fifty-pence piece to one dollar. Something that cost me five pounds would therefore be ten times one dollar.

Once you are familiar with the local currency, glance through your translation dictionary. If there are specific items you need, make a list in both languages. Print this list clearly and in big letters so that when all else fails—when you've tried pronouncing the words with your finest Spanish accent and still can't make your request understood—you can pull out the piece of paper and find someone who can read it. Don't be surprised in undeveloped countries if you need to stop five or six people before you can find someone who reads. Language is a problem, but you'll find that most of your shopping can be done by the point-and-picture method plus a bit of dictionary writeout. If you keep your sense of humor and are patient, this language barrier can add a lot of fun to your day. I remember my very first encounter with a big Mexican public market. It took five or ten minutes of strolling around before I was brave enough to approach an uncrowded produce stall. I pointed at the oranges, held up two fingers, and said, "Dos por favor."

The lady behind the stall laughed and said, "Na-ran-ha."

I obviously didn't understand her, so she picked up an orange, pointed at it, and repeated, "Na-ran-ha."

I realized she was telling me the word for oranges. I repeated, "Na-ran-ha."

She applauded, picked up a lettuce, and carefully said, "Lechuga." By the time my basket was full and several other Mexican people had gathered around to encourage and assist me. I left with a basket full of lovely produce, a head swimming with new Spanish words, and my fears of shopping in a public market where I didn't understand the language laid to rest.

You need special equipment to shop overseas, even if you aren't provisioning for a voyage. Few shops in foreign countries provide any kind of bags, so it is usually a good idea to buy stretchy woven nylon bags such as the kind sold in import shops at home or in marketplaces abroad. These bags are easy to carry in your purse. They expand to carry more than you'll be able to lift and are incredibly strong. On the boat they'll store in any corner; six don't fill half a shoebox. They can be washed with the laundry and dried just by shaking. We use them for a dozen things besides shopping.

Woven baskets may look prettier than nylon mesh bags, but they are bulky to store and unsafe to use because they can harbor insects or their eggs. In Sri Lanka a friend loaned us a rattan shopping bag to carry some eggs, tomatoes, and fruit back to the boat. Back on board *Seraffyn,* I grabbed for a tomato and a three-inch-wide tarantella ran out of the bag, over my arm, across the bunk, and down between the frames. Larry heard my screams and came running. He tore the cushions and bunk boards out, found that hairy monster, and killed it with a wooden mixing spoon. Tarantellas aren't the normal insects found in woven shopping baskets; usually cockroach eggs or ants make their homes between the rattan pieces. Washing destroys the shape and beauty of a natural basket, so any leaky packages, squashed fruit, or dirt will create a smell that is difficult to remedy.

We cruised quite happily for six years using only nylon shopping bags. Then we delivered a fifty-four-foot ketch from Spain to the United States with a wheeling, folding shopping cart on board. You've probably seen the type; we used to call them granny baskets. You can find them in most luggage stores or make your own from a collapsible luggage carrier. Get the biggest rubber wheels you can that swivel independently like castors. Try to have a removable bag that you can wash and a top that you can snap shut. These carts are great. They can take the load of shopping off your shoulder. The cart stands on its own four feet while you select your next vegetables. It's easy to lift on board, and if its wheels are good, even a lightweight like myself can pull a fifty-pound load down the street with ease. That's why Larry likes it so much. He says that since I have one for myself, I don't ask him to come along as a pack mule nearly so often. One warning though: watch out for the toes of passers-by.

Each time you are actually on your way to the market, toss a few plastic bags into your cart. You'll find that most public market vendors sell fish and meat wrapped in paper. Without a plastic bag, leakage could spoil anything under or near your fish. Bring some egg cartons, and, if you intend to buy ice, a canvas ice carrier. Many taxi drivers refuse to carry ice loose in their trunks because of the leakage. Though you can usually talk them into it, it is easier to arrive prepared. Besides, it makes transferring ice to the boat simpler.

The chief of police in a delightful small village in Mexico heard that we'd cashed $600 at the local bank. He took us aside and gave us some excellent advice: "Don't come ashore with more money in your purse than you can afford to lose. To our people you look very rich. If they see you opening a wallet with more money in it than they can earn in two weeks, they are only human, they could become tempted and even steal." His counsel is worth heeding. Carry small bills and lots of coins in a separate change purse so that you don't appear to have a lot of money when you are in a public market.

On shopping days most cruising people have found it pays to arrive at the public market early, dressed quite conservatively. *Dress does matter,* not only because you might be the only foreigner but because you'll get better service. Most of the housewives who are out shopping dress very conservatively. More than half of the Spanish women still cover themselves completely in black from stockings to shawl. I've seen merchants resent customers who are too casually dressed shopping at their stall. In Italian, Spanish, and Portuguese markets, tight trousers, shorts, and backless dresses are an invitation to some painful and embarrassing pinches.

If you are planning to buy more than one basketful of food, find a café located in or adjacent to the marketing area. Order a coffee or tea, then ask permission to use the café as a depot for your shopping. Don't be embarrassed; if you look around you'll find many of the local people do the same. Then go out and shop, bring back a load of provisions, and store it in an out-of-the-way corner of the café. If there are more than two of you, the café makes a good meeting-place where you can compare notes, rest over a cool drink, then plan your next move. If there are no cafés close by, ask a stallkeeper if you can leave your purchase with him. They'll rarely say no.

When I am buying for an extended voyage, I plan my shopping so that I get my fresh fruit and tomatoes first, then my meat. These are the items that disappear from the stands first. Then I buy soft vegetables like lettuce and spinach next, and lastly I look for cheeses, sausages, and hard vegetables

Fruit and vegetables are stacked together at this stall in the public market in Mazatlan, Mexico.

such as onions and potatoes. These don't bruise easily and aren't wilted or damaged by the handling other shoppers give them.

When the shopping is done, our corner of the café usually looks like a small army stores depot. After one last cool drink we call a taxi, load the stores in, and head for the ice plant before we go down to the harbor. The taxi may sound like an extravagance when local buses cost only pennies a ride. But I've found that when I'm finished shopping for a week's provisions, I'm too tired and overloaded to handle the struggle of a bus. When we are provisioning for an ocean passage with extra crew, we've sometimes had to hire two taxis to carry the load.

Larry has a problem with taxi drivers. He feels they know he hates to bargain. But he is finally learning. Ask the driver the fare. If it is too high, just walk away and ask another driver. If there is a meter in the taxi, ask the driver to turn it on as soon as you get into the taxi. If at all possible, carry a small map of the town with you and show the taxi driver exactly where your boat is located. That way he will know you have an idea of how far you are going to ride. Don't let unscrupulous drivers ruin your day, and don't think that unscrupulous taxi drivers are only found in foreign countries.

I've had different experiences with taxi drivers. Since many of them pick up foreign passengers, they often speak a smattering of English when no one else around does. They know an area well and can guide you to the one item you can't find in the marketplace.

Rickshaw and tricshaw (three-wheeled, bicycle-powered rickshaws) drivers are the same. In the Far East we found some who actually helped with the shopping. In Penang, Malaysia, the slight-looking tricshaw driver I'd hired for a dollar an hour came into a shop where I was buying seventy-five dollars' worth of groceries and said to the owner, "You have given my friend her proper 10 percent discount, I trust." The shopkeeper handed me back the equivalent of $7.50. The only problem with tric and rickshaws is that I feel guilty asking a man not much bigger than I am to pull me and all of my groceries through steamy, hot streets while I lounge back in the shade of the canopied cart. I asked my favorite driver in Penang about this. His comment was, "This is a good profession. I need a license to do it and I earn a good wage for my family when many people have no jobs at all. I'll tell you if I can't carry any more. But don't worry too much, you should see some of the loads the local people expect me to carry; mother, father, three children, and groceries too. That's a real load."

When you first set off on a long cruise you'll be shocked at how much time you spend shopping. The average North American takes two or three hours a week to buy food and provisions at home. If you have been living in the same neighborhood, it can take even less time. I figure on spending six or seven hours a week buying food in foreign countries and double that when it comes to provisioning for a long voyage. If you are moving from port to port quickly, provisioning will take more time because you won't have time to get to know the local shopping area and markets at all. I've heard women list foreign shopping as one of the main reasons they hated cruising: "My life is one round of shopping, carting food back to the boat, making meals, washing clothes, shopping," I can appreciate the feeling. However, if you can split up the shopping chores and laundry among the crew, arrive with the proper equipment, and learn to shop the way the locals do, using the café as a welcome rest-point, shopping may become one of your favorite cruising events.

CASH AND CURRENCY FOR OFFSHORE SAILORS

Finding ways to have money easily available as you cruise is a problem. It would be ideal to arrive in each new port with local cash, but that's almost impossible, since few banks carry anything but their own currency plus a bit of their nearest neighbor's cash.

The best solution we've found is U.S. travelers checks in small denominations plus some U.S. cash in small bills. We carry $2,000 in travelers checks, twenty- and fifty-dollar sizes, half in Larry's name, half in mine. This way if either of us is too lazy or too ill to go to the bank, there is no problem. The small bills work best in far-off places where there are no banks and the entire cash reserves of the average store may not total fifty dollars. U.S. currency and checks seem to be the easiest to change at this time—merchants know the value of dollars where they might not have the exchange rate for pounds or francs.

A secret reserve of $400 or $500 in small bills has also come in handy. In Egypt we had no choice: bribery or "baksheesh" is the unofficial law of the land, and to get through the Suez Canal we had to pay off the pilot. No pilot or official will accept a travelers check, so American cash came in handy. There have also been times when some Mideast banks had boycotts on certain brands of travelers checks, so our cash tided us over.

Don't change much money the first day you arrive in a new port. Hotels or banks and moneychangers right at the harbor often give lower exchange rates. People who come up to you and ask to change money secretly could be a source of trouble. We only change enough money to take us out for dinner our first night in port; then we check around among local sailors, at the banks, and with businessmen. We change money where we can see the rates posted and get a receipt. In some countries there are strict laws against changing money except at authorized places. We have sometimes sold dollars to blackmarketing locals, but only where this was very common practice and the penalties for a first-time offense were only a warning. In Israel this was illegal but openly done at a special plaza where you could get fourteen pounds for one dollar instead of the eleven pounds banks offered. In Communist countries, do not change money illegally—you may forfeit your boat and spend time in jail.

Exchange rates are usually posted at banks. One column says Buy, the other Sell. Banks earn 1 to 2 percent by charging for each transaction on foreign currencies. In Canada, for instance, you will pay $1.18 Canadian for an American dollar, but if you cash in an American dollar, you'll only receive $1.16 Canadian. The rates listed in newspapers under the foreign exchange listing are usually somewhere in between. So avoid having too much foreign currency toward the end of your stay in any country.

On the other hand, unless there is a large daily fluctuation of value on local currency, change enough money to last at least a week at a time. It's a nuisance having to start each day at the local bank.

Choose a quiet time at the bank to make a large exchange transaction, being careful to avoid local paydays. Do not put your cash in a pants pocket. Pickpockets hang out around banks on payday and often watch where you put your cash. For men, the European custom of carrying a small clutch bag is a good idea; for women, don't exchange large amounts alone in big cities with bad reputations. Manila, Mexico City, Acapulco, Cairo, Rome, Hong Kong, and Djakarta are ones we've been warned about. We saw firsthand proof of this problem when our host in Manila arrived at the yacht club with slashed pants and no money after cashing his monthly paycheck.

Carry only enough money with you for your day's purchase; hide the rest in a carefully chosen spot on board. Locals feel uncomfortable when they see you handling one or two hundred dollars in cash. Their prices sometimes increase in response.

Getting your twice-yearly supply of cash can be a real problem. We've tried every conceivable method and still have occasional problems. Letters of credit work only in large cities and require that you leave a large credit rating with your hometown bank. Cashiers checks are good only if they are drawn on a well-known bank and have two signatures. The best banks to use are Bank of America, Crocker Bank, or New York Bankers Trust in the United States; National Westminster or Barclays for English accounts, and Sydney Bankers Trust for Australians.

The best solution is to have your bank telex funds to the bank you will use when you arrive. There will be an eight- or ten-dollar charge, but any way you go it will cost you almost the same amount. Before you set sail bound for your refunding port, send your bank two separate letters stating the amount you want and the address and name of the bank you'll use. Two separate letters guarantee that at least one will get through. To get the address of a bank in your next port, ask the local bank for a look at their list of foreign banks. Have the money wired to the person on board who is most likely to cash the check. If it is addressed to two people, have an *or* inserted between the names or both signatures will be required. Have it written exactly as your names appear on your passport, otherwise you could have problems.

Often you'll find there is a one-week delay while the local bank clears your request for money. So we plan our twice-yearly refunding to coincide with a haul out and refit. That way all the messy work and delay come together. You'll avoid a lot of frustration when dealing with a foreign bank if you put yourself in the teller's position. Remember, you have no local address; the teller may never have seen a foreign draft or a foreign passport; the amount of money you are asking to have handed over to you may be many times more than her whole year's salary. So be extra patient and ask for the bank manager before you lose your temper. We find it pays to ask for the bank manager first, explain our situation, present our passports, ship's papers, and any other form of identification we have and then ask him how best to handle the situation. He often takes all of the hassle out of the transaction. If you have a local friend, ask him to introduce you to his bank manager.

Credit cards and bank check-cashing cards can be helpful overseas, but don't depend on these for large amounts of cash. Our National Westminster check guarantee card allowed us to cash a check for fifty pounds twice a week in twenty-eight countries. But when we needed $1,000, we still had to wire for it. Several small villages just wouldn't recognize the card, so we had to bus forty miles or more to the next larger town. My mother found the same problem with her Bank Americard when she visited us in England. Also, the foreign exchange rate offered by credit cards may be up to 2 percent less favorable than that you receive for travelers checks.

There are no ways we know of to avoid losing money on foreign exchange. We find it costs us about seventy to eighty dollars a year in exchange differences and charges. Travelers checks are the best bet. Thieves rarely take them, and despite rumors to the contrary, American Express or other travelers check dealers are very helpful in refunding your money and helping you find lost papers unless they suspect a client has sold his checks and is trying for a false refund. This has actually occurred with young backpackers in places like Thailand or India. But we've heard of no problems involving cruising yachtsmen.

Small foreign shipyards have had some poor experiences with cruising yachts. Offer to leave a deposit before you start using their facilities. We've found it's a good policy to leave a fifty-dollar deposit with local shipyards where we plan to stay a month or two, then run a tab. The deposit establishes our legitimacy (and other local merchants seem to hear about this through the local grapevine) and eliminates time-consuming transactions and paper work when we run in for one roll of masking tape or a gallon of paint thinner.

Spend any coins before you leave for a new country, or toss them in a jar to give to other yachtsmen going the opposite way. Moneychangers won't accept foreign coins, but yachtsmen find a gift of coins for their next port of call a treat.

Day 4

185 miles noon to noon (90 miles due to Japanese current), miles to date 280

smooth broadreach

sunny and warm

Breakfast—apple, orange juice
bread and jam
coffee, tea
Lunch—scrambled eggs
tomatoes and cabbage salad with mayonnaise
coffee, tea

Snack—potato chips and cheese
Dinner—Chinese-style shrimp on instant mee noodles

CHINESE-STYLE SHRIMP

5 garlic cloves, chopped
1 onion cut in chunks
½ bell pepper in chunks
Sauté in 2 tbs. butter until onions brown slightly.
Mix 1 tbs. soy sauce
1 tsp. MSG (Accent or monosodium glutemate)
2 tbs. cornstarch
¼ cup water
Pour over onions and stir gently until gravy thickens.
Add 1 tomato cut in chunks (skin still on)
1½ cups uncooked shrimp
Cover and cook one minute. Remove from heat and let sit for three or four minutes. Then toss and serve over rice noodles.

PREPARING FOR THE FIRST FEW DAYS AT SEA

During the first three or four days of every offshore passage I feel tired and clumsy. We're usually recovering from farewell parties, the mentally exhausting job of shopping for stores, and the physically tiring job of storing them away. Then there is the motion to get used to, and the rhythm of changing watches. This has been a calm voyage so far; the sea is almost glassy. Even so, because of the swell, other ships' wakes, and *Seraffyn*'s motion, we have to brace ourselves as we move around. All night our bodies tense, then relax, as the boat rises and falls over each wave, and though we've slept like rocks on each of our off-watches, seven hours' sleep doesn't seem like quite enough. I think this initial tiredness, which in my case causes me to lose most of my initiative, is even worse than seasickness. For these first days at sea I have to force myself to do something besides lie in the bunk and read. Cooking is about the limit of my self-starting ability, and the idea of opening up my egg locker and checking over 120 eggs doesn't appeal to me at all.

Had the Sea of Japan been known for heavy winds or rough seas, I'd definitely have prepared several meals ahead of time. When we sailed out of Cartegena, Colombia, eight years ago bound north for Jamaica, I'd known and worried about the fact that we'd be closehauled with twenty- to twenty-five-knot tradewinds to contend with. At Larry's suggestion I cooked up several main courses before we left—beef stew, chili and beans, a pork roast. These stayed right in their pots when we left port; thus, in spite of a rude bout of seasickness and really rough seas, I was able to heat something Larry enjoyed even though I was myself having trouble keeping down dry biscuits.

A WORLDWIDE GUIDE TO BUYING PROVISIONS

Thank God Rosalind Foo, a delightful member of the Perak Yacht Club in Lumut, Malaysia, had been to Japan only a few months before we met her. When we told her we were planning to use Yokohama as the jumping-off point on our Pacific crossing, Rosalind warned us, "Stock up here and in Singapore. You won't be able to afford a chocolate bar in Japan." We took her advice and stocked up in Singapore. When we reached Brunei we filled up the empty spots in our lockers, and in Manila we bought everything we could carry, fresh, canned, and bottled. Rosalind's warning wasn't far off. By stocking up where prices were reasonable, we probably saved $400 to $500 just on one passage, and we had an assortment of stores that just weren't available in Japan.

Fortunately, cruising friends all along our route have traded information on buying stores in the countries we are bound for. But it is hard for the new voyager who hasn't become part of the ocean-cruising community to know what to expect. So we've compiled the following list with the help of several voyaging friends.

The list includes the year the information was gathered. The countries are listed alphabetically with a separate section for each person who is contributing information. This list can only serve as a guide, since prices and availability are constantly changing. Last year in Sri Lanka (Ceylon) all canned imports except Australian cheddar cheese and French corned beef were banned. This year the government is allowing three different brands of corned beef into the country plus canned butter. When we state prices are reasonable or high, we are basing our estimate on a set cruising budget of $350 to $400 a month (1978) with $160 set aside for food.

The list is broken into three sections: the countries we personally visited, the countries for which we have only hearsay information, and those countries visited by friends. It is impossible to get absolutely current information on every port of call you are likely to visit, but the list does include those countries most often visited by cruising sailors.

FROM *SERAFFYN*

Based on cruising with a crew of two, or delivering boats with crews of three or four

Aden, South Yemen 1977

Surprising supply of English canned products, frozen meats, and duty-free liquor at slightly higher than English prices. Fresh fruit and vegetables always in limited supply. While we were there onions and eggs were completely unavailable from normal sources. We managed to buy some from a ship. Water taken on here can be brackish during the summer months, but it is safe to drink. It pays to shop with the help of a ship chandler, especially for vegetables.

Antigua 1974

The small store at English Harbor is handy but very expensive. Individual vendors sell a limited supply of local fresh fruit and vegetables just outside the port area. But for real stores shopping it is necessary to take the bus or taxi across the island to town. The open market has a mediocre supply of fresh food early in the day. The large supermarket has a good variety of English and Commonwealth canned and packaged goods, but prices are high. The supermarket does offer case-lot discounts. Be sure to taste canned goods before buying a case.

Azores–Faial 1972

Prices for everything are low, but fresh food supplies are limited. Only a few canned foods are available. Peter or his son at the Café Sport can arrange for enough local fruit and vegetables to stock your boat if you give him four day's warning. The few Portugese canned stores we bought here were exceptional. The canned ham was the best and least expensive we've ever found.

Bermuda 1972

Everything is expensive here because it is an island with little farm land. Costs are at least 25 percent higher than in the United States. But many good English canned meat varieties are available and worth the price for a cruising boat on a long passage, including stewing beef, meat pies, Shipham brand canned chicken products. Duty-free liquor is reasonable and easy to obtain.

Brunei 1978

Fresh fruit and vegetables are very expensive here and in limited supply. Canned Australian and English goods are reasonable as are frozen meats and fresh seafood. The public market has no meat available because of the Muslim health laws. But the minisupermarkets have freezers with all sorts of Australian meat in them. The stores near the port area have only limited supplies, but a bus runs each half-hour to the capital at Bandar Sere Begewan.

Canada 1979

Prices in any of the small ports in the Gulf Islands and smaller towns are usually 20 to 40 percent higher than those in the United States. Supermarkets in Victoria, Sydney, or Vancouver proper are excellent; prices are 10 to 15 percent higher than in the United States. Dairy products, cheeses, and sausages are lower priced and exceptional in quality. Fresh vegetables are much more seasonal than in the southern United States. But it is worth shopping here for many of the English brands of canned meats and meat pies which are helpful for offshore cruisers. Shipham brand stewing beef, chicken in supreme sauce, many meat patés, Tyne brand meat pies, and several types of canned cheeses are worth a try. For onshore fine eating stop fishermen and buy dungeness crabs, oysters, clams, and delicious fresh salmon.

Cayman Islands 1971

Everything is imported from Miami by air. Everything is outrageously expensive. The selection is all right, but I'd avoid having to buy much here.

Columbia 1971

Cheapest fresh food in Latin America, but the most primitive marketing conditions we've seen outside of North Africa. Excellent variety of fresh vegetables, meat, and seafood, but very few imports and not much in the way of canned goods. Soft drinks such as Coca-Cola were delivered to the boat at only pennies a bottle in the case. Duty-free stores are not available and all shopping must be done early in the morning at the public market. By early we mean 0600.

Costa Rica 1970 (Punta Arenas only)

Canned goods cost three times as much as they would have elsewhere and very few were available. Liquor and soft drinks were very costly and no duty-free stores were available. Fresh local foods were all very reasonable; the beef was often excellent if you selected carefully. Pork was always very good. Seafood selection was great. There are only open markets. Flour and grains are only available from fifty-pound sacks, making weevils a problem. (See weevil control in bread-baking section.) Don't plan on stocking up for an ocean passage here.

Denmark 1973

Very expensive. The Danish Plumrose brand bacon we bought in England cost only one-third as much as in Denmark. Even bread and staples were 50 to 80 percent higher than in England.

Egypt 1977

Almost no canned stores are available here. Flour and rice come from open fifty-pound sacks and become full of weevils quickly. Fresh food and vegetables are reasonable but of low quality. The markets are very dirty. You must bargain for prices. It pays to learn Arabic numbers as this is the way prices are written and marked. Ali at the Port Said yacht club will write down the numbers for you. They are easy to understand. Fifty-pound blocks of ice will be delivered direct to your boat for five cents extra.

England 1973–74

Ice is hard to find but not terribly necessary. Excellent selection of canned goods. Great cheeses. Fruit and vegetables are limited in variety and seasonal. Wine is very high priced. Duty-free stores are available, but liquor is limited to one pint per person per day for the estimated length of time at sea. Supermarkets are excellent and seem to be just as reasonable close to the harbors as they are farther away. For fresh fruit and vegetables, the greengrocer is best bet. Prices are lower than in the United States. Definitely stock up here before visiting the Baltic, Germany, Holland, or France.

Finland 1973

Prices are slightly lower than in England. Quality was superb. There were wonderful new fruits to try, such as cloud berries which only grow north of the Arctic Circle and taste like tangy, golden raspberries. No duty-free stores were available except out of Helsinki. Most supermarkets in coastal towns have someone on hand who speaks English and is willing to translate the labels on the cans.

Germany–Kiel Canal 1973

The food here is the highest in Europe. But duty-free liquor is reasonable and easy to obtain.

Gibraltar 1976

Excellent wholesale prices on English cheeses, packaged and canned goods, especially beef. Vegetables, wine, and fruit are very poor quality. If I were planning an Atlantic passage again, I'd buy canned stores and cheese, meat, and paperback books in Gibraltar, then sail across the straits to Spanish Ceuta for fresh provisions and wines. It is only sixteen miles.

Greece 1977

The yogurt, feta cheese, wines, and olives are a treat. A few main towns such as Corfu, Rhodes, and Athens have a good selection of imported canned foods, but the prices are 50 percent higher than in Malta. There is a small selection of local canned fruit and vegetables. Do as much of your shopping as possible in the bigger villages as many of the beautiful, inviting small islands have almost nothing to offer but onions, yogurt, and feta cheese.

Italy 1976

Sardinia, Sicily, and Italian Islands Prices here are about 20 percent higher than in Spain. The cheeses are completely different and delightful. Wine is priced at sixty to seventy cents a bottle and can be very good, but lower-priced ones tend to be rough. Italian canned goods are excellent. Beef and pork tend to be good quality but pricy. Beware of the pastries if you are watching your weight. Shopping is in small private stores; one sells cheese, another fruit. All Italian ice cream is delicious, some is even better.

Italian mainland In a few cities there are fine supermarkets being built. The large one in Trieste has a tremendous stock of Italian packaged goods. Prices are higher than in the United States. Quality is good. But most towns still have small shops instead of supermarkets. Shopping in small towns tends to be best after siesta; often the finest produce arrives at 1700 hours.

Israel 1977

Shockingly expensive, but a 30 percent devaluation of the Israeli pound occurred a week after we left, so prices may be better. The supermarkets in Tel Aviv had a good selection of fresh and packaged foods. But the prices at the Carmel open market, twenty minutes from the yacht club by bus, were 25 percent lower on vegetables and meat. Because of dietary laws, pork and many familiar cuts of beef are only available at the Carmel market. Israeli canned products are first rate, as are the dried fruits and nuts.

Jamaica 1974

Liquor, canned local fruits and vegetables, coffee and tea are cheap. But fresh vegetables and fruit are expensive compared with Latin America. There are supermarkets for meat and packaged goods, but it is best to visit the public market for fresh items.

Japan 1978

Everything here is very expensive by American or European standards, but the quality is exceptional. Eggs are reasonable, but otherwise figure prices averaging double those in the United States. The best shopping is in the small public markets or the supermarkets located under many large shopping malls. Chinatown in downtown Yokohama has many Chinese canned goods at much lower prices than the comparable Japanese goods. Check with the chandlers when you are stocking up. They offer a good selection at low prices, tax-free. Meat in fifteen-kilo packages is available at Australian prices. Don't buy fresh vegetables from the chandlers; you save some money, but the quality is not nearly as good as at the public market.

Madeira 1975

A wonderful variety of locally grown fruits, vegetables, and meats was available at very reasonable prices in the public market before noon. The beef was exceptional. Very few canned or packaged goods are imported. There are only a few minimarkets. I depend on replenishing my fresh stores and wine here but nothing else.

Malaysia 1978

Penang Imports of all sorts available here at reasonable prices. Excellent selection of fruit, seafood, and meat. Shopper's paradise, especially for cruisers coming from the West. We saw foods here we hadn't seen since we left the United States. Malaysian canned goods tend to be excellent. The canned meats are spicier than those sold elsewhere. Fill up here if you are not bound direct for Singapore. Definitely fill here if you are headed north or west.

Malaysian mainland Prices are all very good. Pork is sold in separate markets because of Muslim dietary laws. It is usually at least a block away from the main market. Shopping is much cheaper in the open market. Fewer imports can be found here than in Penang.

Malta 1977

Very low-priced meat. English imports of all types reasonably priced and readily available. Local wines coarse but cheap. Small supermarkets with good selections. Duty-free stores available. Wholesalers here will sell partial cases and are worth visiting. Vegetables that are grown locally are reasonably priced, but imported vegetables and fruits are too expensive. There is a large selection of American canned goods available in special markets used by U.S. oil men's families—the prices are slightly higher than in the United States. Stock up here for all of the Mediterranean, but avoid taking on water as it is poor tasting though safe to drink.

Mexico 1979

Fruit, vegetables, and ice are very low-priced, and in the larger towns the variety is quite good. Beef, though cheap, was tough and rangy tasting, but the pork was excellent. Fresh chickens tended to be tough but tasty. Beer and liquor was so inexpensive that there were no chandlers around. Imported canned foods were becoming available, but local canned goods were limited. Open markets were by far the best place to shop, early in the mornings but not on Saturdays. La Paz, Baja California, Guaymas, Manzanillo, and Acapulco on the mainland are good ports for shopping. Salina Cruz is not a good place to shop for lengthy voyages.

Panama 1978

The Canal Zone commissary is not available to visiting yachtsmen, so stores must be bought in Panama City. Fresh food and produce is very cheap, but shopping must be done early in the day. Some small supermarkets have a good selection of canned goods from other places, but prices were higher than they should have been. Meats vary in quality, so careful shopping pays off. This is the best place to stock up between Mexico and Puerto Rico. Stock up here for sure if you are bound for the Pacific Islands. Shopping is easier in Cristóbal than in Panama City, but the variety is better in Panama City. Duty-free stores must be loaded at the Canal Zone Yacht Clubs. It is well worth looking at duty frees not only for liquor but for canned stores in case lots.

Philippines 1978

We can only speak for Manila. But we found pickpockets to be rife, especially on the first and fifteenth of each month, traditional paydays. Food is exceptionally low priced. The quality is good. Philippine canned and packaged goods, done under license for U.S. companies, were very good quality and cheap. Coffee is cheap here, but very few teas are available. Local rums cost as little as fifty cents a bottle; the best is about $1.50. The supermarkets in large shopping centers offer the best place to buy meats, packaged goods, and liquor. For fresh vegetables the open market is a must.

Poland 1973

Owing to the black market rate on dollars, prices were extremely reasonable. Fresh meat was scarce—vegetables and chickens were good but had to be bought in the public market before 1000. State-run ship chandlery supplied excellent sausages, smoked bacon, cases of peanut butter, and several American brands, including Scott paper towels at half the American prices. Excellent Crimean champagne cost eighty-five cents a magnum, Bulgarian wines forty cents a liter. We filled the boat to the brim.

Portugal 1974

There are no imported goods available and few canned goods. Wines, fresh vegetables, and seafood are good quality and cheaper than in Spain. Meat is low quality. The markets are quite primitive compared with other European countries, and we found no supermarkets at all except for a tiny one in Caiscas outside Lisbon.

San Blas and Panamanian Islands 1971

No stores are available except for a few onions, coconuts, fresh fish, lobster, and yams. Ice cream can be bought once a week from the interisland ferry that brings refilled butane tanks from Panama.

Singapore 1978

If you have patience and are willing to spend a lot of time looking for what you want, this is a shopper's paradise. The prices for almost everything are 20 percent cheaper than in Penang. The variety is even better with goods from Australia, England, the United States, and Communist China topping the list. The Chinese Emporiums offer real bargains in canned goods, the open markets are breathtaking, and the supermarkets just like home. The market chains have wholesale departments that are willing to sell case lots at 20 percent discounts. So if you are filling the boat, it pays to shop around for a week before actually buying anything major. It also pays to shop in central Singapore, even though it is twenty miles from the two yacht clubs. Many people found it worthwhile to rent a low-priced hotel room in the central area (near the Thieves Market a modest room could be had for four dollars per night). That way the forty-five-minute bus ride to and from the yacht anchorage can be cut out while you organize your shopping over the hotel telephone. Do not plan on buying charts in Singapore. Although the supply is excellent, the chart agents charge eleven dollars each. Light lists and almanacs cost 2½ times their cover prices. But you can trade for charts with other cruising boats with some success.

Many people have avoided Singapore because of rumors about unfair and extremely high port charges. These can be avoided by arranging for a deratification certificate in Malaysia or Indonesia, where they cost only fifteen dollars. Then *without fail* pay for the Singapore garbage fee for a month in advance as soon as you sign for your entry papers.

It will cost four dollars per month if you pay in advance, two dollars per day if you don't. Keep the garbage-payment receipt; you'll be asked for it when you clear out. This solves all paper problems in Singapore!

Spain 1975

The wines, local cheeses, and sausages are all delightful and reasonably priced. Seafood is exceptional. Meats can be good if you choose carefully. Canned food other than seafood is not high quality, so try any Spanish brands before you buy a case. Try Spanish mejillones en escobeche (mussels in Garlic and Tomatoe sauce), a canned delicacy we ate by the case. The best marketing is in the public market, although a few cities are getting supermarkets now. Palma, Mallorca, is an

During our stay in Andraitx, on the island of Mallorca, Spain, we often used a motorcycle to make the weekly expedition to the farmers' market more pleasant.

excellent place to shop, as is Vigo in the northwest. All of the coastal villages have lovely open markets. Ice is usually available right at the port where the fishing boats tie up. In Palma, two different people help cruisers do their shopping. The prices are the same as in the market, but the assistance in finding oddball items is great, and these people deliver right to your boat. Ask at the yacht club for further information. Stock up here if you are bound for African ports or France, Corsica, northern Sardinia.

Spanish Morocco—Ceuta 1975

Superb wines, brandies, Spanish sparkling wines, and liquors at untaxed, rock-bottom prices, especially if you bring your own containers. Excellent low-priced vegetables, fresh pork, and fruit. Butane and ice are relatively easy to get. Spanish canned goods, cheeses, and sausages are easily available. The harbor is a safe place to tie up, and taxis to get you to the main marketplace are cheap. Shopping is in a huge public market with small specialty shops surrounding it. Dried fruits and nuts of all sorts are an exceptional bargain here.

Sri Lanka 1977

Almost no packaged goods available. No imports at all. Fresh food is amazingly low-priced, but the selection is limited, you have to bargain, and you have to be there by 1000. Rice and flour bought here is already full of weevils. Don Windsor, who greets yachtsmen in Galle Harbor, will help you shop. His prices are lower than those we would have paid by ourselves and his help is invaluable.

Sweden 1973

We couldn't afford to eat here. We went on a diet.

Tangier 1975

This would be a good place to shop except that the problem of thievery in the yacht harbor makes staying here uncomfortable. Keep someone on board at all times. Bargaining is necessary, and street urchins can make life unpleasant.

U.S.A. West Coast 1978, East Coast 1972

Excellent selection of canned and packaged foods available at prices that offer good value for money spent. But the selection of main-course meats in cans is not as good as that found in England and Australia. Because of the huge variety, all brands should be tested beforehand. Fresh fruit and vegetables are best bought from places other than supermarkets. Dried fruits are good quality but expensive. Supermarkets near most harbors are much more expensive than those found five or six miles inland. Prices in Key West and San Diego are higher than those farther north. Cash-and-carry outlets are available to quantity buyers, but since most supermarkets will give case-lot discounts, it is wise to compare prices before purchasing. Ship chandlers in San Diego, San Francisco, Norfolk, and Charleston can provide duty-free liquor and cigarettes but don't offer much value for stores of other types. Ice is easily available but somewhat expensive. Prices on the average run slightly lower than Europe and England, much lower than Japan. U.S. prices run 30 to 40 percent higher than in Singapore.

HEARSAY

The following countries are not ones we have visited. The information is from conversations with other cruising sailors.

Channel Islands 1975

Alf Taylor, who cruises his thirty-two-foot cutter out of England, goes to Saint Peter's Port on Guernsey Island to stock up. Imported goods cost 30 percent less than in England. Wines are half the price.

Djibouti 1977

Both the crew of *Girl Morgan* and *Shikama,* two Australian cruising boats, visited Djibouti on their way up the Red Sea. They said the selection of foods was quite good but double the prices found elsewhere. But the independence granted Djibouti and the French withdrawal in 1977 made supplies difficult to obtain. When we were in Aden, we spoke with commercial ships captains who said they couldn't get any fresh vegetables in Djibouti.

France 1977

According to Jo Forrestal, who was cruising the Mediterranean on board her fifty-foot sloop with up to nine crew to feed, food and stores here were the most expensive in the Mediterranean. It paid to get away from the main ports to do the shopping.

Guam 1978

Linda Balser replenished the stores on forty-nine-foot *Styx* here after a voyage from Honolulu. She found the prices about 20 percent higher than in the United States, but the supply was quite good. Fresh local vegetables were reasonable.

Hawaii 1978

This is Linda's home. She says to expect prices to run 10 percent more than they do on the U.S. mainland. Try to get away from the harborfront to shop. Look through Chinatown for Chinese canned goods at lower prices.

Hong Kong 1978

Fill up; the prices and varieties surpass those of Singapore, according to Lois, who is cruising with Ron Amy on his forty-footer. Moreover, the transport to and from your yacht is easier, and the yacht club is only minutes from the shopping areas. Chinese products are exceptionally low priced.

Maldives 1977

Marion on the forty-foot cutter *Joya* spent four months in the Maldives. Nothing was available other than onions and fish in the outer islands. She did all of her shopping in the main port of Mali. She found a good selection of canned foods at lower prices than she expected. But fresh food supplies were limited. She recommended stocking up here if you are bound for Sri Lanka, India, or the Red Sea Countries.

Sudan 1977

According to the crew of *Girl Morgan,* there are no imported goods here at all. The local food is good and reasonably priced. Much of it still comes to the market on camels. All shopping is done at rather primitive marketplaces and requires bargaining.

Taiwan 1978

Lydia Tangvald on *L'Artemis de Pytheas,* the forty-nine-footer she and Peer have cruised on for seven years, lived in Taiwan for a year before stocking up. She says the food prices are low, but one is limited to local foods only. No whole-grain rice is available unless you go direct to the mill accompanied by a translator who really understands what you are after.

Hal and Margaret Roth, who cruised around Cape Horn on board *Whisper,* their thirty-five-foot sloop, during 1974 and 1975, sent the following information:

Argentina

This would be a good place to stock up for a voyage. Food prices were less than in the United States, but the currency fluctuations day to day were so great that it paid to shop for the best exchange rate before shopping for food. Fresh beef and excellent tinned fish were available in Mar de Plata. Wholesale grocers sold food in case lots. All shopping was in open markets and small shops, which had a good selection of fresh fruit and vegetables. Wines were of fair quality.

Brazil

This is a good place to stock up. Prices were generally less than in the United States depending on the currency exchange rate. Fish and shellfish were of superb quality and sold fresh daily. Open markets offered good fresh produce. Wines were excellent.

Julius Wilensky, author of *The Yachtsman's Guide to the Windward Islands,* is constantly revising his books and sent this information based on his travels during 1976–77. "Most of the things that come from the States have a duty which is as high as 30 percent added on to the wholesale price. British items enjoy half that duty so are generally favored over U. S. imports in Saint Lucia, St. Vincent, and Grenada."

Martinique

The best place to stock up here is in Fort-de-France. Almost everything is available, though shops are scattered.

Saint Lucia

Castries is the only port that has much available as far as supplies.

Saint Vincent

There are some groceries available in Kingstown. The best shopping is in the public market on Friday and Saturday morning.

Bequia

Admiralty Bay (Port Elizabeth) has groceries and supplies just a short walk from the dock. You also find an excellent supply of fishing, diving, and marine supplies at Lulley's, up the hill from Princess Margaret Beach.

Mustique

No water, no ice, a few supplies at a small store north of the dock.

Cannauan

Only a few minor groceries and drug items are available.

Union Island

Liquor, beer, grocery staples, bread at the Grand Union Supermarket near the customs house.

Palm Island (Prune Island)

There is a little supermarket with frozen meats, canned goods, liquor, general staples, toilet articles, and a limited supply of ice.

Petit Saint Vincent

Excellent fresh bread and ice available from the hotel.

Carriacoa

Hillsboro has a small grocery store on the main street parallel to the beach south of the dock.

Grenada

Saint Georges has excellent supermarkets and a good public market. Buy fresh food at the public market on Wednesday and Saturday for the best selection. The Super Center Market has a good choice of frozen meats. For grocery items try the Cold Store, Food Fair, or Buy Rite Supermarket. This is a good place to stock up, but you will have to take a taxi from the docks to the shopping area.

Gordon and Annabelle Yates, who have cruised for eleven years on three different boats, spent three years on a voyage from Denmark through the Caribbean to the Pacific and north to California, 1973 to 1975. Some of their special comments follow.

Holland

Prices here are very high and all shopping is done in supermarkets.

Tenerife, Canary Islands

This is a good place to stock up; prices are lower than in U.S. Good citrus fruit and wines are available. Shopping is in open markets. Good selection of Spanish-brand cans.

Saint Bartholomew

There is a really exceptional marine store here with prices from several years back. But food supplies are minimal.

Tortola

This is a friendly place with a supermarket and good fresh food available.

Barbados

Inexpensive food supplies available at the supermarket.

Nicaragua

Minimal supplies are available at very low prices in Corinto, but there is a distinct feeling of hostility here and many gun-toting police. I wouldn't recommend planning to stock up here.

Jim Hollywood, who completed a circumnavigation in three years on board his thirty-four-foot *Sea-goer* ketch, contributed the following information about classic round-the-world ports of call.

South Africa

Capetown and Durban are excellent places to stock up; in fact, they are the best stop after Australia for westbound cruisers. Ship chandlers visit each new yacht and take orders for bonded liquor and cigarettes plus some stores. Prices were similar to those in the United States in 1974. Special good buys were eggs, meat, tinned food, sterilized milk, and liquor in bond.

Saint Helena

Prices for available supplies were high. There is little to choose from other than a few daily necessities. Fuel and water must be rowed out, telegraph is available to United States and Europe. Good rest stop but not a place to count on provisioning.

Ascension

The anchorage is subject to rough seas, water is only available if no one is in prison. All provisions are flown in, and prices are high. Frozen meat is available, but prices are outrageous. Only a few onions, tomatoes, and cabbages were available as a gift from a local gardener.

Eric and Susan Hiscock sent us the following information from their latest cruise from New Zealand to Canada on board *Wanderer IV* in 1978.

New Zealand

Most voyagers leave New Zealand in April or May at the end of the southern summer so that potatoes and onions are freshly harvested and of excellent quality. Citrus fruit is difficult to get at that time of the year, but one can get delicious oranges, grapefruit, and lemons earlier in the summer, not with particularly good keeping qualities. Dairy produce and meat are first-class and not expensive. Meat bought in ten-pound lots is more economical; we bottle it. There is little demand for canned goods; the population is so small, and practically all households have deep freezes. The only canned meat worth buying is corned beef (get the most expensive, Helaby's Sterling, as many other brands are exported to the Pacific Islands and they like fat) and ox tongue. Sheep tongue is rubbishy. Canned butter, the best in the world, is only obtainable from the creameries—and you must buy a case. This year I salted down enough to take us to Tahiti and then bought New Zealand cans there. Canned soups, vegetables, and fruits are not as good quality as elsewhere. Most yachts use Northern Foodstuffs, Ltd., a wholesale outfit in Whangarei, the most northern fair-sized town. Bonded stores are obtainable in Whangarei, Auckland, and elsewhere. Propane is twice the price of United States or Canada.

Rarotonga, Cook Islands

New Zealand canned goods are available but more expensive. They offer duty-free stores, but they take off the import duty and impose a steep "levy" so there is little advantage; but many yachts are taken in.

Tahiti

Papeete has at least two very sophisticated supermarkets loaded with goodies. But most are flown in, even potatoes, and prices are high. If you expect to buy only tropical island stuff, it's still expensive. But friends usually put one on to reasonable homegrown produce. Pamplemousse is our favorite citrus fruit.

Rica Laymon, who was wintering in the Solomons in 1978 on board *Ocarina,* sent the following information:

Solomon Islands

Stock up in Pago Pago or Fiji before cruising here. Canned goods were available in some of the six islands we visited, but the prices were unbelievably high. Bring along all the mayonnaise and peanut butter you plan to need. Fresh vegetables are cheap but only on Honiara did we find a good selection. On Gizo there was nothing. On Kieta and Kira Kira there was nothing but lots of coconut and betel nut. People on the more isolated islands would sometimes paddle out to greet us and bring a limited supply of produce. Some of the coconut plantations had private *abattoirs* [slaughterhouses] and would sell excellent meat for very low prices. Local canned tuna fish and sugar were very good buys. Duty-free stores were only sold to multiton commercial vessels.

John Mathias on board *Coryphaena* spent part of 1977 and 1978 in American Samoa; his report from Pago Pago:

American Samoa

Almost everything is available here at one time or another. The maxim is, "When you see it and the price is right, buy it, for it won't be there next week." The problem with shopping here is that in the open-air-market prices are fairly standard, although unmarked, and it takes a bit of art for the "Palagi" (non-Samoan) to find out what they really are. So shopping around is only necessary to get the quality you desire and/or the price at what it should be. It seems sometimes that haggling is possible, but in reality you are just getting the price down to what it normally is. Prices in the supermarkets vary widely for the same item, so it pays to make the complete rounds before stocking up. Prices are higher than in the United States generally, but New Zealand dairy products, frozen meats, and liquor are very good buys. Duty-free liquor is available but only at a slight reduction from the already ridiculously low prices. Try to bring coffee, cocoa, and any marine hardware and fittings with you, plus glass cloth, resin, engine parts, and sailcloth.

Jim and Cheryl Schmidt, cruising in the South Pacific right now on board the seventy-foot steel ketch *Wind'son,* sent the following information on two important Pacific ports:

Galapagos

We entered at Wreck Bay in February 1977, and at that time yachts were only permitted to stay for three days. Officials were courteous. Water on the dock was not safe for drinking; washing only. We were told you could probably go to individual homes with jerry cans and obtain water. We did not. This is a small place and very few provisions were available at high prices. The only fresh food we could buy was onions, potatoes, dried beans, grapefruit, and bananas.

Guam 1979

We provisioned for a voyage here and found prices much higher unless you could use the military commissary, where prices are the same as United States. Duty-free liquor is the exception; it is very inexpensive. There is an excellent supply of U.S. products but no native markets, as all food is shipped in from the United States and sold in large supermarkets. J and G Payless in the Agana shopping center has a wholesale division where stores can be bought in case lots for 15 to 20 percent discount. Some good hardware and boat supplies are available here. There is a coin laundry and several good restaurants, including Chuck's Steak House for excellent steak and salad.

Mary Baldwin, who hitchhiked through several groups of South Pacific Islands in 1977–78, worked as cook and privisioner for three different yachts. Her comments on the ports where she stocked up:

Australia

We stocked up in Darwin, where prices seemed higher than in the United States, but then I'm told prices here are slightly higher than they are in the rest of Australia as everything has to be trucked up. Everything is available here except canned butter. Wine is good and cheap, canned goods are fairly reasonable relative to Fiji, New Hebrides, and New Guinea. Fresh produce is easily available through supermarkets but prices are high. It may be worth investigating the various organic farms in outlying areas. Duty-free stores were very reasonably priced and no problem to obtain. The officials were casual about sealing them. We bought all of our nonperishable stores through "Jack the Slasher," an open-to-the-public wholesaler where you mark your own prices, box your own purchases, and save up to 25 percent. It's not near the harbor but worth taking a cab. You don't have to buy in case lots. Australia is a cruiser's/provisioner's paradise. Because a large percentage of the population lives in the bush, they have developed packaging and processing so foods can be kept unrefrigerated for long periods of time.

Fiji

Suva is a shopper's delight; almost everything you want is available; the open market downtown is wonderful. Indian merchants there are not as willing to deal as are the Fijians. Much of the fresh produce sold here has been brought in chilled from New Zealand and doesn't keep too well. Duty-free stores were not available. But fresh Australian meats and New Zealand dairy products were excellent and cheap—less than half of U.S. prices. Bring wine—the local stuff is poor-quality Australian wines at nine dollars for a half-gallon—and canned meats—all that is available here is canned corned beef, canned mutton, and sheep's tongue.

Stephen and Linda Dashew are spending this winter (1979) in Papua, New Guinea, on board their yacht *Intermezzo* after a voyage through the Tuamotos, Marquesas, and various South Pacific Islands groups bound for New Zealand.

Marquesas

Don't plan on buying anything in the Marquesas or Tuamotos. Their limited supplies come via copra boat from Tahiti and are very expensive. Occasionally they slaughter a cow, but don't count on it. Eggs, when we could get them, cost three dollars a dozen. Some fruit was available from private parties.

Tuamotos

Only coconuts and fish are available here. The coral soil won't support gardens or fruit trees. You can get flour, sugar, and some canned goods at the local store.

New Hebrides

In Vila we found a fair open-air market with local beef and veal at good prices. There is some selection of canned and packaged goods, but because of the high prices we bought only daily supplies. There are many French products plus excellent yogurt. Duty-free stores are available.

Papua, New Guinea

Everything is available in Arowa and Pangreini. The supermarkets stock American products for the Americans who work at the big copper mine on the island of Bougainville. Kieta is the main port; the prices are high but not out of sight. Kieta has a fine open market. Prices are better in the Solomon Islands, so I'd recommend bringing everything with you.

Don't be ashamed of appearing constantly cost-conscious as you cruise. It's necessary to research and find the best value for your money. In fact it's a matter of survival if you are on a cruising budget, because food and drink are most sailors' single largest cruising expense. Locals already know the angles, just as you do in your hometown. You have to learn or pay as much as double for your stores.

Joan Reynolds, on board the yacht *Utahna,* visited many of the places I've listed already and had one final comment worth passing on. She said, "Don't take a food list from someone else unless you know you like and eat everything he eats. Would you do that here?" I can't help but agree, and after looking over this list I find that most long-distance cruisers soon come to the same conclusion. Stock up every time you see things you like. Use your boat as a pantry-warehouse. With a twenty-four-footer like *Seraffyn* we find it pays to plan a stop at one of those ports where we know stores are easily available twice a year. In between we've found we can make do. But just before we arrived in Singapore I remember longing for a peanut butter and jam sandwich, aluminum foil to bake in, and good paper supplies. I think that is one of the joys of cruising—it's either feast or famine as far as stores shopping goes. But when it's feast, you really appreciate and remember it.

Day 5

noon to noon 90 miles, miles to date 370

Closehauled, just making our course in an eight-knot breeze. Cloudy.

Breakfast—whole tomatoes
Japanese pastries
tea and coffee
Lunch—chef's salad with shrimp, cheese, ham, tomato, onion, lettuce, cucumber, and Thousand Islands dressing
Dinner—pork chops in sweet sauce
boiled potatoes

steamed cabbage
camembert cheese
red wine

PORK CHOPS IN SWEET SAUCE

Sauté pork lightly in oil
Add ½ cup catsup
1 tbs. vinegar
3 tbs. sugar
Simmer slowly for 15 minutes if chops are thin, longer if chops are over ½" thick. This same sauce can be used for any sweet and sour dish.

COOKING AHEAD

We were becalmed when I was preparing dinner, but there was a large swell from the east, dead on our nose. A swell like that can be the forerunner of a good blow. There were no other signs of a storm; the barometer was high, the clouds settled-looking. But just to be safe I put several extra potatoes into the pot when I was making dinner. Then after we'd eaten and before I cleaned up the galley, I made the extras into a potato salad for the next day. I've learned the lesson the hard way about preparing food ahead whenever there are signs of a storm. In fact, I've come to the conclusion that whenever I am in the mood to do a bit of extra cooking, it pays to make up something fancy for the days ahead. If the weather stays fine, I end up with some free time to enjoy it. If the weather deteriorates, Larry and whatever crew I'm with thinks I am a magician when I produce something more than soup in a mug.

Rudi, the Filipino cook on *Deerleap,* a beautiful cruising power yacht, told me, "It is always calmer in the morning at sea. Either that or you have more patience in the morning.

So if you want to cook up something elaborate, do it as soon as you get up or before you wash up the breakfast things."

One other hint he mentioned came to mind today as I was making up the potato salad. "I only peel potatoes when the owner is on board or when we are entertaining fancy," Rudi told us. "When we are at sea I think the crew needs all the vitamins they can get, and the vitamins in a potato are all near the skin." I agree wholeheartedly and also feel the skins add flavor to any salad. Besides, peeling potatoes is a drag.

SPECIAL PROVISIONS

Certain nonfood items are vitally important to long-term cruising people. These include toiletries, medicine, paper products, cleaning items, and boat supplies.

Most people who have traveled in foreign countries already know that toilet paper in almost every country other than the United States, England, Australia, and Singapore is rough as can be, poorly packaged, and very expensive. In some places such as India, Sri Lanka and the South Pacific Islands, Africa, and the poorer South American countries, it is almost impossible to find except in the largest cities. The same is true of that indispensable item, paper towels. So I would advise finding someplace in your boat where you can store a case of toilet paper and a case of paper towels. We find that the odd-shaped area around the water tank under *Seraffyn*'s cockpit can hold thirty-six rolls of plastic wrapped paper towels plus eighty rolls of toilet paper. These last us about five or six months. Every time we are low we start looking for another case.

Special cosmetics, shampoos, and lotions should also be bought in quantities to last for at least a year. These along with sun-protection lotions are most easily found in resort areas, or if necessary in the fancier hotels. But, if there is a brand name you vastly prefer, stock up when you see it. I know that between Israel and Malaysia there are absolutely no places to find toiletries we recognized, and the quality of local products like hand soap and shampoo are poor. Tampons and sanitary napkins are the one exception. Mary Baldwin, who hitchhiked around the South Pacific Islands for a year on board three different cruising boats, laughed when she told me how she'd given up valuable space in her rucksack for a year's supply of sanitary products, only to find that they were easily available even in more primitive places. One comment on tampons: be sure to store any opened package in a sealed plastic bag or the cotton will absorb moisture and the whole tampon will become useless.

Birth-control pills and medicines for your medical kit are actually easier to find and buy in primitive countries than they are in the United States, England, or Europe. They are also much cheaper. Be sure to have your doctor give you the generic name of any drugs you may need, as brand-name items are rarely available in foreign ports. Then go directly to the pharmacy in almost any country, and you'll find you can buy drugs without prescription at about one-quarter to one-half the American price. I have asked doctors from various countries about the advisability of buying medicine in foreign countries. They all assure me that drugs worldwide are carefully prepared mostly by American, British, German, or Swiss companies. Ask to see the package from which you are buying your pills. The generic names are the same no matter where the pills were packaged, so you can make sure you are getting the right package. At the same time check the expiration date on the label, if there is one. Carry a written perscription for any narcotic-containing drug on board alongside the container. This way officials will know your drugs are for legitimate uses.

Standard household cleaning products such as scouring

soap, dish soap, and scouring pads are easy to find worldwide, though you'll often have to use local brands which may smell different than those you are used to. Scott Bright pads are available worldwide and in primitive places are sold by the square meter. But bleach is one item that you should buy when you see it—especially in the South Pacific and Indonesia where you'll probably want some for water purification.

Buying boat supplies and parts is one of the real curses of the cruising sailor's life. Even in the United States it's difficult to find the specialized items needed for yachts in any ports that aren't specifically yachting ports. Stock up with spares before you leave; carry a magnet with you whenever you shop for any nonferrous items. The only places where you have a good chance to find items such as stainless steel bolts or screws, bronze or stainless rigging items, bronze screws, sailmaker's dacron thread, or sailcloth are Southern California, East Coast U.S. yacht harbors, Puerto Rico, Antigua and Saint Thomas in the Caribbean, England, the Baltic countries, northern Italy, Gibraltar and Malta in the Mediterranean, Singapore, Australia and New Zealand in the South Pacific, and Hawaii in the North Pacific. With boat parts and supplies even more than with food items, it's a real case of "it's cheaper to carry extra." I know we've found any spare bits and pieces that we didn't use made great gifts or trading items as we cruised. Spare thread and scraps of sailcloth made us several new friends in both Malaysia and the Philippines.

Basic electrical repair gear is much easier to find. Electrical tape, simple connections, and various gauges of wire are available worldwide. But any boat specialties such as electronic taffrail logs or the special circuitry to keep them running and twelve-volt light bulbs are difficult to find when you go foreign. Simple batteries for flashlights and such are cheap and available in the more primitive places. But if you use any sizes other than C, D, or square six-volt batteries, bring along spares.

Don't depend on being able to get any engine parts as you voyage. Even engine oil can be a problem, and transmission oil should definitely be bought by the case and carried with you. Write to the manufacturer of your engine before you set sail and ask him for a list of parts dealers in the area in which you plan to cruise; if there are no dealers, find out who you write to to have parts shipped when you require them. Then visit a shop that repairs engines such as yours, ask what parts are likely to give trouble as you voyage, and carry spares and any special tools required to change them with you, *and then double-check to make sure you have the right spares and tools.*

I know this list seems to have gotten out of the domain of this book. But I know of several hundred sailing people who have spent three times as long looking for engine repair parts as they did shopping for all the food for a 2,000-mile voyage. Some foresight in this area will free the whole crew for that sightseeing tour during the last few days before you set off from another interesting port-of-call.

Day 6 The first ten days at sea you feast on fresh food, trying to use perishables before they go bad.

Day 6
noon to noon 40 miles, miles to date 410

becalmed—sunny and warm

Breakfast—melon
cheese
coffee and tea
Lunch—hard-boiled eggs
potato salad
tomatoes and lettuce
orange juice and nougat candies
Teatime—last Japanese cakes

Dinner—homemade tomato-vegetable soup
salisbury steak (just thick hamburger patties with no bun)
potato chips (canned ones)

TOMATO-VEGETABLE SOUP

Put 4 large (6 medium) tomatoes in a soup pot
add 1 cup salt water
1 cup fresh water

Bring to a boil for 5 minutes. Remove tomatoes and let them cool until you can easily remove the skins and stems. Return all tomato meat and seeds to the pot.

Add 12 garlic cloves, chopped
4 scrubbed carrots cut in 3/8″ slices
1 large onion, chopped
¾ cup of shredded cabbage
1 tsp. oregano
3 tbs. sugar
3 cubes beef bouillon

Simmer slowly for 45 minutes, stirring occasionally. Thicken slightly with cornstarch.

ON WEIGHT LOSS

I spent part of this morning checking over the vegetables in the forepeak. We had all of the hatches open, the sea was very smooth, and I'm starting to get my energy back.

One thing I'm sure of is that I'll never buy vegetables of any kind from a ship chandler unless there is simply no other choice. The cabbages the chandler sent are already starting to show signs of rot where they got bruised in handling. I peeled off one layer of outer leaves on each cabbage, cut a thin sliver off the bottom of the stem, and turned them so they rested on a different spot in their basket. I took careful count of my tomatoes. Because of the gift crate that arrived the morning we were setting sail, I know we will have too many to last. That's why I decided to make up a soup.

I'm starting to lose a bit of weight now just like I always do at sea, no matter how much I eat and no matter if I am seasick or not. Larry isn't quite so lucky, and when I read this last paragraph to him today during our cocktail hour we got into a discussion of why some people lose weight on sailing voyages.

From the moment you leave harbor on a yacht, your body is moving, even though you aren't aware of it. Your muscles are tensing and relaxing to each bit of motion. Even when you are sleeping, sitting, or lounging on deck, you are using up calories that you wouldn't use on land. Of course, the amount of weight you'll lose, or the extra quantity of food you'll eat to maintain your weight, depends on how long you've been sailing, how big or complicated the boat is, how many sail changes you have to make, and what kind of wind and sea conditions you meet.

On *Seraffyn*'s first few voyages, we were busy all of the time we were at sea, changing, modifying, experimenting. Larry would be adjusting the sails every half-hour to get more speed out of whatever wind we had. He spent hours playing with the adjustments on Helmer, our self-steering gear, and tore through our spare junk collection almost every day looking for the right piece of gear to make a different adjustment lever or a better bracket for something on board. So he tended to lose weight on any voyage over five days long. Now, ten years later, all the bugs are worked out of the rig. The windvane works perfectly, our spinnaker pole arrangement is so simple I can handle it alone, the reefing gear is really "jiffy." Larry knows the exact adjustment that gets the most out of the sails. There is almost nothing to do on the boat at sea other than routine checking of gear and changing of sails. So Larry rarely loses a pound. (This may also be the reason he is building us a new boat—he misses having problems to solve.) On the other hand, when we were delivering a fifty-ton ketch from the Mediterranean to New Orleans, Larry lost weight even though he ate like a horse, including eggs, toast, and pancake breakfasts. He spent two or three hours a day in the engine room of that sixty-footer, he varnished, he spliced up rigging replacements, he had to horse up a temporary four by four, twenty-two-foot-long, sixty-pound whisker pole, and he had to stand behind the wheel steering six hours a day just like the rest of the crew.

When we did an inland waterway delivery, powering most of the way, both of us gained weight. We sat and steered all day with no sail changes to make. There was no sea motion to keep our bodies active. Because of the constant steering necessary in the canals, meals were all that broke up the day, so we ate more snacks and meals.

One lesson we've learned the hard way is that an exercise program is a must when cruising is a way of life. On any small boat at sea, your legs just don't get used enough. Your knees grow weak, while your arms and shoulders get stronger. A continous program of knee bends and leg exercises for ten minutes each day on long passages really helps. I do mine on my night watches on deck in calmer weather. If we are on a delivery and have to steer each watch, it's easy to exercise right at the helm. When you reach port after a long passage, try to get a bit of extra leg exercise, walking without carrying a big load, bicycle riding, or even dancing to the local disco band.

BUYING MEAT IN FOREIGN COUNTRIES

Jill and I were walking down the main street of Turtle Bay in Baja California last week (April 1979), exploring while her crew took on diesel. She was on a northbound delivery trip. I was on one going south. Around one corner we spotted the local equivalent of the butcher. A man stood on the dirt road in front of his home, splitting a side of beef into chunks with a hatchet. The beef lay on an old wooden spool that had once held telephone cables. Snarling dogs fought for chunks of bone and fat only inches away from the pile of yellow and maroon meat. "Sure glad I don't have to buy meat here," Jill commented. Both she and I still had loads of fresh food from the supermarkets of Southern California.

Turtle Bay's butcher was one of the worst I've seen. But as you cruise you'll find that few countries outside the United States, Canada, and Australia have butcher shops like we are used to. Very few use standard cutting methods, and almost none age beef beyond the time it takes to carry the slaughtered animal to the marketplace. Certain pointers will help you select usable meat no matter how primitive the marketplace is.

Pork (see fig. 1) is by far the safest buy in any country. I have never bought a tough piece of pork. Though foreign pigs rarely have as much fat as U.S. pigs, the flavor is usually the same. Any cut of pork other than the lowest part of the leg can be barbequed or fried for tender, tasty chops. To preserve the pork fresh for more than a day, rinse any bone chips, blood, or foreign matter off with fresh water. Dry the meat completely. Then store it in a metal or ceramic container that is loosely covered and set it right on the ice. I use a large salad bowl for all of the meat I buy at one time. Various types of meat are separated in the bowl with sheets

FIGURE I
PORK CHART
Wholesale and Retail Cuts*

1 HAM
a. Butt end or half
b. Shank end or half
c. Center slices

3 BELLY

4 SPARERIBS

6 PICNIC
a. Picnic roasts
b. Arm steaks

2 LOIN
a. Loin chops
b. Rib chops
c. Loin and rib roasts
d. Canadian-style bacon

5 BOSTON BUTT
a. Boston butt roast
b. Blade steaks

7 JOWL
a. Jowl bacon square.

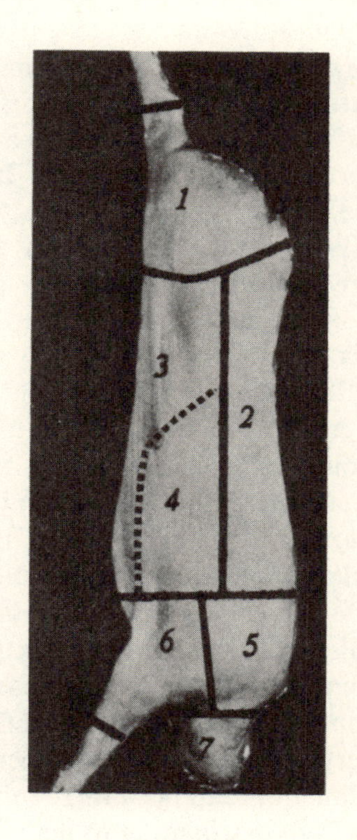

Section 2 would definitely be my first choice for barbecue or grilling. 5 and 1 bake quite nicely. But 7, 6, 3, and 4 tend to be quite fatty.

of aluminum foil; then the whole thing is covered lightly with a paper towel. Do not use plastic bags for any meat you plan to keep more than three days. It will hasten decay. Pork will last up to seven days at the thirty-four- to thirty-eight-degree temperatures found close to the ice in your cold box. If the pork should get yellow slime on it, wash the meat in fresh water and rub it with a dishcloth dipped in half-vinegar, half-fresh water. Pat the meat dry, and, if it is fresh smelling, cook it within twelve hours. If the meat itself takes on a green hue, discard it.

Trichinosis bacteria die at 140°F. This is the same temperature as the middle of a rare piece of beef. So as long as you cook any pork products until the meat is white throughout, this disease is no problem.

Beef (see fig. 2) lasts longer on ice than pork does. But it is far more difficult to get a piece that is sure to be tender enough to fry or barbeque. American and English cattle are usually grain fed and confined in pens for at least a month before they are slaughtered. Everywhere else, including Australia and New Zealand, cattle is range fed. So the meat tastes different. It has less fat and little marbling. I've come to really like the flavor and texture of Australian beef, which is what you find frozen in most parts of the Orient. But the uninitiated will notice the difference. Fresh beef from almost every other place we've been tends to be tough. Even the sirloin cuts can need forty minutes of stewing or twenty-four hours of marinading to make them tender. The only cut that is usually tender enough for frying is the fillet, the 2- to 2½-foot-long cigar-shaped strip of meat found inside the rib cage next to the backbone of the animal. Don't pay the price for fillet unless you've actually seen the butcher remove it from the ribs. Otherwise you might end up with a piece of extremely tough leg muscle that looks similar. Second choice would be the sirloin, which comes from the opposite side of

Whole carcasses of pork lie on the counter waiting for your order.

the rib bones and is halfway back from the shoulder of the animal where the saddle would sit. Anything else is bound to be stewing or grinding meat. Whenever possible, avoid buying leg meat unless you plan to cook it for a minimum of 1½ hours. Even if you grind leg meat, it can be springy and tough.

Almost any cut of beef other than leg meat can be used for ground or minced beef. If you are having the butcher grind it for you, make sure he doesn't put it through the grinder more than once. Otherwise it is finer than the hamburger North Americans are used to. Also, ask the butcher to add some fat. Hamburger patties will not hold together and will tend to be much too dry if they don't have at least 15 percent fat ground into them. The fat adds more flavor as well.

FIGURE 2

BEEF CHART

Wholesale and Retail Cuts

Numerals in circles ◯ refer to wholesale cuts and major subdivisions of such cuts. Letters refer to retail cuts.

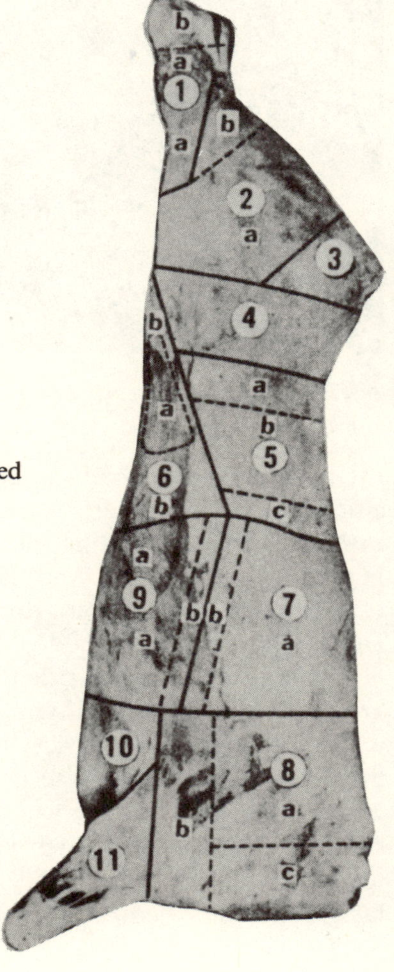

(1) HIND SHANK
- a. Soup bones
- b. Hock

(6) FLANK
- a. Flank steak
- b. Stew or ground beef

(9) PLATE
- a. Stew, ground beef, or boned and rolled pot roasts
- b. Short ribs

(10) BRISKET
Stew or boned and rolled pot roasts

(11) FORE SHANK
Soup bones or ground beef

② ROUND
a. Round steaks or roasts
b. Pot roast

③ RUMP
Roasts or steaks

④ LOIN END
Sirloin steaks or roasts

⑤ SHORT LOIN
a. Porterhouse steaks
b. T-bone steaks
c. Club or Delmonico steaks

⑦ RIB
a. Rib roasts or steaks
b. Short ribs

⑧ CHUCK
a. Chuck rib roasts or steaks
b. Arm pot roasts or steaks
c. Stew or ground beef

Section 4 and 5 are the most tender meat on range cattle. Anything cut from 1, 2, 8, 10, or 11 should be avoided

Hamburger or ground beef will not keep as long as whole pieces. I find regular beef keeps eight days on ice, ground beef only four or five. That is one of the reasons I recommend carrying a portable hand-operated meat grinder, which you can buy for less than twelve dollars in the United States.

Beef will turn a darker color as it ages, but is safe to eat as long as it smells good and has no green or mold on it. Cut off any green parts, and if the inside meat looks and smells good, use it. Beef liver and kidney also keep very well. Try to buy pieces that come from a young-looking animal.

Occasionally, even in countries that usually slaughter only old dairy cows for meat, you'll find a good young animal whose sirloin meat will be very tender. Look for a carcass with very white fat and marbling or white streaks in the sirloin meat. To age the meat yourself, wash any foreign matter off. Dry the meat, then place it in the ice chest on a cloth-covered tray or plate for four or five days, turning it over once a day. This will help tenderize the meat.

Horsemeat is sold in many European markets, usually in a completely separate area from more common meats. The flesh is a deeper red than beef and has almost no fat at all. When cooked, it's much drier but tastes almost like beef. I haven't personally had much experience with horsemeat but did once purchase some by accident. It made a tasty but dry meat loaf.

Lamb (see fig. 3) and goat both look the same once they are cut up. They often taste the same. Only the rib chops are sure to be tender enough for grilling or frying. Once again try to get the chops that are near the saddle of the animal. Marinading other cuts in a mixture of half-oil, one-quarter vinegar, one-quarter white wine plus any spices you prefer for twelve to twenty-four hours in the icebox will make the tougher cuts tender for shish kebob. Otherwise stew them at least thirty-five to forty minutes. Ground lamb or goat is just as usable as ground beef.

FIGURE 3

LAMB CHART

Numerals in circles ◯ refer to wholesale cuts. Letters refer to retail cuts.

WHOLESALE CUTS

①②and⑥ HIND SADDLE
- 1 Leg
- 2 Loin
- 6 Flank

③④and⑤ FORE SADDLE
- 3 Hotel Rack
- 4 Chuck
- 5 Breast

RETAIL CUTS

① LEG
- a. Roast
- b. Chops or roast

② LOIN
Loin and kidney chops

⑥ FLANK
Stew

③ RIB
Rib chops or roast

④ SHOULDER
- a. Roast or chops
- b. Neck slices or stew

⑤ BREAST
Stew

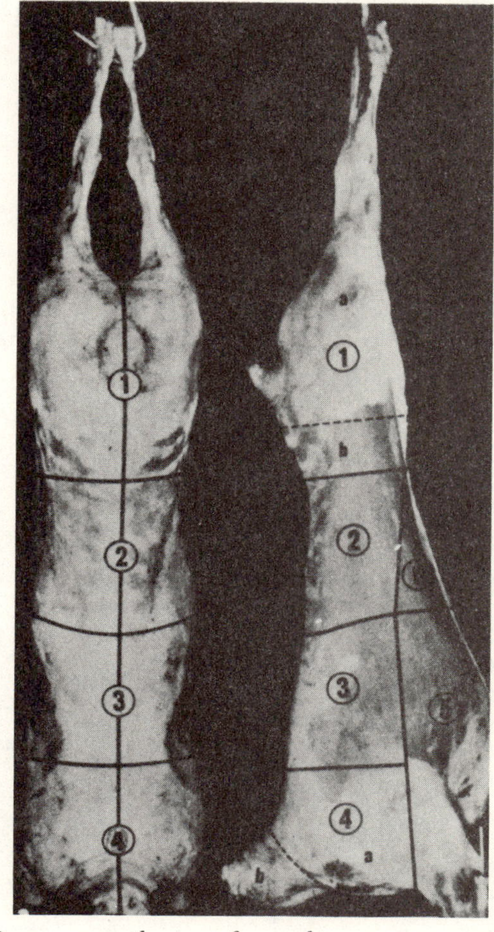

I would prefer cuts from section 2, 3, or the top of 1 as these tend to be less fatty.

Although several countries now sell frying chickens already cut and frozen, you'll find live chickens are normally slaughtered to your order. A chicken that weighs over five pounds live is probably too tough to fry. A live chicken loses a third of its weight when it is plucked and cleaned. They are sold with head and feet intact, since many foreign recipes use these for soups and gravies. If you buy a frozen chicken that is locally grown, don't be surprised to pull out the head and feet along with the liver and gizzards.

If you are buying a ready-plucked chicken, don't be put off by the yellow color of the skin. This comes from different feeding methods. Test the chicken for tenderness by pressing on the end of the breastbone nearest the neck. If it is as flexible as the end of your nose or only a bit firmer, the chicken is young and probably just what you want. If the end of the breastbone is tough, plan on using the meat for stewing, boiling, or slow baking.

Day 6 Where you do find chickens already slaughtered, they'll usually come with their heads and feet still on.

Unless you want small unidentifiable chunks of chicken, learn to section birds yourself. You'll need a good chopping board and a very sharp, thick-bladed knife plus only one or two birds worth of practice. I learned this after I watched in amazement as a Mexican butcher took his hatchet to my chicken and before I could say a word handed me twenty-five or thirty inch-and-a-half chunks when I had planned a southern fry. Chicken rinsed and dried keeps for five or six days on ice.

Cooking sausages in many countries are not seasoned the same as the ones at home, so taste the local ones before you invest heavily. On the other hand, you'll discover many delicious smoked and cooked sausages as you travel. These keep well without refrigeration for up to two months. Hang them in any airy place; if mold starts to grow, wipe the sausage with a rag dipped in half-vinegar, half-fresh water, then let them dry. When we sailed from Poland we had forty pounds of smoked sausage hung in our chain locker. We ate the last in England two months later. On a delivery from Spain we carried thirty pounds of chorizo blanco and ten pounds of chorizo rojo, two types of tasty garlic sausage. They made great snacks, sliced thin and served on crackers. Cut in chunks the sausages added spice to stews and rice dishes. The last piece made a tasty soup sixty days later as we approached the United States. When shopping for sausages, just indicate you want a small sample. Almost any vendor will slice off a small piece for a serious-looking customer.

Sides of smoked bacon are a wonderful addition to an offshore crew's diet. We've bought complete sides, drilled a hole through one corner, and hung them from the beams in the chain locker for four weeks at a time. When mold formed on the outside, we left it until the time came to slice pieces to cook. A vinegar-and-water scrubbing removed the mold. The bacon was great fried, grilled, or added to mixed dishes.

If you don't have room to hang bacon or sausages, dip a rag in vinegar, let it dry, then wrap the meat so it is covered completely. Wrap the resulting package in newspaper and store it in a cool, airy place.

One final word on buying meat and sausages in foreign ports. Few people inthe world can afford to buy large pieces of meat like North Americans do. In most underdeveloped countries, meat is used as a seasoning to be added to rice or beans or as in Mexico to be wrapped inside tortillas. So don't be surprised when you find most meat cut up into tiny chunks, or chops and steaks sliced three-eighths inches thick. With patience and lots of sign language you can persuade the butcher to cut your chops three-fourths inches thick, or to leave on some of the fat when he trims your steaks.

When you are stocking up for a passage, overbuy on meat just a bit. I find we rarely catch fish the first few days at sea, so we welcome the fresh meat for our main meals. The life of excess meat can be extended three days beyond its normal limit or three days beyond the life of your ice. Just cook up any meat you have left and leave it in a pot on top of the stove. Reheat it each morning until the liquid in the pot comes to a full boil, simmer two minutes, and cover tightly. Then let the closed pot of meat sit until the next day. Even hamburger will last for three days without refrigeration. Fourteen or sixteen days after you leave port, the crew will be pleased to be served an Irish stew or spaghetti bolognese that tastes just like the fresh food on shore.

Day 7 Sorting out the various fruits and vegetables only takes a few minutes every other day.

Day 7

noon to noon 40 miles, miles to date 454

light breeze from the south clear—slight surge from the south

afternoon—beam reaching with eight or ten knots of wind

Breakfast—biscuits
cheese
jam
coffee and tea
Lunch—fresh rye bread
ham slices

tomatoes
hot leftover soup
Dinner—tossed salad with the last of our lettuce,
tomatoes onion, shrimp, and cucumber in
Lin's special dressing
pork chunks in wine sauce
rice (cooked up extra to use tomorrow)
white wine

SPECIAL DRESSING

Mix together remains of broken egg (about ½ of scrambled raw egg)

2 tbs. salad oil
1 tbs. vinegar
1 tbs. parmesan cheese
1 tsp. worcestershire sauce
½ tsp. garlic powder
½ tsp. oregano

Let sit 10 minutes before using.

PORK CHUNKS IN WINE SAUCE

Sauté ½ pound pork chunks
1 tsp. slivered ginger (fresh)
in 1 tsp. oil
Add ½ cup white wine
1 tbs. soy sauce

Simmer for 10 minutes.
Thicken sauce with a bit of cornstarch.
Bring to a boil, then add 1 onion, sliced 1 green pepper, sliced
Cover and remove from heat.
Let sit for 5 minutes, then serve over rice. (Onions and peppers should still be crisp.)

I HAD TO THROW OUT ONE canteloupe-style melon today. I didn't think they'd last too well. I should have invested in a thicker-skinned melon like watermelons. I've had three-pound watermelons last up to four weeks at a time in hot climates like the Red Sea in August.

We've been having very light winds since we left Yokohama. To date we've only covered 454 miles in six days. Being a worrywart at times like these, I began to do some arithmetic. If we continued at the same rate, we'd average seventy-six miles a day, and it would take fifty-two days more to get to Canada. Then I began to wonder if I had enough food. Looking back at our worst passage ever, the time we drifted painfully across the Arabian Sea at an average speed of sixty-two miles a day, taking thirty-two days to cover 2,200 miles, I realize my fears are unfounded. Even if we do take fifty-two days more, there is lots of food. The variety might not be too inspired by the time we get there, but we'll keep right on eating.

Just before noon the winds freshened, and we started making five knots through the water. There is a three-quarter-knot current with us. Now I'm dreaming of 120 miles a day; if we can do that it means only thirty-one days to go.

We ate lunch in the warm, steady cockpit. The fresh, hot bread smelled delicious and tasted even better spread with well-salted Australian butter. Two Japanese fish boats passed us while we ate. Seagulls glided over the sparkling swells, diving for any crumbs we threw them. All is right with my world.

CHOOSING AND KEEPING FRESH FRUIT AND VEGETABLES FOR A LONG PASSAGE

The following list of fruits and vegetables is based on my observations and actual experiences both in far northern waters and in the deep tropics. The climate you will be sailing in and the water temperature surrounding your hull will affect the longevity of your produce. Buying direct from the farmer or produce supplier is far better than buying from a supermarket. It is well worth having a chat with the farmer or produce supplier before you buy; he usually knows which vegetables last longest on his shelves. I know that every time I went to the trouble of doing this, I not only ended up with better fruit and vegetables but learned new tips on how to

There were hundreds of fruits that were new to us in the Oriental markets.

keep them. Everyone loves to be asked questions about his profession, and the farmer or supplier you will be dealing with is no exception.

Whatever you do, don't buy from ship chandlers if you can avoid it. First, they think you are like a big ship and have a refrigerator or cold room to store your produce in. Second, they do not handle produce nearly as careful as the retail man, since most ships are only keeping produce for two or three weeks between ports.

Mike Greenwald in his excellent book, *The Cruising Chef,* recommends soaking all fruit and vegetables in a light solution of chlorine bleach and water to kill skin bacteria, then drying each piece before you store anything away. Although this works well in the temperate climates of the Mediterranean and North Atlantic, I don't recommend it for tropical voyages. If any vegetable is not absolutely dry before you

These ladies sold completely peeled pineapples in the market at Ipoh, Malaysia, for only four cents extra.

store it away, decay will set in even sooner than if you hadn't dipped the produce. The other problem with this method is that it is time-consuming just when you are busiest, the day before you set sail.

FRUITS

Apples

Green ones keep the best, red, hard varieties next, yellow least well. Buy small apples without any bruises. Wrap each one in tissue and store in a dark place. They will keep up to eight weeks if they aren't jostled. Check them over every week, cut off bruised spots, rub the spot with lemon juice. Use the bruised ones first.

Oranges

Thick-skinned varieties keep best. Keep them in a cool, dark place with lots of air. Check every three days. They keep well for twenty to twenty-five days.

Tangerines

Great if you can get them. Last better than oranges. Leave the stems on them if they come that way. Keep as cool and dark as possible, but give them lots of air. Good for twenty-five to thirty days. Be sure and inspect every three or four days and toss out bad ones.

Melons

Canteloupe, honeydew, and mush types are only good for six or ten days. Check them carefully for bruises, keep them in a cool place.

Watermelons

The thick-skinned, red-fleshed variety keeps for up to a month if bought carefully. They ripen slowly. Buy the smallest ones you can. In the Far East, two-pound watermelons are readily available. They are perfect for two people at one sitting. Ripe watermelons sound hollow when you tap them with a knuckle. Store watermelons in a place with lots of air where they can't roll around. I kept four in the chain locker on top of some newspapers when we sailed from South Yemen in September 1977. We ate the last one twenty-one days out. We cooled it by lowering it twenty feet over the side in a net bag. What a treat!

Peaches, pears, grapes

Too much trouble because they bruise so easily. I only buy enough for two or three days at the beginning of a voyage.

Lemons

Real lemons with thick skins should be bought slightly green, wrapped in aluminum foil, and stored in a cool, dark place. They last about twenty to twenty-five days that way.

Limes

Small, green hard ones kept in a basket and turned over every four or five days will last thirty to forty days and are good even when the skins go hard and brown.

Bananas

A cruising boat sailing off into the blue; stalks of green bananas hanging from the boom gallows—what a romantic sight. But the picture eight or ten days later has no romance at all. The crew is fed up with trying to eat the damn things before they go bad. Overripe bananas are falling off the stalk, making the after deck a danger zone at night. A stalk of bananas, containing usually up to 150 individual fruits, will all ripen within four or five days. Sunlight will hasten the process. It is better to buy individual hands of bananas from various stocks and set them in a dark, cool place below decks. Large, thick-skinned varieties ripen more slowly. Very dark green, hard bananas will keep for approximately fifteen days. Hang hands of bananas overboard for two minutes, then rinse well with fresh water before storing them away to avoid carrying spiders on board.

Plantains

These look just like bananas but aren't at all similar. I think they could better be classed as a vegetable, since they require cooking. Plantains require the same care as bananas, but they last twice as long. They can be cooked green, yellow, or overripe looking black. I've kept plantains for thirty days and then fried them in slices for a sweet treat with cocktails.

Coconuts

These keep indefinitely but are bulky to store. The meat and milk taste great thirty days out.

Pineapples

I've had no luck keeping pineapples on board for more than six days without refrigeration. The same goes for mangoes, papaya, and starfruit.

Limes keep wonderfully just stored in a basket. Great for cool drinks at sea.

Mamones (Rambutan)

These delightful tropical treats will keep for ten to fifteen days if stored in a dark, dry place. They are both the same fruit. One has a red, hairy-looking skin, the other a smooth, green skin. They are similar to lychee and taste just like grapes when fresh. Store them right on the branch they come on. Lay them in a basket or hang them in bunches. Once the skins become tough (eight or nine days), split them open with a knife instead of with your thumbnail.

VEGETABLES FOR THE OFFSHORE PASSAGE

Lettuce

Tightly packed iceberg and romaine lettuce purchased with as many outside leaves still intact as possible, then stored in a very open place wrapped in newspaper, will sometimes keep up to ten days. In the tropics, six days is usually the limit.

Cabbages

Buy these fresh from the farmer's field if you can. Preferably buy on a dry day, as moisture inside the cabbage from a recent rainfall will cause it to decay faster. Have the stems left as long as possible, and keep all of the outer leaves intact. Store so that cabbages are not touching each other. Check every three days and remove any mildewing or rotting leaves, but don't remove leaves that are getting dry. Cut one-eighth inch off the bottom of the stem if it is black or soft. I have kept cabbages as long as thirty-five days. They last better in hot, dry climates than in cold, damp ones. If the cabbage becomes dry, steam the leaves for half a minute to restore moisture, then cool to use in salads.

Onions

Dry yellow or purple onions should be squeezed before buying. If they are solid feeling in all directions (test both longitudinally and latitudinally), they should keep for two months or more. Store them in a dry, dark place. I use a plastic shopping basket to keep mine. Buy more than you think you need; they may be the only fresh vegetable you have toward the end of a long voyage. Check every week.

Potatoes

New potatoes keep best. Try to buy completely round ones. The irregular ones rot faster. Keep completely dry and in a dark place. Inspect once a week. Good for two months.

Tomatoes

The longest we've ever had tomatoes keep on board without refrigeration is twenty-four days. We purchased them through Jurgenson's grocery store in San Diego, a specialist who used to outfit sport-fishing boats bound for Mexico. They sent us a carefully packed crate of very round tomatoes which ranged in color from extremely green to ripe and red, with the greenest on the bottom of the crate. Each tomato was wrapped in tissue paper and fitted securely in the box so it couldn't roll around.

Carrots

In the tropics, carrots go limp in about eight days. In northern climates they stay crisp for two weeks and usable for about three. Select large carrots. Keep dry and well aired. Check every three or four days and remove any spots that are going black.

Squash

Butternut, acorn, pumpkin, and other hard squashes are great. They need no special care other than a secure place to stay so they don't break. Buy small squash, ones you can use up at one or two meals; once you cut into them, they rarely last for more than four days. Squash has kept on *Seraffyn* for up to seven weeks.

Turnips

Good for four weeks if kept in a cool, dry place.

Yams

Buy solid, regular shaped ones. These last as long as potatoes with the same kind of care.

Cucumbers

Buy very dark green ones. Keep them out of the direct sunlight and turn every four days. Use any that feel soft right away. (They can be preserved in any pickling mixture such as one part vinegar, one part oil). Good for twelve to fourteen days in the tropics, longer up north.

Green peppers

Keep cool, avoid bruising. In the tropics they last eight to ten days. Up north, twenty days. They may dry out a bit, but their flavor perks up most cooked mixed dishes.

Bean sprouts

These can be great fun. I've personally only used mung beans, which I sprout in bread tins in the oven. They take four days to mature and are good added to salads and Chinese-style cooked dishes.

Brussels sprouts, cauliflower, green beans, and asparagus

These vegetables don't keep well, so enjoy them in port or on the first few days at sea.

Jicama

Just like turnips, it will keep up to a month if kept dry. This is a Mexican root vegetable that tastes like sweet carrots. Great raw or cooked.

Plantano (Plantain)

See fruit section.

Checking and turning vegetables and fruit may sound like a tedious job, but in reality it only takes about ten minutes a day, and at the same time you can be choosing the vegetables you plan to use for the next few meals. Even when I was feeding a crew of seven on a fishing trawler offshore for twenty-eight days, caring for our produce took less than twenty minutes a day on the average.

My general philosophy on buying fruits and vegetables is that it's better to carry too many and throw away a few if necessary. Fresh produce is much less expensive than canned. If it is ripening faster than you'd hoped, you can often find ways of using it for snacks.

Day 8

noon to noon 108 miles, miles to date 562

beam reaching, sunny and warm

Breakfast—orange juice
bread, peanut butter, and jam
cheese
coffee and tea
Lunch—soup
shrimp salad on cabbage leaves
apple
Dinner—garlic and onion omelet
grilled tomatoes

rice salad
white wine

RICE SALAD

1 cup leftover white rice
1/2 small onion chopped
1/2 green pepper chopped
1/4 cucumber diced
3 tbs. mayonnaise
2 tbs. vinegar
1 tsp. sugar
1/2 tsp. garlic
1/2 tsp. MSG
1/2 tsp. dill weed

Mix well and let sit one hour in a cool place before serving.

THIS MORNING LARRY HAD TO ADD five gallons of water to our header tank. That means we've used about eight gallons so far, not bad. We've got sixty gallons more on board and only 4,000 miles left to go.

We ran out of ice, and at noon I cleaned out the icebox and wiped it down with bleach so that it wouldn't take on any odors. Normally our ice lasts ten to fourteen days, but the price of meat was so high in Japan that I only bought enough to last a week. Then I bought forty pounds of plain ice and twenty-five pounds of dry ice instead of the usual fifty and fifty. After ten years of cruising on *Seraffyn,* I'm still sold on an icebox. (See discussion of refrigeration that follows.)

Well, from now on it's sea cooking. No more fresh meat. We're moving well, the sailing is unbelievably smooth, sky is clear, Canada doesn't seem too far away.

Just before dinnertime the wind freshened, the seas built up on the quarter, our speed was up to almost six knots, and the motion was definitely getting uncomfortable. Larry suggested I hold dinner for a few minutes, and together we took down the nylon drifter and set the smaller number-two genoa in its place. Cooking and eating was more pleasant. That is one of the big differences between cooking on a cruising boat and cooking on a race boat. No racing skipper would give up a half-knot of speed just to gain a bit of comfort.

In spite of changing sails, the building seas created more motion than we'd had the past seven days. Tomatoes slid off the plates, my omelet tried to crawl over the edge of the pan. Larry put a damp towel on the table before I set dinner out, and we used coffee mugs for our wine instead of our pewter goblets.

TO ICE OR NOT TO ICE

Refrigeration on board a cruising boat is one more subject on which opinions reach from extreme to extreme. The average English sailing person, used to shopping daily and a climate where the idea is to keep as warm as possible, looks on any form of refrigeration as a nuisance, a waste of time and space. The average American, pampered by freezer foods, can't imagine living without at least a small deep freeze. Somewhere in the middle lies the long-distance cruiser, who spends much of his time in the tropics where fresh food spoils in a day if it isn't kept cool.

I was chatting with an English couple who had just started cruising on board a thirty-five-footer and were wintering near us in the Mediterranean. The husband asked, "Is an ice chest really worth the bother, doesn't it just take up good storage space?" Larry answered, "Lin only has to go shopping once a week if she has ice, and if someone asks us to join them for dinner, the food we have on board can keep until the next night. Most important, fresh food costs less than canned and is certainly more interesting. If you do run out of ice, that box can still be used for storage." His answers must have impressed them because they were building an ice chest the last time we saw them.

On the other hand, Larry and I were lounging comfortably under our sun awning in La Paz, Mexico, about nine years ago when the launch off a luxurious fifty-foot cruiser approached. "Do you like roast lamb?" the owner asked. "Who doesn't," we replied. He handed us a semifrozen leg of lamb and explained, "My freezer broke down two days ago, and we can't use up 200 pounds of thawing meat, so I'm giving it away." That was only the first time we were on the receiving end when someone's freezer gave out. It happened again in Acapulco, Panama, Gibraltar, and the Suez Canal. We were told about the crew on *Windward Passage* threatening to mutiny when their freezer gave out three days after the start of the Bermuda to Spain transatlantic race.

Like everything else on board a long-distance sailing yacht, your food-cooling system should be extremely reliable and simple to repair. We were having dinner with a couple who had just taken delivery of a thirty-five-footer last month. They were moving on board, and the wife looked at us in exasperation and stated, "I've had refrigerators in my house all my life. Not one has ever given any trouble. What is so special about a refrigerator on a boat?" Larry answered, "On shore the electricity company makes sure the power gets to your house at a constant and steady voltage. The electricity company stores the power for you when you don't need it. The community household wiring codes assure your electrical system is properly installed, and finally, there must have been 30 to 40 million household refrigerators built in the past few years; that is enough to make sure all of the bugs are worked out. Compare that to the refrigeration unit on a sailboat. *You* personally have to convert the power to run your refrigerator. *You* have to store it in your own batteries or run your compressor twice a day. *You* have to be sure power is available on demand. *You* have to wire it all up or be sure that the shipyard does it correctly. And there are few companies that have built more than 1,000 refrigeration units of the same model for sailing boats. Most have probably built fewer than 100 of the same type in the past year. So the actual units aren't as well tried or as reliable. And finally, not one household refrigeration unit is asked to stand up to saltwater corrosion, constant motion, and unlevel working conditions. You'll have to face it, there are a lot of links in the chain that can break down and leave you with a freezer full of thawing meat. No fuel, water in the fuel lines, broken-down alternator, unreliable generator, broken compressor, freon leaks, all mean no refrigeration. When this happens *you* have to provide the servicing and repairs. There are few professional refrigeration mechanics in primitive places and almost none at all at sea."

That is why a properly insulated ice chest is our choice. It's easy to install and costs very little. With proper packing and careful use, we can keep food cold for ten or twelve days with eighty-five pounds of block ice. During the past ten years we've found ice available in every country except the Baltic and England, were there really wasn't much need for ice. It has been cheap to buy, from fifty cents to two dollars for 100 pounds. Figuring that at an average of a dollar every ten days, we spend about thirty-five dollars a year on ice. Materials for our box cost about thirty-five dollars, so our complete refrigeration bill for the past ten years hasn't been over $390.00, probably less. We have heard that ice is more costly in some parts of the Caribbean and Bahamas, but the cost of repairing your electrical or mechanical system would probably be extremely high in those places also. Since ice is used for fishing boats in most warm countries, it's usually just a pleasant row to the docks to ice up.

For long-distance ocean passages, we buy all frozen meats and bring them on board as late as possible. We ate our last lamb chops ten days out from Bermuda and had only five days on cans before we reached the Azores. Even when we can't get ice, the box is still useful. A frozen three-pound chicken will cool down a bottle of wine and be fresh and perfectly thawed three days after it is bought in most temperate climates. And because the lid seals well, fresh food and leftovers stored in the icebox will be safe from flying and crawling insects in tropical ports.

For those willing and able to have a bit more complicated system, one that requires more maintenance, the second most successful refrigeration unit is a top loading box with a holding plate and refrigeration unit run off a compressor on your engine. By using your engine to drive this compressor (most home builders use one off an automotive air-conditioning unit), you avoid the energy loss of converting mechanical power to electricity which is stored in a battery and then converted back to mechanical power to drive a compressor to cool your refrigerator. Your freezer holding plates can take up very little space, and with a properly insulated box you should only have to run your engine thirty minutes twice a day in the tropics. The only problem with this system is that you must be around the boat to start the main engine that drives your compressor. If you decide to go away from your boat on the spur of the moment to explore Madrid for four or five days, you have to arrange for someone to come on board twice a day to run your engine and protect your fresh or frozen food.

A final very good system we've heard about but never used or seen on board a boat is a kerosene-burning freezer unit with a gymballed burner. We have seen a nongymballed version of this system in use on an island in the southern

Caribbean. The owners had a box that kept 200 pounds of meat deep frozen on a pint of kerosene a day. The unit did create a lot of heat, which could be a nuisance in a galley. This is one system we are considering building into our next boat. We'd combine it with the ice chest described in the next pages. That way, if the kerosene freezer unit failed, we could simply use ice.

A butane refrigerator does not belong on a boat. Even if the burner has an emergency heat-activated shutoff, it is dangerous. I have seen these shutoff valves fail in household refrigerators. Consider that to meet the demands of a butane refrigerator you must leave your butane tank and lines open at all times. It is just a matter of time before your system develops a leak, or a gust of wind puts the pilot flame out. As opposed to stoves that don't have pilot lights and can be easily checked each time you use them, a butane refrigerator system is too dangerous to use on a boat.

Compressed natural gas may someday be the answer. This gas is lighter than air and dissipates easily. Unfortunately, it is only available in the United States. At present it is five times the cost. It is also inefficient to get the equivalent amount of fuel as butane requires six times the number of tanks. But the gas systems people, promotors of CNG, say that there are improvements on the way.

No matter what type of refrigeration you choose, the design and insulation of the food box will determine how well your unit works. The following article, which Larry wrote for *Boating* magazine, *Seacraft,* and *Practical Boat Owner,* describes how to build and insulate your own.

HOLD THAT COLD!

When I asked, "What is the best way to build an ice chest?" everyone I spoke to said, "Ask Vic Berry." Vic's sheet-metal shop in Newport Beach, California, had made hundreds of the stainless steel liners for ice chests, refrigerators, and deep freezers on local yachts and also on the sport-fishing boats that went south to Cabo San Lucas, Mexico, for marlin. Vic told me how he had made deck freezers for some of these sport-fishing boats that could hold the cold so well that the compressors would only run for twenty to thirty minutes a day, even though these freezers were sitting out in the Mexican sun.

Vic said, "The trick is the design and insulation of the chest, whether you use ice or a compressor." He told me the chest should first and foremost be top opening. A front-opening design just pours all of the cold on your feet and rarely seals perfectly—the cold leaks out all day long, melting your ice or causing your compressor to work overtime. Even with a top-loading chest, the cold will seep out if the lid doesn't have a good, airtight seal. A top-loading chest is definitely safer at sea. Unlike the side-opening box, things can't come sliding out just because you are on an unfavorable tack.

Your chest can be built with a complete top-opening lid, with or without a wedged access plug, or a combination of both as shown in Figure 4. The combination is best for large freezers or ice chests as it makes cleaning and storing big items like blocks of ice easier, while the smaller plug for everyday access allows less cold to escape each time you go for a drink. The complete lid should have good seals with firm latches so you can't feel any cold escaping when you put your hand at the lid to box joint. The wedged plug should also be well sealed with two or three soft, compressible gaskets.

FIGURE 4

FREEZER OR ICEBOX WITH COMPLETE REMOVABLE LID AND ACCESS PLUG

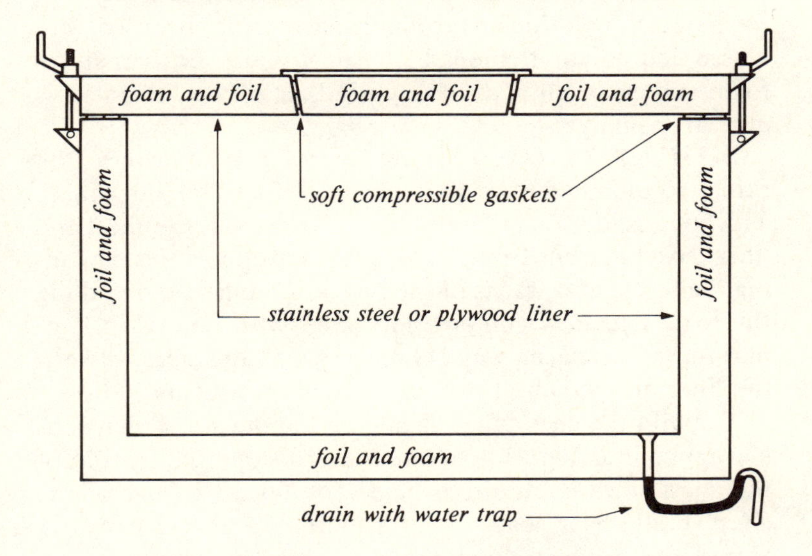

A good-sized drain (three-eighths of an inch inside diameter minimum) with a screen to catch food particles is essential. It will allow you to wash the chest and drain off ice water easily. A water trap or valve in the drain will stop cold air from leaking away into the bilge (fig. 4). The water from the ice chest shouldn't be allowed to drain into the bilge at any rate as it will soon cause odors and, in wooden hulls, rot. On *Seraffyn* we drain the water from our ice chest into a bucket, then use it to chill our wine, champagne, or bottled drinks.

Vic went on to say, "Next to top opening, the most important thing is the thickness and type of insulation you use." He recommended several layers of half-inch-thick closed cell polyurethane sheet foam with ordinary household aluminum foil between each layer. First a layer of foil shiny side to the outside of the chest, then a half-inch layer of foam, another layer of foil, foam, foil until you have a three-to-four-inch insulation barrier. The shiny side of the foil tends to reflect the initial heat and creates a barrier between each layer of foam. Half-inch-thick styrofoam sheets can be used, but closed cell polyurethane is better as it is denser than styrofoam and each cell holds a tiny dead-air pocket. Dead air is a great insulator.

In his book *The Ocean Sailing Yacht* (W.W. Norton), Don Street recommends two part Freon II foam for insulation. This sounds like a lot of hassle. Don warns that the chest and liner have to be built extra strong just to support the expanding foam. He also warns of the physical dangers of handling the toxic chemical combination. And with poured-in two-part foam, there is no way of knowing if all the areas between the liner and ice chest are properly filled with insulation.

To build the chest, first decide on the outside dimensions and make it as big as possible. Plan to slope the bottom of the chest toward the drain hole. The lowest corner of the chest should have space under it to fit a water trap or valve. Now build a quarter-inch-thick plywood outer chest. This chest should be capable of holding water. Use 3/4″ × 3/4″ corner pieces fastened with screws and glue to achieve this, or use a simpler method—fastening the corners of the plywood chest with copper wire and sealing each joint inside and out with two-inch-wide fiberglass tape.

Use glue to secure the first layer of foil to the plywood chest, then cut the half-inch sheet of foam slightly oversized and jam it snugly against the sides. A handsaw and plane will shape the foam easily. Repeat this layer of foil, layer of foam until you have the desired insulation thickness.

Vic used eight layers of half-inch polyurethane foam with foil between each layer to get four inches of insulation on his Mexican deep freezers. You can use as little as two inches of

FIGURE 5

ASSEMBLING THE GLASS-LINED CHEST

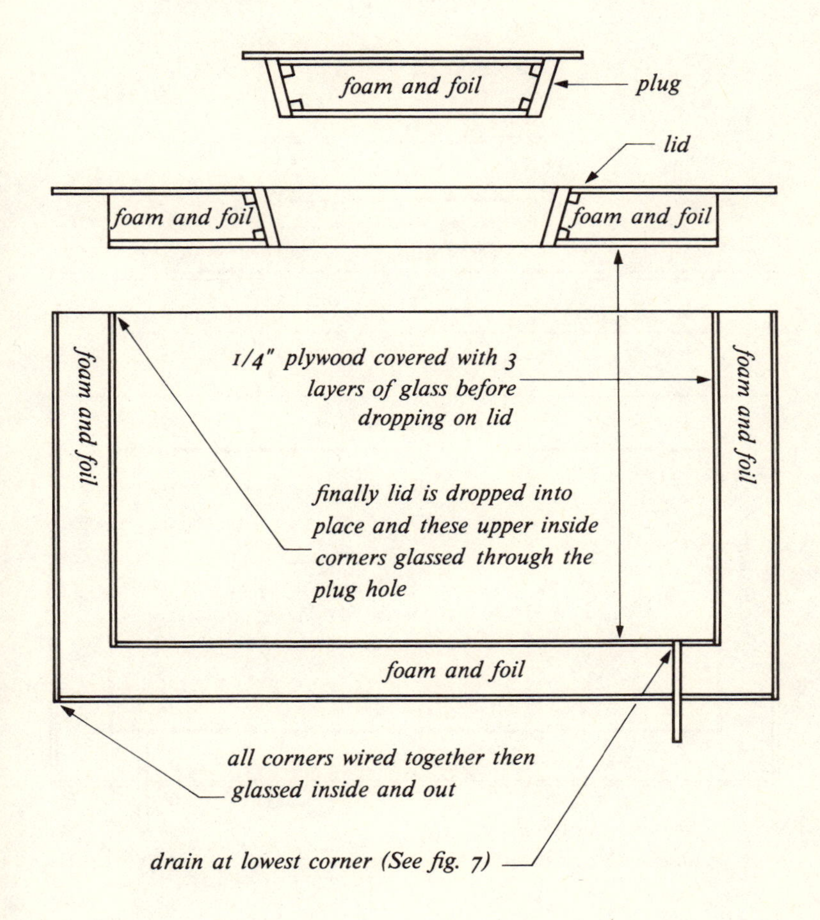

FIGURE 6

ASSEMBLING THE STAINLESS STEEL LINED CHEST

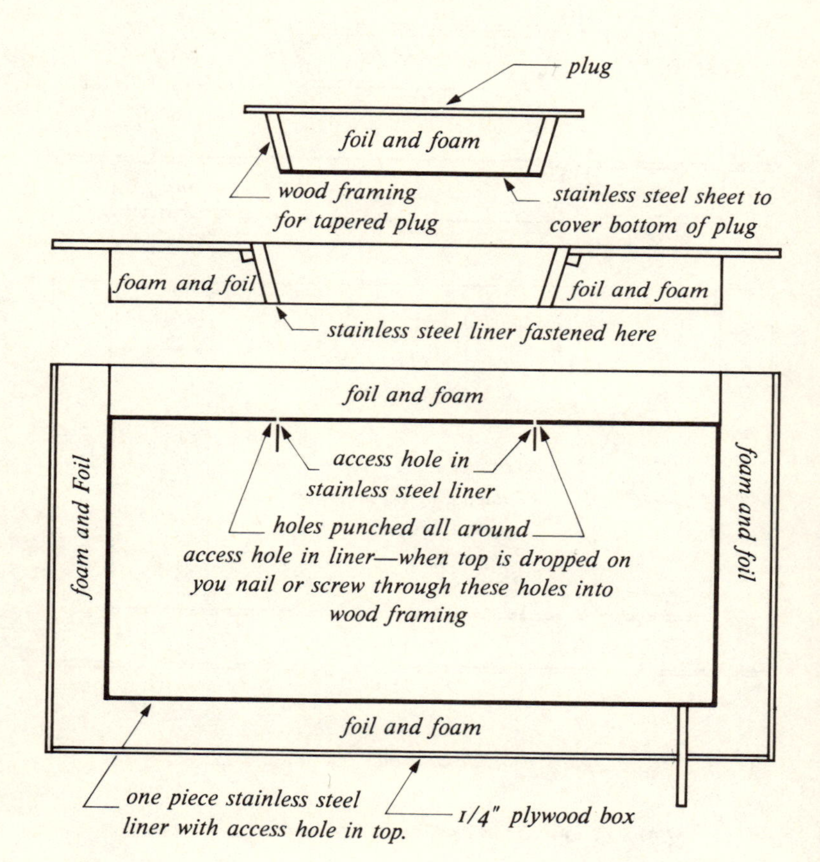

FIGURE 7

MOLDING A DRAIN FOR A GLASS LINER

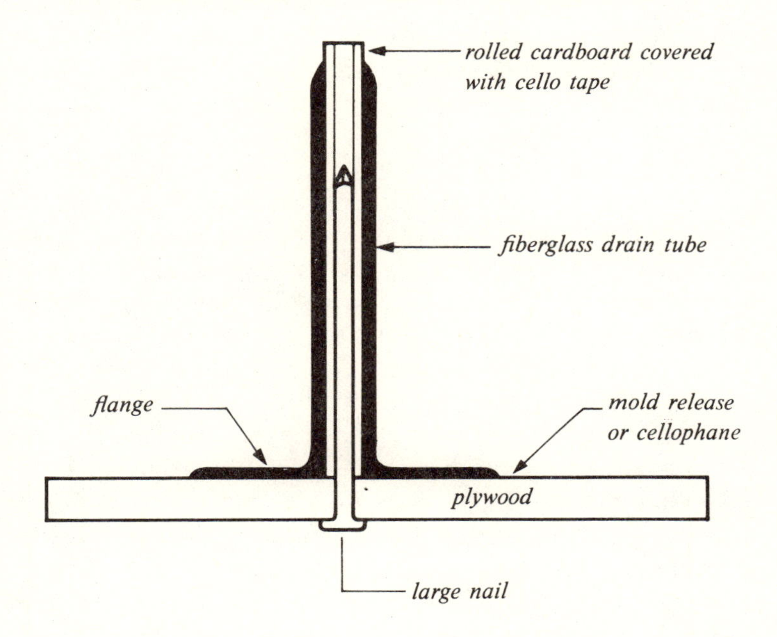

foam and foil for refrigerators, and this is usually enough, but the cold holding efficiency will drop proportionally.

The chest liner comes next. To fit a professional-looking stainless steel one, you'll have to make an accurate pattern that suits the inside dimensions of your insulation. A cheaper liner for the home builder is quarter-inch plywood fitted to the inside of the insulation and wired together at the corners. After the plywood is wired and the corners glassed with tape, drill a hole at the lowest corner of the chest through the liner, insulation, and outer chest. Make a mold for a fiberglass drain tube by rolling thin cardboard into the desired shape and size, then covering it with cellophane tape, as illustrated in Figure 7. Fiberglass around this mold and form a flange at one end. When the glass tube is set up, the cardboard mold can be removed by soaking it in water. Fit the tube into the drain-hole position in the chest, then glass the whole inside of the chest, bonding the flange to the bottom layers of glass. If you choose a stainless steel liner, have a drainpipe connection soldered to the liner by your sheet-metal man. The pipe should be long enough to extend through the bottom of the insulated chest so you can clamp a plastic drain hose to it.

The liner for your chest should be strong and slightly flexible. If it is glass, it should have three layers of heavy cloth and resin. Otherwise, when you drop ice or heavy frozen food into the box it could crack the liner, and polluted water will leak into your insulation and foul it. I would use epoxy resin for this job, as it is more flexible and less likely to crack than polyester resin.

When all the cloth is bonded in, sand the inside of the chest smooth and paint on a flow coat of finishing resin to give a smooth, odorless, easy-to-clean interior surface. Then fit the top and glass the upper corners. Whatever type of top you decide to use, it must be as well insulated as the sides and bottom.

In addition to being easier for the home builder, a plywood and glass liner has other advantages over the stainless steel one. It is simple to screw wooden supports on the inside for sliding food trays. It's also easier to drill and seal snug, airtight holes for refrigeration pipes.

Proper placement and usage of your cold chest or freezer can help hold the cold. If you want a deck or cockpit freezer chest, paint it white to reflect the sun's heat better; if the chest is located below, try not to position it next to the stove, heater, or engine. If possible, place it below your load waterline, where the boat is kept cooler by sea water. On long passages plan your meals so that you open the lid to your chest only one or two times a day. With an ice chest, use the drain water to cool beer, soda, or wine so the guests don't open the main ice chest every time they want a cool drink. Don't leave the melted water standing in the bottom of your chest in a seaway—it will melt your ice faster. If you have spare room in your compressor-driven refrigeration box, fill it with blocks of ice. This will help keep the temperatures down. For safety, if you have a deep freeze, carry extra nonfrozen stores in case your unit quits working.

The ice chest on *Seraffyn* is ten years old and has one of Vic Berry's stainless steel liners, a double seal on the plug, and only two inches of foil and foam insulation. I could have lengthened the life of our ice greatly if we'd had room for four inches of insulation, but *Sereffyn* is only a twenty-four-footer. With seventy-five pounds of ice we can have fresh food and cold drinks for ten days in the tropics—not bad for a home-built ice chest.

Day 9

noon to noon 106 miles, miles to date 668

sunny and warm, reaching in seven or eight knots of wind, seas very calm

Lunch—tuna salad sandwiches
leftover rice salad
soft drinks
Dinner—spaghetti bolognese
red wine, camembert cheese
canned peaches

TUNA SALAD

1 can of tuna, drained and flaked
1/2 onion chopped

2 heaping tbs. pickle relish
1 tsp. vinegar
3 tbs. mayonnaise

Mix well and let sit for a while before serving.

SPAGHETTI BOLOGNESE SAUCE

Place the following in a deep saucepan:

3 Very large tomatoes (pulp and seeds only)
10 crushed garlic cloves
1 chopped onion
3 tbs. sugar
2 tsp. oregano
1 tsp. marjoram

Simmer slowly for 30 minutes, stirring occasionally.

Add can of corned beef, break the meat up into small chunks, stir well and serve over noodles with parmesan cheese sprinkled on top.

MEAL SCHEDULES AND DIVISION OF LABOR

This afternoon I found some tomatoes that had been split because they rolled out of their basket. I used them up to make spaghetti, a real at-sea favorite for us. I love spaghetti; Larry loves the chili and beans I make with the extra sauce. If we have ground beef we use that instead, but the corned beef tastes almost as good. When I'm not trying to use up overripe or bruised tomatoes, I use a can of peeled tomatoes plus a can of tomato paste for this recipe.

After I cleared up dinner dishes I put a cup of dried beans in fresh water to soak for tomorrow. I really prefer canned beans not only because they are already soft and ready to use but because they don't take extra fresh water to prepare. You can't soak or boil dried beans in salt water—their skins stay tough. So to prepare three cups of beans takes a quart and a half of fresh water plus a cup of dried beans. But I couldn't buy any type of canned beans in Japan for under two dollars a can, and dried pinto and brown beans only cost fifty cents a package and yield as much as four cans of beans would have.

As you may have noticed, Larry and I don't have any formal breakfast at sea. There are several reasons for this. When we are making a passage on board *Seraffyn* there are just the two of us. We always stand night watches of three hours on, three hours off, usually starting about 2000 hours. Larry sleeps the first three hours, so his day starts at about 0500, while I sleep on until 0800 or 0900. Rather than wait for me to get up and feed him, he makes a snack for himself —coffee, bread and jam, a piece of fruit. He usually makes a cup of tea for me when he sees me stirring.

This casual breakfast works well for us since it eliminates one set of dishes and gives our mornings at sea a more leisurely schedule. The rest of the day's schedule goes like this: after the casual breakfast, Larry takes a morning sight and checks the rigging while I spend some time cleaning up the boat. Then, just after Larry takes his noon sight, I record the noon-to-noon run on our small-scale passage chart and enter it in our log, then serve lunch.

We have tea at about 1600 if neither of us feels like taking a nap. Then at 1730 or so we have cocktail hour, when we get together and practice the guitar, watch the birds fly by, or play our favorite tapes on the cassette stereo. This is an important part of each day, because, as surprising as it may sound, it may be the only time we really get to discuss our plans and schemes.

We eat dinner about 1830. Then Larry helps me wipe the dishes and goes on deck while I clean out the sink and galley. After a final check around, he brings the oil lamps in and I clean the chimneys as he fills and lights each one.

All of the cooking at sea on board *Seraffyn,* including

taking care of stores, baking, doing the dishes, and cleaning up the galley, rarely takes more than three hours of my time a day. On delivery trips when we hire crew, we serve a formal breakfast, lunch, tea with snacks, dinner, and snacks for the night watches. If there is no self-steering on the boat, meals have to be staggered, so cooking, cleaning, and so on takes five to six hours of my day even though one of the crewmen helps in the galley each day.

I stand no watches during the day if we have two extra crewmen on a delivery. At night I take the 2400 to 0200 watch, my favorite. This works well because it means each crewman gets six hours of sleep in an uninterrupted stretch, while I end up with a good four or five hours of uninterrupted rest before my watch and again before it's time to start breakfast. With only one extra crewman on shorter deliveries, I stand two two-hour watches, which means nine hours of my day are full. But these deliveries rarely last more than ten or fourteen days.

When we are at sea on *Seraffyn* Larry takes care of all of the navigation and most of the sail adjustments during the day while I do the cooking and care for the inside of the boat. At night we each take care of any sail trimming that is necessary during our own watch. If there is a sail change because the wind is dropping, we almost never wake the other person. But if the wind is increasing and a sail change means going out on the bowsprit, we usually wake the person who is off watch, just to be safe. The noise of my changing from big genoa to small genoa would wake Larry anyway.

This schedule seems to give both of us plenty of time for reading and doing any little tasks we want during the day. With the vane steering, the night watches are a great time for writing letters, reading, or doing projects like this one.

Day 10 The secret to successful egg storage is buying them correctly.

Day 10

noon to noon 68 miles, miles to date 736

very light winds, calm seas, cloudy

Lunch—chili and beans
bread and butter
soft drinks

Dinner—huevos rancheros (scrambled eggs topped with ranchero sauce)
bean salad
camembert cheese and saltines

CHILI AND BEANS

1 1/2 cups leftover bolognese sauce
1 1/2 cups boiled beans
1 1/2 tsp. chili powder
2 small green peppers, chopped

Simmer for 15 minutes, then serve in bowls.

BEAN SALAD

2 cups cooked beans (or canned if available)
1 small chopped onion
4 chopped garlic cloves
1/2 cup salad or olive oil
1/4 cup vinegar
1 tsp. sugar
1/2 tsp. oregano
1/2 tsp. dill
salt and pepper to taste

Mix and let sit at least 4 hours. To keep for periods longer than 2 days, put the bean salad in a clean jar until 3/4 ″ from the top. Add half-oil, half-vinegar until the jar is full. Put the lid on tightly and store upright. Will last 15 to 20 days and works great as an addition to any kind of salad.

RANCHERO SAUCE

2 tbs. butter
1 onion cut in strips
1 green pepper cut in strips
5 cloves of garlic
1 chopped whole tomato

1 tsp. sweet basil
1 tsp. lemon juice
1 tsp. worcestershire sauce
1/2 tsp. chili powder

Simmer together slowly for 15 minutes, then serve over scrambled or fried eggs.

In the morning while we did our morning chores, I boiled the beans that had been soaking since the night before. They took about thirty-five minutes to become tender. Half went into the bolognese sauce and half became bean salad, which I let soak for dinner. Then I checked the eggs and turned them over. Three of the eggs had cracks in their shells that hadn't been there three days before. A bit of investigation showed that those eggs were slightly larger than the rest, so they must have cracked when I closed the plastic cartons more securely. One of today's meals has to be eggs so that I can use the cracked ones up.

The last two days of light winds, with over 3,700 miles still to go, have been wearing on our nerves. Today was muggy, cloudy, and hot; our moods matched the gray color of the sea. I must admit that I'd have given anything for a restaurant to run to. Cooking dinner was the last thing I felt like doing. Paul Simon sang sad songs on the stereo. The mainsail slatted back and forth in the windless swell. I was nearly crying by the time dinner was over, and the idea of scrubbing up a sink full of pots had little appeal. Larry offered to wash them up on deck and rinse them overboard while I final-rinsed them in fresh water and wiped them below. A bunch of mother carey's chickens fluttered and chattered near our taffrail log spinner. The clouds turned crimson as the sun set, and Larry broke the gloomy spell of the day when he said, "We sure have small problems, we could be commuters fighting our way on to a train from Tokyo everyday."

ON PRESERVING EGGS

Every cruising cookbook will mention some way of preserving eggs for long voyages. I've personally heard of five basic ones; the choice depends on your pattern of thinking.

1. Grease each egg carefully and thoroughly with vaseline.
2. Paint each egg with sodium silicate (water glass).
3. Boil each egg ten seconds.
4. Deep freeze the eggs.
5. Turn the eggs over every two or three days.

The first three methods are slightly messy and consume time when you are busiest, preparing to leave port. Greasing must be carefully done as any void in the coating will allow the eggs to rot. Overboiling will cook the eggs so they are no good for cakes or baking, and you won't find this out until you actually break an egg open. These methods require no extra maintenance once you are at sea other than removing the Vaseline if you choose method 1. Neither Vaseline nor sodium silicate is dangerous to your health if a small amount should get into your food while you are breaking an egg.

Deep freezing works perfectly and is in fact how eggs are kept in many countries where they must be imported. You can tell an egg has been frozen by its pale yellow yolk. If your freezer fails and the eggs defrost at all, they'll start going bad in five or six days.

Turning the eggs is the method I always choose. All I have to do before we leave port is store the eggs away in regular egg cartons. Then at sea it's necessary to remember to turn each carton over three times a week. There is a chance of failure with this method. If the eggs aren't turned over because you forget, or because you are too seasick, they'll start to deteriorate. If they sit for a week without turning, they'll start to go bad after twenty-five days or so.

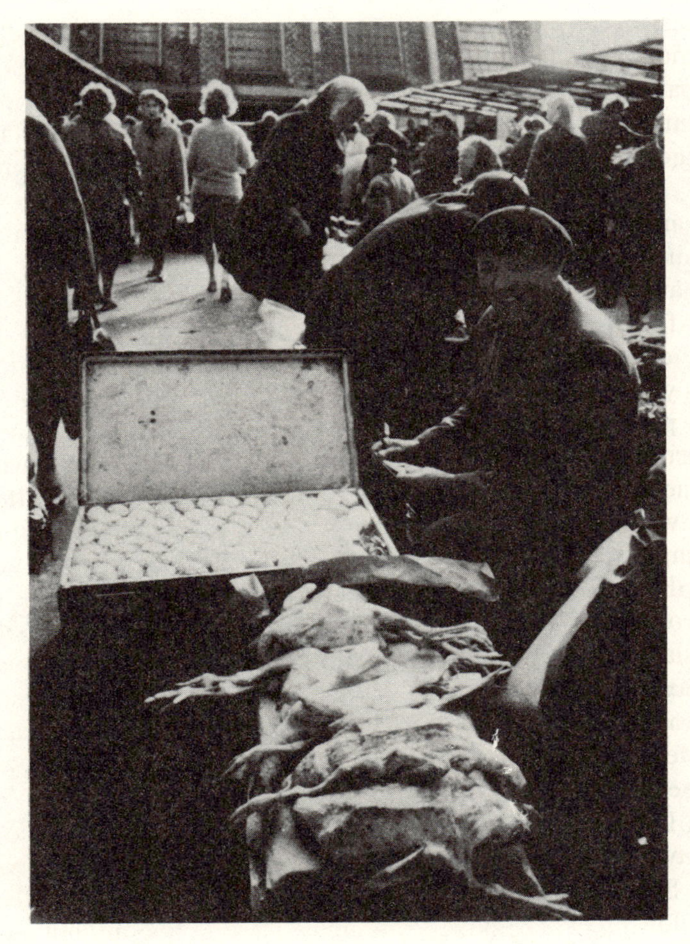

These eggs, bought in the Polish Peoples' market, had I'm sure never been refrigerated.

The reason all these methods work is that they keep air from entering the semiporous eggshell. When an egg is absolutely fresh, its shell is well coated inside by the clear egg fluid, and air can't get through. As it ages, the shell dries out inside where the air space sits, and then the shell becomes more porous. Vaseline and sodium silicate add an airtight barrier to the outside of the egg. A ten-second boil adds an internal barrier. Turning the eggs works the same—it keeps the whole inside of the shell moist.

Whichever method you choose, buy the freshest eggs you can find, ones that have never been refrigerated or kept in an air-conditioned room. Two- and three-day old eggs tend to have lumpy shells that are absolutely white and opaque. After five or six days of storage, even in refrigeration, the shells start to develop small, slightly gray spots, easily visible if you hold the egg up to a strong light. Supermarket eggs are a poor choice, first because they are usually bought from a central egg distributor and are at least three days old when they reach the store, and second because they are almost always transported in air-conditioned trucks. This is vitally important. A twenty-degree rise in temperature will drastically affect the keeping qualities of eggs. If you are sailing from a cold climate such as England, New England, or Canada, bound for the tropics, your eggs won't last much longer than twenty-five days. So buy just enough to last until you reach warmer waters such as Spain, Bermuda, Hawaii, or Mexico, then buy your egg supply. Going the other way, there is no problem.

Don't wash your eggs before you store them away. They have a natural protective covering, and it's water soluble.

Store your eggs in the coolest part of the boat, somewhere below the waterline if possible and close to the hull but away from the heat of the engine. Water temperature in the tropics rarely gets above seventy-six degrees, and eggs kept naturally at this temperature with no preserving methods at all last nicely for two or three weeks.

No matter how you keep your eggs, they will change slightly as they age. After twelve to twenty-five days, depending on the temperature of your storage locker, the yolks will become fragile and making sunnyside-up eggs will be a challenge. After twenty-five to thirty days, the eggs will only be good for scrambling, boiling, or baking. After thirty days, the whites of hard-boiled eggs may have a slightly yellow or brown tinge and the yolks will be pale in color. This doesn't change the eggs' cooking value nor does it affect the flavor. But if the egg is cracked, or has a dark appearance right through the shell, I wouldn't use it. I'd also suggest breaking each egg separately into a cup after fifteen days so that a bad egg won't spoil a whole cake mix or a ten-egg omelet.

The longest I've had eggs last by turning them over three times a week is three months. Then I ran out of eggs. Out of the 144 eggs I'd started with, 5 went bad, the first one twenty-five days out, the second after forty-five days. But either of these eggs could have had a small crack in their shells.

Don't throw away egg cartons. They might not be available in the next country you visit. Save any styrofoam ones you get; they'll last better than pressed paper ones and can be washed if necessary. In Mexico, the Mediterranean, and Far East, you can buy plastic egg carriers in one dozen and two dozen sizes. These are great. They're sturdier than styrofoam, have a good carrying handle, and are quite crush-resistant. I still have one I bought in Mexico nine years ago.

As for quantity, I take as many eggs as I have room for. Eggs are a real bargain worldwide. A dozen cost less than one twelve-ounce can of corned beef, yet can be a main course for five or six people. I figure on a minimum of two eggs a person per day on real long passages, one and a half a day on 1,000-mile voyages. Eggs and, egg salads, deviled eggs, omelets, custards, soufflé, cookies—when most of your other perishables are an ancient memory and cans are the reality, eggs in all forms still taste fresh.

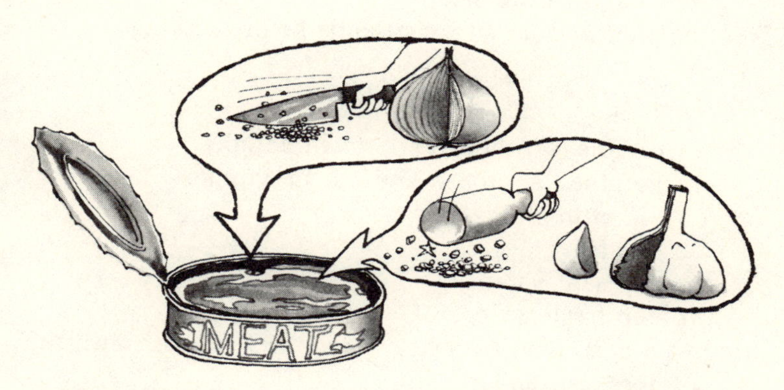

Day 11 Dressing up canned meats will require all the spices and imagination you possess.

Day 11

noon to noon 73 miles, miles to date 809

light north breeze, close reach, cloudy skies

Lunch—liver paté sandwiches with tomato slices
cabbage salad
Dinner—pork stew
bread and butter
red wine

CABBAGE SALAD

1 1/2 cups chopped cabbage
1/2 tomato in cubes

1/2 cup of bean salad

Toss together and let sit for a while before serving.

PORK STEW

3 carrots, scrubbed and cut in chunks
4 potatoes, scrubbed and cut in chunks
1 onion in chunks
2 bay leaves
1/2 cup salt water
1/2 cup fresh water

Bring to a boil, then turn heat down and simmer until the potatoes are tender.

Add 2 cans (small size) Chinese Great Wall brand pork chunks
1 tsp. sweet basil

Bring to a boil.

Mix 3 tbs. gravy mix or 3 tbs. flour into 1/2 cup of red wine

Thicken stew by adding wine and gravy mix slowly, stirring constantly for two minutes.

WE ARE MOVING ALONG A BIT BETTER today, and our noon sight confirmed that the Kurishio current is giving us a free twenty to twenty-five miles a day. So at worse we could take thirty-six or thirty-eight days more to reach land. That's well within our planned, good-eating stores list.

Several years ago we read a delightful true sailing story in *Sail* magazine called "The French Nudist and I." In it Kay Cartwright describes Rosie, a hitchhiking French sailor who joins the Cartwrights on board their ketch in the Canary Islands for a voyage across the Atlantic. Rosie comes complete with her own sextant, life raft and a bag of 99 spices with the ability to use them. I wonder if Rosie brought her own wine too. Every bit of spice and wine magic you can think of is necessary when it comes to cooking from cans. Even if we didn't carry drinking wine on board, I'd still want some to cook with.

WINE AND LIQUOR AROUND THE WORLD

As we were reaching Spain after six years of cruising on *Seraffyn,* Larry told me about his skiing days with his cousin Marybelle in the mountains around Vancouver. She was just as fond of wine as he, and they'd talk of going to Spain someday, where good wines cost a dollar for a whole gallon. Ten years later Larry was surprised to find that many tasty Spanish wines were still available for about the same price if you brought your own bottle to the local bodega or wine warehouse. This became one of the delights of cruising in Europe: discovering new wines, trying to taste as many as we could while we savored the unusual and delicious foods that the country people served.

Almost every country we've visited has its alcoholic treats, and since voyaging yachts can often buy beer and liquor duty-free (Black and White Whiskey two dollars in 1978), few cruising people sail with a dry ship. Even when we lived in California, wine had its place on the table each evening, so it's natural that at sea it's the same. Cocktail hour is a special part of our offshore day. We turn on the stereo or play guitar and sing. I enjoy a sherry or rum and coke while Larry has a scotch or a rum and water. At dinner two or three nights a week we share half a bottle of wine. It is rare during an offshore passage or even a long-distance race when the pleasant, relaxing effects of a single drink can be any danger.

On delivery trips we include one drink before dinner, some wine, plus beer for lunch in hot climates. Even when Larry joined Leslie Dyball of England for the two-man 'round Britain race in 1974, cocktail hour was observed. Obviously its effects were beneficial, because they took the fleet handicap prize in thirty-foot *Chough.* I guess it's a case of moderation. On a long passage like this one, there are lots of small inconveniences. The custom of wine with dinner adds sparkle to meals and days that would otherwise be pallid.

A list of the interesting beverages we've encountered during our years of sailing follows. We are not connoisseurs, and you may not agree with our favorites. We tend sometimes to choose quantity instead of quality when it comes to wines for cruising get-togethers. Our cruising budget of $350 to $450 a month during the 1970s definitely affected what wines we bought. We did learn that prebottled wines kept far better than wine bought in bulk. I cannot truthfully say that we found any difference between the keeping qualities of red or white wine during long voyages, but then we have rarely kept wine for more than three months at a time. We have found that all sealed liquor keeps well for up to a year.

Mexico

Tequila, rum, and gin are one-fourth the price found in the U.S. Larry's favorite beer, Bohemia, costs about twelve cents a bottle when bought by the case, even today in 1979. There are some interesting local brandies to try plus chocolate liqueur. Be careful of margaritas and frozen daiquiris, two local mixed drinks. They are much more potent than they taste. If you are not used to drinking tequila, go easy.

Costa Rica

Very little local liquor available. The white rum produced here is coarse and expensive. Mixers are also very expensive, so bring your own Coca-Cola and other bottled or canned beverages with you from Mexico or Panama.

Panama

Local cheap rum, called "white lightning" by yachtsmen, is very rough. But Ron Cortez at two or three dollars a bottle is excellent. There is a great selection of duty-free wines and liquors; we bought a case of 1965 Côtes du Rhône wine in bond for fifteen dollars. At the yacht clubs, which are in duty-free areas, a drink of rum still cost twenty-five cents.

Columbia

A surprising collection of imported wines were available when we were in Cartagena in 1970. The local rum was O.K. in mixed drinks. Mixers such as Coca-Cola or Seven Up cost less than a nickle a bottle if you bought a case at a time and returned the empties.

Jamaica, Cayman Islands, and Caribbean in general

Finest rums in the world. Mount Gay Rum from Barbados is an international favorite among sailors. At the source it costs about eighty-five cents a bottle. In Jamaica, Appleton Estate Golden Rum was Larry's choice. (I mix mine, so I can't tell the difference.)

United States

We are prejudiced. Even after two years of traveling in Europe we think California wines are some of the finest in the world. Rough California mountain burgundies start at about four dollars a gallon on the West Coast, $5.50 a gallon in the East. Carlo Rossi brands are our favorite at this price. For six dollars a gallon you can buy some fine wines such as Inglenook Navelle Chablis, Burgundy, or Sebastiani Mountain Burgundy. I'd match these with almost any moderately priced wine in the world. For those very special occasions, Wente Brothers chablis or chateau at $2.50 to $3.00 a bottle are great complements to those lobster you'll catch when you sail south to Mexico. We took a case when we first sailed, and six months later the last bottle was magnificent.

For sherries and brandies we depend on Christian Brothers. Sherries sell at about two dollars a bottle, brandy is six dollars. Other brand-name liquor sells at six dollars a bottle on up.

Azores

The wines grown on Pico and Faial are unique—volcanic soil, cool, damp, but very sunny climate. The red wine is coarse and hardy. The white wine, really gold colored, is extremely potent. From latest cruising reports, the better vintages now sell for sixty cents a bottle. Mainland Portuguese wines in five-liter carafes are also available at about the same price per liter.

England

If you like beer, this is the place for variety. But wines and liquor are heavily taxed. Guinness stout must be tasted draft, in a fire-warmed, sixteenth-century pub, to be appreciated.

Scandinavia

Liquor in all the countries of this area was very expensive, even the local aquavit, a potent vodkalike drink costs eight to ten dollars a bottle. Beer starts at seventy-five cents. Duty-free liquor can be bought outward bound in the Kiel Canal.

Poland

Wines from the Iron Curtain countries were exceptionally low priced. Bulgarian red wines were excellent; in fact the Red Gamza wine we have on board for this North Pacific voyage is one we first tasted in Poland. Russian pink sparkling wine from the Crimean area is a real favorite of mine at ninety cents a magnum.

Spain

Wine-tasting adventures start here. Every town has a bodega where wine and liquors are sold from the barrel. If you arrive with five or six empty bottles, the proprietor will usually hand you a small glass and invite you to taste some from each barrel. In some bodegas we visited there were as many as fifteen different red wines ranging from twenty-two cents to two dollars a liter. There were fifteen more white wines and twenty types and qualities of liquor. In smaller villages the bodega was usually part of the local café. Selections in these village cafés were much more limited and tailored to local tastes. Tasting ideas from some of the different regions we visited follow.

Galicia (Northwest Spain) People here prefer a very young white wine, which is drunk from low, handleless cups. I particularly liked this light wine. Local brandies were good —fundador being the bottled version of the type Larry liked best. Bottled fundador cost $1.85. At the bodega, bring your own bottle—fundador cost ninety cents a liter from the barrel!

Southern Spain—Costa Del Sol Even if you don't like sweet wines, you must try medio-medio, a combination of half-muscatel, half-young white wine. Wonderful aperitif. It cost about sixty cents a liter in 1974. We also discovered that Spanish sparkling wines could be as good as French champagne. A brand we came to like was Carta Blanca Sec at $1.30 a bottle.

Mallorca There is a very special wine made in the valley of Andraitx and sold in the shop that sells tobacco and stamps. The locals call it summer wine, vino de verano. It's a light red wine with only 10 percent alcohol. Smooth, perfect chilled for lunch on a hot summer day.

In Palma Mallorca there is one of the most complete bodegas we've ever visited, and it's less than six blocks from the yacht club. Go to the small public market nearest the club—the bodega is one street past the Southwest corner of the market. Our favorite was the red wine used to make local sangria at thirty cents a liter. They will provide empty bottles if you have none.

Italy

Unfortunately, bodegas don't exist in Italy. Almost all wine is sold already bottled and labeled. We found some wonderful wines here by asking local people for recommendations, but we learned that wines available in one part of Italy couldn't be found in another only 100 miles away. Wines were about 50 percent higher priced than in Spain. Most table wines came in returnable bottles. On the island of Lampedusa we found a wonderful dry white wine called porto palo, vinted in Sicily at fifty cents a liter. We bought two cases to tide us over to Malta. A month later we sailed to Sicily, landed in Porto Palo, and found their entire supply goes to Lampedusa. Never found another low-priced wine as nice anywhere in Italy.

Portugal

No cruise in this area is complete without a visit to Oporto. Visitors can choose from five different cavés (wineries in caves) and take a delightful tour that ends with a chance to sample the cave's supply of port wines. Eat a good meal before you go. There are at least twenty different varieties of port offered, and the sample glasses aren't small. Sample and tour are free, the prices for bottled port are irresistible.

Vinho verde is the favorite Portuguese wine on the coast; the wine is called green because it is not fully aged and not as potent as most wines. Supply your own bottle at the local café for good wines at low prices.

In Lisbon, a local yachtsman, Jose Ventura, took us for a ride out to his farm, forty miles east of the port. With him we visited three different farmers and tasted the wine they save for their own consumption, all hearty red wines. At the third farm we filled the eight bottles Jose had told us to bring and had to almost force forty cents a bottle on the farmer.

Greece

Greek wines are sold bulk, but unlike in the Spanish bodegas, wine dealers usually only have two or three varieties to offer. So here it is a matter of visiting each of the local dealers, tasting their two or three varieties, and then trying to remember which dealer's wine you liked best. Retsina is the most common wine. It is aged in resinous pine barrels and to me tastes like turpentine. Larry likes it (but then he likes anything alcoholic other than gin). Chilled well I find it just drinkable.

Malta

The only place we've been where wine was delivered to your door or ship's boarding ladder just like milk. Unfortunately, the local wines can be of poor quality—good enough for meals but not much to remember. Fewer than 100 acres of grapes grow on Malta. As one local story goes, an old Maltese winemaker is lying on his death bed; he calls his oldest son over and whispers, "Son, I want you to know . . . they do make wine from grapes too." In actuality Maltese wine is fermented from grape juice shipped in from Sicily. Some of the higher-priced local brands are quite pleasant at seventy-five cents a bottle. Excellent duty-free imported liquor and European wine is available when you set sail.

Israel

Most expensive wines in the Mediterranean. Nothing less than a dollar a liter. The local wines at three dollars a bottle were excellent at times.

Egypt, South Yemen, Aden, Djibouti

There are no native wines or liquors, but duty-free liquor at standard prices (two dollars a bottle) can be obtained through the chandlers.

Saudi Arabia

If you visit any ports here, all of your liquor will be put in a sealed locker. The seals will be checked frequently, and consequences can be very grave if you are found with illegal liquor. Do not be tempted to smuggle liquor to oil rig personnel in this area. You may earn fifty to sixty dollars a bottle, but you could possibly lose your boat. Liquor to strict Muslims is like hashish or marijuana to Christians.

Sri Lanka

Arak, made from coconuts, is similar to white rum and usually served straight or with ginger ale. A potent punchlike drink is also made using Arak, papaya juice, and lemons, delicious over ice. Local soft drinks are excellent, the dry Elephant Brand ginger ale being the best of the lot.

Malaysia and Singapore

No local beverages except for pleasant beers. But there is an unbelievable variety of imported wines and liquor available in major cities, though prices for a bottle of wine start at four dollars. Duty-free liquor is available in Penang or Singapore through ships' suppliers. We found Mount Gay Rum in Penang for $1.50 a bottle and laid in two cases.

Brunei

We were absolutely amazed to find a large supply of pleasant Australian wines available here. This is a strictly Muslim sultanate, and the door of any business that offers wine and liquor for sale has a sign that says, "It is against the law to sell alcoholic beverages to any person of the Muslim religion." The huge number of foreign oil company employees are the main purchasers. Prices are 50 percent lower than in Singapore. We discovered and purchased a great Australian invention—wine in a box! Sold under the name of Coolabah. We had a choice of five varieties—two red wines and three different white ones. One imperial gallon of wine (six normal bottles) comes in a heavy plastic coated box 9″ × 9″ × 4″ with a plastic carry handle. To serve the wine you open a flap on the side of the box, pull out a spout, and pour. There is a heavy-duty plastic sack inside the box which collapses as you use the wine, so no air can start deterioration. The chablis was the best of the lot, a light, not-too-dry wine well worth seven dollars a box. The boxes stored wonderfully, and the wine traveled well—seven weeks and 3,500 miles later we found no difference in flavor.

Philippines

Excellent selection of rums and gin. Locals prefer the expensive five-year-old rum at $1.50 a bottle. After careful taste tests we found the unaged, gold label seventy-seven-cents-a-bottle rum to be our favorite. The local drink, calamancy and rum over ice, is a treat. Calamancy are tiny fruits that are a cross between lemons and oranges in flavor.

Japan

We had quite a surprise here. We knew the Japanese made sake or rice wine. But we never suspected that the local breweries would be copying European wines. They are and as usual, Japanese copies are meticulous. Prices are low compared with most items in Japan. We had some really pleasant Suntory wines at three dollars a bottle. Suntory whiskey is good. Sake takes getting used to. Served warm it is extremely intoxicating, but the local custom of drinking warm sake from tiny cups while seated barefoot on cushions in a house made of paper screens is a special treat. Thank you, Sanae.

Canada

We were both pleased to find that Canadian wines have definitely improved over the past ten years. They cost from six to ten dollars a gallon, and it's a matter of tasting each one to find your favorite. Wine here is sold in government stores and labeled with numbering system for dryness. Zero means extremely dry, 5 means sweet. We found those labeled 1 or 2 were the ones we enjoyed most. The cream sherry made by the Okanagan wineries rivals Bristol Cream Sherry, my favorite. The Okanagan sherry costs two dollars a bottle in Canada, while Bristol Cream costs seven.

The previous list is very incomplete, only mentioning the highs or lows of our round-the-world cruising adventures with wine and liquor. If it sounds like a lot of drinking, remember, it must be spread over ten years of cruising. Shopping for interesting local wines can be an adventure.

A wonderfully informative incident happened while we were delivering a fifty-four-foot ketch from Palma Mallorca to New Orleans. We'd found a five-gallon pine barrel on board, marked "Grog Keg." It had never been used. You could see light through its staves. So we filled it with water and set it in a large plastic bucket in the shower stall for the three weeks it took us to prepare the boat and sail from Mallorca to Madiera. By then the keg was good and tight.

I didn't take the keg with me when I did my stores scouting in Madeira, so it took quite a humorous mixture of Spanish, English, and hand signals to explain to the Portuguese-speaking taxi driver that I was looking for a wine shop that sold bulk wine. When the taxi driver started driving away from the market district and straight up the hills toward the outskirts of town, I got a bit concerned. One mile later he drew to a stop in front of a vine-covered gray stone warehouse. He led me inside, and all around were beautiful old oak barrels and the aroma of wine.

A gentle-faced middle-aged man in a gray business suit saw us and came down from his office. He spoke English, and when I explained my quest said, "Bring me the barrel. If it is sweet, I will sell you some good wine to go in it. But if it has been used for bad wines, that will ruin it."

The next morning Larry and I carried the keg with us. As soon as we arrived at the wine warehouse, the same gentleman appeared and called to a diminutive, gnarled-looking man who was working around the huge barrels at the back of the warehouse. Together they opened the bung in our little barrel; each smelled it carefully, conferring seriously in Portuguese for several minutes. Then the proprietor turned to us and said, "Yes, it is a sweet barrel. What kind of wine do you prefer?"

Larry asked for a dry, red, hearty dinner wine and we were led along the rows of barrels until the proprietor pointed one out. The gnarled wine taster climbed a short ladder and pulled the bung from the top of a five foot in diameter barrel. Then he dipped a long, thin-handled ladle, made from a four-foot length of bamboo with the bottom six inches left round to scoop up the wine through the bung hole. The wine he brought out was excellent, like a hearty French burgundy. With our approval he climbed down and opened the spigot on the huge barrel, poured a liter of wine directly into our small keg, swished the keg around for a minute, then, to our horror, poured the wine out on the floor. He proceeded to fill our keg then, taking wine from the large barrel and measuring it in two-liter bottles. As we watched, the proprietor explained that these wines were from his family vineyards, eight miles outside the city on the hillsides of southern Madeira.

"Now you must be careful about how you decant this wine," he told us. "Do not take off one bottle at a time. Instead keep four or five bottles with you and decant a whole week's supply. Then take a small square of clean cotton and dip it in pure alcohol; a piece twelve centimeters by twelve centimeters is enough. Place it just inside the bung hole, light it on fire, drop it into the wine barrel, and seal the bung. That small fire will burn all of the oxygen out of the barrel and your wine will last perfectly for up to a year, even on your ship."

As we were thanking him and paying the forty-seven cents a liter he charged for his wine, I asked, "Do you have a real fine bottle of Madeira that we could buy?" He excused himself and climbed the steps down to the cellar below the warehouse. A few minutes later he emerged with two unlabeled bottles marked with hand-painted numbers. Their tops were sealed with a heavy ceramic coating. As his taster finished wiping off our barrel and finding a box to carry the two bottles of Madeira, the proprietor ran his fingers down the pages of a much-used notebook. Finally he pointed to some numbers, turned to us, and said, "Each year our family stores away 200 bottles of the finest wine from our vineyards. These were bottled twenty-four years ago. Please take them as a gift and listen carefully to the radio as you sail. In seven days there will be the first Portuguese election in fifty years. If we do not become a communist country, then open this wine and drink to our success. If our people choose the communists, then please do not drink this wine until Portugal is again free."

Eight days later, 1,200 miles from Madeira, we heard the BBC radio reports of Portugal's election results. Larry opened our first bottle of Madeira wine, and as the mellow, full-bodied sweet wine first began to work its magic inside my throat, we toasted the winemaker who cared so much about his family's product and the now-free country he came from.

Day 12

noon to noon 96 miles, miles to date 905

cloudy, occasional drizzle, eight-knot headwind

Lunch—leftover stew
bread and butter
hot chocolate
Teatime—raw carrot sticks
cheddar cheese and biscuits
Dinner—Greek salad
fried sliced canned ham
canned sweet potatoes
white wine

FIGURE 8

Pardey's Unpatented Nearly Perfect Passage-making rain catcher

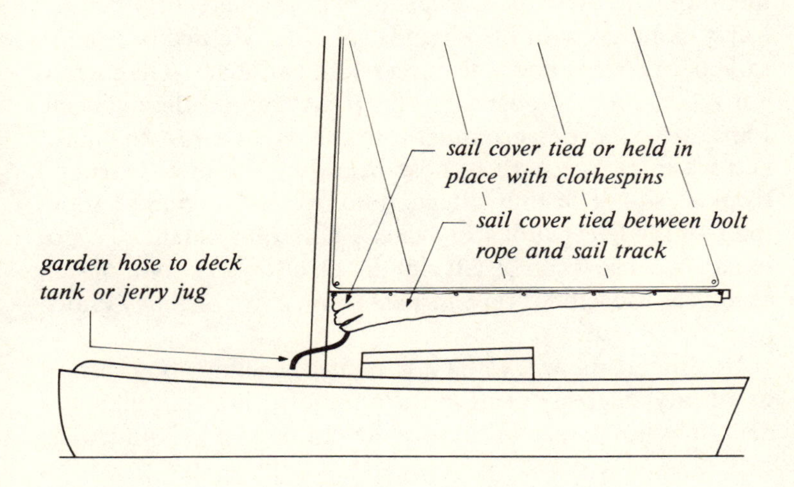

GREEK SALAD

tomato slices
thin onion slices
green pepper slices
cucumber slices
Arrange on a plate and sprinkle with olive oil, oregano, garlic, salt and pepper. If you have any feta cheese, sprinkle a generous amount over the salad.

ON CATCHING RAIN

Larry woke me during my morning off-watch with a shout, "It's raining!" He struggled into his wet weather gear, and I soon heard the sounds of our rain catcher being tied in place. I looked out the companion way and saw only a slight drizzle. But when I awoke three hours later, Larry told me he'd caught three or four gallons of fresh water. Once again we laughed about the eight years we'd spent experimenting with all sorts of ideas for rain catchers until the day Larry came up with the obvious solution. He tied our mainsail boom cover under the main boom and it acted like a rain gutter, catching almost every drop that ran off the mainsail. Larry sewed a rope grommet into the part nearest the mast, and we insert a length of hose into the grommet. During a tropical squall lasting fifteen minutes, we've caught more than thirty-five gallons of water. This rain catcher is also handy because it can be left right in place on any point of sail, as long as the winds don't surpass twenty-five or thirty knots. (See figs. 8 and 9.)

By dinnertime we were close hauled, heeling about fifteen or twenty degrees, beating into a short chop. Dinner was definitely not as elaborate as it would have been otherwise.

WATER!

We've seen offshore sailors run out of water more often than they run out of food. When we were on the race committee for the 1969 Los Angeles to La Paz race, which was supposed to be a run but turned out to be a beat for the first five days, two boats came in without fresh water. One crew just hadn't had enough water on board. The second had a broken pressure system and couldn't get at the twenty gallons stored in the bilge tank. We've met cruising people in the Mediterranean, Mexico, or Bahamas who had to cut short their stay in a fish-laden, magically deserted anchorage when their water supply ran short. But the people who must be most concerned about water are the ones bound across an ocean where there are no escort vessels to come to their rescue. The passage maker bound for the Marquesas, South

FIGURE 9

Details for the Passage-Makers' Rain Catcher

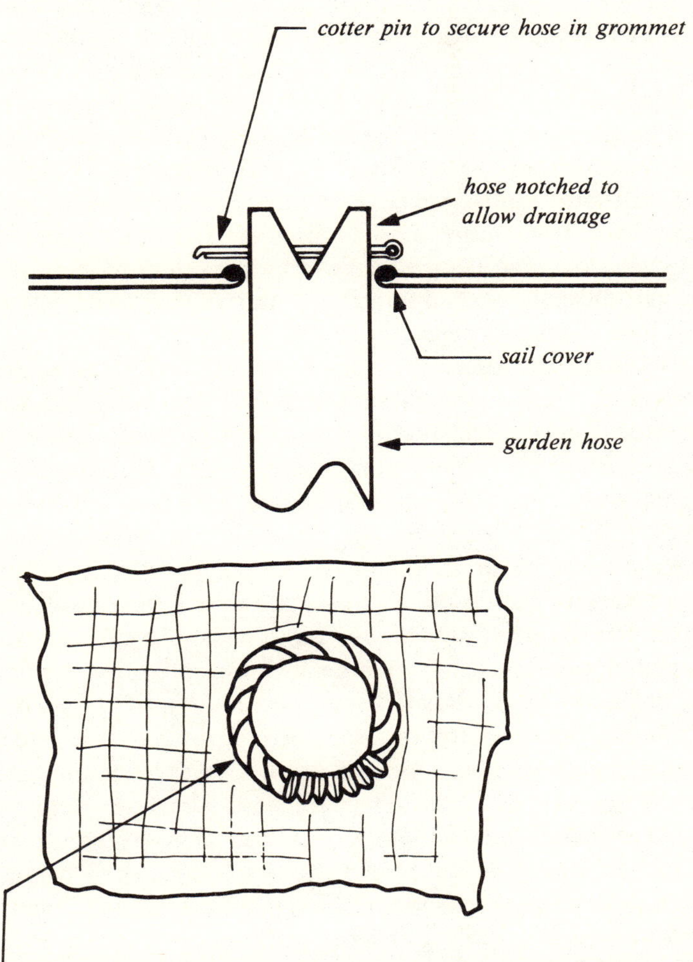

3-strand marlin laid back into a grommet and sewn to sail cover at the lowest point—should fit snugly around the garden hose

Africa, or, like ourselves during summer 1978, from Japan to Canada, must carry water to last the crew for more than forty-five days. As with food stores, you must carry 30 to 50 percent extra water for such unforeseen possibilities as unfavorable winds, storms, or gear failures. But unlike food stores, water needs special taste-proof containers. It is also far bulkier and heavier than food.

The average island hopping, onshore voyager needs one and a half gallons of fresh water per day per person. This is higher than for offshore passage making, first because water supplies can be more easily replenished and therefore it's hard to convince people to ration themselves as carefully; second, because the salt water around you in port may not be clean enough to use for washing and cooking.

On most passages, two and a half to three quarts per person per day is the minimum for safety and comfort. I know that many cruising manuals state one-half gallon per person. But most of these guides were written by Britons and Canadians—the Hiscocks, Smeetons, or the Guzzwells. They refer to the imperial gallon, which is one-fifth larger than the American gallon.

The average daily use of water per person on an offshore passage is: one cup per day for tooth brushing and morning washup; two cups per person per day for cooking; four cups for coffee, tea, hot chocolate, or fruit punch. With two and a half quarts or ten cups of water, this leaves less than a quart for other uses such as a twice-a-week rinsedown or the occasional rinseout of clothes that are necessary on a passage.

During particularly warm weather passages you need more fresh water. When we ran down the Red Sea in August, the temperatures never fell below 95°, even at night, with ten days at 110°. We each drank one gallon of water a day just to keep up with our perspiration.

Beer, soft drinks, and canned fruit juices are important to

carry, but it's safest to figure these items as additional liquid sources, not part of your freshwater supply. But if you are on a very weight-conscious boat, or if your water-storage capacity is extremely limited, it is acceptable to carry two cups of water fewer per day for every quart of other drinks you carry.

The most dependable and often least expensive water tank building material for any boat other than a steel-hulled one is marine grade stainless steel. Manufacturers of some glass boats don't use stainless steel because it is easier for them to just glass a cover over some suction of your boat's keel, or to glass up a portion of the area under a bunk. They also complain that separate tanks can't be fully shaped to fit each curve of the boat, so they end up with a slightly smaller water capacity. But unlike fiberglass tanks, stainless steel doesn't impart a flavor to your water supply. It is relatively easy to build with the proper baffles; it's lighter than a separate properly constructed glass tank and, surprisingly, less expensive. Stainless steel is subject to electrolysis. If your tank shows signs of pitting on the outside, be sure to check and find what is causing the flow of electricity. Also include your water tank when you are wiring your hull fittings together to avoid electrolysis.

One of the most reputable fiberglass molding shops in the Newport Beach, Costa Mesa area, Crystalliner Corporation, explained that fiberglass water tanks can be constructed so that they are taste-free. To do so, they must be coated inside with finishing resin. The only problem is that when you secure the top of the tank in place you have to use laminating resin. This two-or-three-inch-wide strip that goes completely around the inside of your tank will impart a flavor to your water unless you cut an inspection plate in the top of your tank, then cover the inside joint with a coating of finishing resin. If the tank has baffles in it, this can be a difficult job.

If you have fiberglass tanks on board right now and your water tastes bad, Crystalliner recommends steam-cleaning the tanks. In the United States there are often outfits that bring a steam-cleaning unit right to the dock to clean bilges and engines. They'll know how to help your situation. A product called Aqua-Chem disguises the fiberglass flavor in water. There are also water-filtering systems which can be installed in your water-pressure line. But for the discriminating water drinker or the person who brews mild tea, there is no real answer if your fiberglass tank isn't properly built in the first place. Even after two or three years, your water will still taste bad.

Steel boats of course use steel tanks, the cheapest way to go and best way to avoid electrolysis. For the first ten years of a steel boat's life, tanks welded right in place work great for water. But after that you may wish you'd had separate tanks, as you may start to suffer from rust-red water or holes caused by corrosion and electrolysis.

While I was preparing this chapter I spoke with Vic Berry's sheet-metal shop in Newport Beach, California, the people who built all of *Seraffyn*'s successful stainless steel tanks ten years ago. Tom Berry, Vic's son, who now runs the shop, made a comment that surprised me. "We use 5052 marine alloy, the coast guard-recommended, saltwater-corrosion-proof aluminum," Tom told me, "and it is absolutely no good for freshwater tanks. The aluminum builds up calcium deposits that not only make the water taste bad, but after six or eight months these deposits will start to foul up your plumbing. These tanks are slightly cheaper to build and lighter. They cost the boat manufacturer less and are great for some purposes but not for storing fresh water."

I was completely unaware that anyone used aluminum tanks for fresh water, so I called Doug Muir, head of sales at the Westsail Newport Beach Cruising Center, and asked him about the aluminum water tanks used in all Westsails.

He agreed that the tanks had a flavor and said that it is necessary to empty them and flush them out every two or three months to avoid calcium buildup. And in fact Doug, who like me drinks light-flavored tea, recommends that people with aluminum water tanks carry a separate drinking-water supply in plastic containers. Doug said, "Westsail switched to aluminum water tanks three years ago so we could standardize our tank building materials. Westsail will supply stainless steel water tanks at no extra charge if the customer requests them."

Molded polyethelene tanks have become popular with production boat builders in recent years. They are seamless and have molded-in fittings. Such tanks can be fabricated in complex shapes to take more complete advantage of available space. They may cost less than other tanks to produce since they are made in molds. They are lighter but they must be carefully supported, not only on the bottom but on the sides, or they will work harden and eventually crack. Baffles cannot be installed in molded tanks, and for this reason we would choose another type of tank material. Though polyethelene tanks can be repaired by heat sealing right on the boat, you must have the tank absolutely dry and oil-free to do so. Taste should not be a problem with polyethelene tanks, but often a plastic flavor is imparted to the water by the hoses and fittings used in your system. Be sure to use all high quality vinyl and polyvinyl chloride (PVC) hoses and fittings to produce the taste-free results. Tanks should not be stored in the sun before installation, or they will deteriorate and work-harden sooner than normal. We personally have had only one experience with polyethelene tanks during a 5,800-mile delivery from Palma, Mallorca, to New Orleans. The connections leaked and the tanks bulged badly. We lost more than 100 gallons of fresh water during a 2,800-mile passage. This convinced us the tanks weren't strong enough, should have had baffles, or needed extra external support.

FIGURE 10

Proper water tank construction

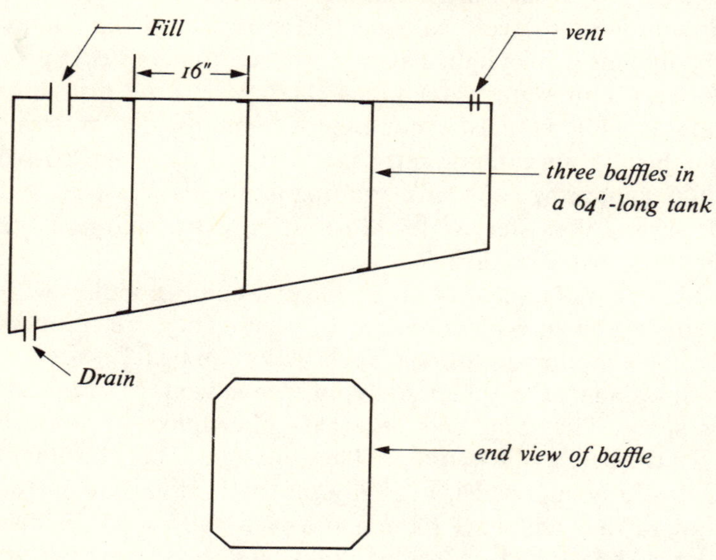

Whatever type of tank you use, if it doesn't have sufficient baffles or cross plates built into it, it will drive you crazy at sea. Eric and Susan Hiscock had water tanks welded into the large space under their sea berths on forty-nine-foot steel *Wanderer IV.* The builder did not put proper baffles in, and the water in their tanks sloshes around so much in a seaway that they can't sleep on those bunks. Baffles help prevent the oil canning that semi-empty tanks cause and cut down the flexibility of the tank. Stainless steel tanks that aren't properly baffled and supported will eventually work-harden and crack. Tom Berry recommends a baffle every sixteen inches on tanks 24" × 24" × 48" and slightly closer if the tank is much larger. I saw tanks in their shop as small as 8" × 10" × 18" with baffles built in. (See fig. 10.)

FIGURE 11

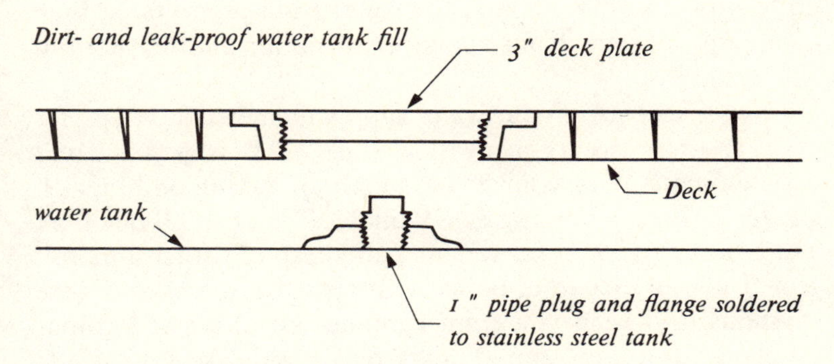

If your tanks are in the bilge, be sure you have an alternate way of getting to them. If your pressure or pump system breaks down, you could be stuck without fresh water even though there are fifty gallons beneath your feet. An inspection plate and portable hand pump are the best bet.

If your water filler is on deck, be sure that it is clearly labeled. A dose of diesel in the water tanks will take months to clear up. One way of avoiding contaminating the water tank is to have a large opening such as a three-inch bronze inspection plate on deck, then the opener to the water-tank fill below that (fig. 11). That way the dirt that builds up around the edges of the opener won't go into the tank each time you fill it. Also, by having a type of opener different from the normal fuel fill, accidents will be less likely. On a long ocean voyage, contaminated fuel would be an inconvenience, but contaminated water could be a disaster.

If your water tanks do not have easy-to-reach deck fillers, consider changing them now. When water is not easily available from a garden hose at the dock, you'll find those under-the-bunk fillers a nuisance. I know that Mary Baldwin, who crewed on *Peloris,* resented catching rain water because they had to channel it into five-gallon jugs, carry the jugs below, move the cushions, siphon the water from jug to tank, then wipe up the spills before going on deck for another jug full of water.

Never keep all of your water supply in one tank. We prefer two or three twenty-five-gallon tanks. This way you won't contaminate all of your water supply by taking on brackish water if there is nothing else available. You can fill one tank with brackish water for washing and keep the other tank full for drinking. Separate tanks with separate valves and hose systems also keep you from running out of water without warning. If a tank should crack or a hose leak, your whole supply won't be lost.

Most of us bound on a long voyage resort to carrying extra water in five-gallon plastic jugs. Smell the jugs before you buy them. Avoid any that aren't specifically made for water. We learned this the hard way when we bought four five-gallon jugs in the Philippines. Our water was almost undrinkable if it stayed in the jugs more than twenty-four hours. We cured much of the problem by adding one cup of chlorine bleach to each five gallons of water and letting it sit for a week, then rinsing the tanks four or five times.

We store our spare water jugs on deck lashed to the bulwarks and shrouds and have been surprised to find that black plastic water jugs outlast white ones three to one. The white jugs grow brittle and crack within one year in the tropics. Our black jug, originally used for battery acid, is now three years old and in fine condition. The dark color has an added benefit—the jug acts as a solar heater, so we have warm water for showers after four or five hours of direct sunlight.

Collapsible water jugs are convenient to store below decks when they are empty. But we found they deteriorate rapidly in direct sunlight. The handles generally seem to pull apart within six months. If your jugs are used only for transferring water from shore, I'd use collapsible ones. But if you plan to store water on deck in the jugs, invest in good firm plastic.

Even if you don't need spare jugs to supplement your water supply, plan on carrying at least two five-gallon ones for those times when the nearest fresh water is three blocks away from the waterfront. Once you leave North America, I'd estimate you'll find a watering dock in less than 10 percent of the ports you visit even alongside a fuel dock.

The Goodyear rubber company makes several sizes of collapsible extra storage tanks. These are great, but once again, be sure yours is rated and built for water storage.

When it comes time to fill your water tanks, sample the local water supply first. If you are bound on a long voyage, it may be worth your while to go somewhere else to fill your tanks. I know in Malta the water in the city mains tasted terrible. In fact, people collected rainwater on their roofs or off awnings to drink. Yet a friend told us about one of several small artesian wells on the island, and there we found superb spring water. Though we had to tote our five-gallon jugs a quarter-mile, we felt it was worth it. In Gibraltar most water is made by converting sea water and is extremely brackish-tasting. Ceuta, only sixteen miles away on the tip of North Africa, has excellent drinking water. If you are bound for the Canaries or Madeira, I'd plan to stop there. But there are times when you have no choice. In Aden we had to put up with water that was safe but tasted as bad as any we'd ever sampled. We drank it halfway across the Arabian Sea until we replaced it with rainwater.

I know one of the things that worries many new cruisers is the idea of taking on water in a foreign country. They have heard the warnings issued by travel agents about drinking only bottled water, or boiling water for five minutes, or adding tablets to the water to purify it. For the average tourist whose resistance is low because he is usually rushed and tired, eating all his meals in restaurants, and sleeping poorly in a strange bed every night, this may be a good precaution. But for the cruising family the best solution is to check for any cholera or typhoid warnings. If there are none and the local people drink the water, then drink it yourself. If you are still concerned, chlorinate the water. (See Table 1.) Add one teaspoon of any 5.25 percent solution of sodium hypochlorite such as Clorox, Purex, Sani-Chlor, Hy-pro, or Super-X to

TABLE 1

PURIFYING FRESH WATER

Chlorine bleach

Use liquid chlorine laundry bleach. Read label to determine percentage of chlorine available.

Available chlorine	No. of drops to be added/qt. Clear water	Cloudy water
1%	10	20
4–6%	2	4
7–10%	1	2
percentage unknown	10	20

1. Mix thoroughly.
2. Let stand for 30 minutes with maximum ventilation.
3. If you cannot detect slight chlorine odor at end of 30 minutes, repeat process and let stand for 15 minutes.
4. Water is safe to use.

Tincture of Iodine

Available iodine	No. of drops to be added/qt. Clear water	Cloudy water
2%	5	10

1. Let stand for 30 minutes, after which time water is safe to use.

Information courtesy of U.S. Department of Health, Education, and Welfare, Public Health Service every five gallons of fresh water. Let it sit with the cap off your tank for at least thirty minutes so that the chlorine has a chance to work and the fumes dissipate. This not only kills almost all bacterial contamination but also helps keep your tanks free from green or brown slime. When I called the Orange County, California, Health Department to confirm these facts, Mrs. Mazer, who works in the environmental health agency in charge of water sanitation, confirmed that this simple chlorination is equivalent to boiling all your water for five minutes. She also told me some interesting facts about water worldwide. "Most people who get upset stomachs from water in a place they are visiting really are reacting against the different trace chemicals and elements, not any bacteria. Water in some places has more salinium, or more magnesium or more calcium. That doesn't make it dangerous, just different. Some people are more sensitive to water changes than others. Children notice changes because of their smaller body size. People who travel a lot grow more used to the changes. Don't think that bottled water is going to prevent problems. There is no way of knowing how sterile the containers the water is going into are, nor how good the water that is being bottled is. What it comes down to is, you can't be sure of the water purity even right here in the United States." She went on to tell me about two Orange County health officials who went into the San Juaquin area of California, part of the watershed for Orange County. "They were there to test our water's primary sources. Found them great. But both officers picked up a water-borne bacterial disease from the San Juaquin county water supply."

To enjoy cruising worldwide, you have to avoid being a hypochondriac about water. People fully adjusted to a cruising life rarely suffer from stomach upsets, at least no more than they would have at home.

Rainwater makes the best drinking water in the world. If you are in a tropical area, your sun awning could probably catch all the water you'll need with only a bit of conversion. At sea your mainsail cover turned upside down under the mainboom can catch a tremendous amount of water in a short time. (See Day 12.) Taste the rainwater running off your catchment before you put it in your main tanks to be sure your system hasn't any salt on it. The saltiest mainsail or awning will run clean after two minutes of a tropical downpour. Some people just close their bulwark or toerail scuppers, then open their deck fill plates and let the rainwater run in. I don't trust this system as there is no way to be sure the water is salt-free or dirt free.

No matter how you get your water, fill your tanks and keep them topped up every chance you get. If you are at sea, this is really important. Catch every bit of rain today, because tomorrow it might be blowing too hard, or the rain squalls might pass you by. Island and harbor hoppers soon learn that water isn't always easy to get in the next port.

To preserve the water you carry and to extend your cruising range, turn off your pressurized water system when you leave port. Use a hand pump or gravity day tank or daily jug to make people aware of just how much water they are really using. We speak from experience. We were delivering a large ketch with two extra crewmen on board who were not used to ocean passages. The boat had ten forty-gallon water tanks and a pressure system. Twenty days out from Madeira and 210 miles from Antigua, the pressure system ran dry. Fortunately, we had thirty gallons of water in a separate shutoff tank. Where did the water go? The crew had let the tap run while they brushed their teeth. They'd showered for five minutes with the taps on full. We'd used only fresh water in the galley. That and a dozen other bits of wastefulness used up an average of five gallons of water per day per person. In the United States the average person uses sixty-five gallons of fresh water a day. So the measures necessary to conserve water for an ocean passage are far from the average shore dweller's experience.

Whatever system you use to get water from your tanks, once you head offshore, isolate each tank. Then when one runs out and you have to turn on the next, you'll be aware of your rate of consumption. If you have a gravity header tank such as we use, transfer water from the main tank in a five-gallon jug and mark each transfer in the log.

On a long voyage where your tank capacity is near the minimum requirements, we find it works well to figure consumption as a ratio of gallons to hundreds of miles left to go. If the ratio drops, we tighten our water usage. If it increases, we take a shower. In other words, if we start out with sixty-eight gallons of water for a 4,500-mile passage, that's 1.5 gallons per 100 miles. If fifteen days later we've covered only 1,200 miles and consumed twenty-two gallons of water, our ratio becomes 1.4, so it is time to cut back. If, on the other hand, we've covered 1,900 miles during the same time, our ratio becomes 1.77, so we can indulge just a bit. This way our water conservation happens all through the voyage, not just toward the end.

For that ultimate emergency we carry an air force-surplus portable freshwater still. It is a small, plastic sea water converter that comes in a 4″ × 6″ × 6″ container. It will convert about a quart of water per day. It's kept in our abandon-ship package but is available if all else fails on board. These stills are often advertised in yachting publications and cost less than ten dollars.

To actually save fresh water, install a saltwater tap conveniently placed right in the galley area. The simplest way to do this is to put a three-quarter-inch thru-hull fitting below the water line with a hose to a convenient tap near the cook. This will only work if the water line on your boat is near knee level or higher. On *Seraffyn* our saltwater tap has a hose fitting on it so we can use it for scrubbing and rinsing out the bilges.

If your boat floats too high for this method, you'll have to install a pump in the galley. Choose a pump that is obviously different from the freshwater pump, or a complete meal can be ruined when a new cook adds a pump full of salt water instead of fresh.

Salt water can be used for cooking. One cup of sea water has approximately two rounded teaspoons of salt in it. For bread baking, substitute one cup of salt water for one cup of fresh. Boiling vegetables, use one-quarter salt water and three-quarters fresh. Boil eggs in 100 percent salt water, cook rice in one-third salt water, two-thirds fresh. For dried beans, don't use any salt water at all or they'll stay tough.

Wash all your dishes and pots in salt water. We often do this right in the cockpit instead of below decks. Then we rinse them in a basin with one or two cups of fresh water. This is important as salty plates or pans will not only flavor other food but will start to grow mold after eight or ten days in the tropics.

Wash yourself in sea water, then rinse in fresh. Liquid dish soaps or hair shampoo work fine as a body soap in salt water. My thick, long hair feels great if I wash and rinse it with salt water, then shake out the excess and rinse over a bucket using a quart of fresh water. I run the fresh water through my hair three or four times, then use it to rinse my body.

Some people don't feel the need to rinse with fresh water at sea, but this can be unwise as it leaves you susceptible to skin diseases. Salt attracts moisture; moisture on your skin attracts fungus. Several types of skin problems can develop quickly in the tropics, ranging from itchy rashes to skin discolorations. Almost all are aggravated by salt deposits on your skin, either from perspiration or from salt water. Cruising people are particularly susceptible to this as they can't bathe twice a day.

Washing clothes in salt water doesn't work well at all. If they aren't thoroughly rinsed in fresh, they won't dry completely, they'll be stiff, they'll soon smell, and they'll cause salt rashes, especially on your bottom and under your arms. If it is necessary to wash out some clothes or towels during a long voyage, use a small amount of dishwashing liquid in fresh water, then rinse the clothes just once. The small bit of soap left in the fabric won't hurt at all.

Don't try to conserve fresh water by drinking salt water. Bombard, the scientist who tried to prove that man could live on salt water and cross an ocean, did survive his Atlantic crossing. But he obtained most of his liquid from the raw fish he ate.

Fresh water is the most important store you carry on board. If your food supplies run out because you lose your mast and have to limp along under jury rig, or if you hit a bad weather system, your water supply could save your life. The average healthy person can live for thirty days with no food and only one and a half pints of fresh water a day to drink and still suffer no irreparable body damage.

Day 13 Some days nothing seems to go right in the galley.

Day 13

noon to noon 46 miles, miles to date 951

brisk east wind, closehauled

It's a dead muzzler (wind dead against us), but skies are sunny.

Lunch—fried ham slices
fried tomato slices
bread and butter
canned rambutans stuffed with pineapple (a Chinese-Malaysian treat similar to lychees)
Tea—butter cookies and a pot of Earl Grey tea
Dinner—chicken in sage sauce
mashed potatoes
white wine

CHICKEN IN SAGE SAUCE

Sauté 1 onion cut in strips
8 cloves of garlic, chopped
2 small green peppers in chunks
in 1 tbs. butter until the onions start to lose their opaqueness.
Add 1 tsp. rubbed sage
1 14-ounce can of chicken in supreme sauce (this is an English product that is similar the chicken in white sauce).
Heat slowly for 5 minutes, stirring lightly so as to not break up the chicken chunks.
Serve over mashed potatoes

CAN OPENERS

Larry was in a fix-it mood when I woke up this morning, and almost before I'd really opened my eyes asked, "Need anything done?" "Can opener isn't working too well," was the only thing that came to mind. Larry disassembled it, greased the moving parts with Luberplate waterproof outboard motor grease, and sharpened the inside edge of the cutting wheel with a fine file. It works like new. Ours is the same hand-held, chrome-plated, heavy-duty $2.98 Sears and

Roebuck swing-away can-opener we've used for nine years. It has a replaceable cutter and plastic-covered handles. I find it much handier in a seaway than a wall-mounted model because I can operate it right in the sink, so any overflows go down the drain. Besides, bulkhead models are subject to being ripped off in a seaway if the boat lurches while you are using them.

We are beating again, and it's a time for spills. Yesterday it was one rum and water and a deck of cards. We lost one of the cards somewhere in the bilge. Today it was one-half bottle of Coca-Cola and the tea leaves from the teapot. The spills were only an additional irritant. Just beating to windward bugs me.

Day 14 If only once Larry would get seasick! Then he'd know what the rest of us feel like.

Day 14

noon to noon 32 miles, miles to date 983

sunny but very cool

still beating against a fifteen- to eighteen-knot headwind

Lunch—hot dogs
baked beans topped with chopped onions
Cocktail time—biscuits and cheese
rum and water
Dinner—cook's night off, cold canned corned beef and
canned beans crackers

WE ARE STILL BEATING to windward with the reefed jib, staysail, and main set. It's a dead muzzler, a cold east wind right out of Vancouver. Larry took the staysail down just before dinner to cut some of the violent motion down. But still I felt just on the edge of seasickness. The thought of cooking dinner made me blue—my imagination as a cook deserted me completely. So when Larry suggested, "Cook's night off," I took two seconds to agree. He opened a can of corned beef, another of beans, and ate right from the cans. I ate nothing. Primitive, yes. Nice rest for the cook, though. On the average the need for cook's night off on board *Seraffyn* seems to happen after about twelve to fourteen days at sea.

I'd say I've been too seasick to enjoy cooking once or twice a year. Only two times in ten years have I actually been too sick to cook anything at all, and both times were during the same voyage south down the Adriatic in winter. (See below on seasickness.)

Meanwhile, back to tonight. Larry took care of his own dinner and produced no dirty dishes. I had a few saltines and cheese. Then we cuddled together under a blanket on the settee and listened to Beethoven's 4th piano concerto on our stereo. For a little while, beating over the cold gray sea didn't seem so frustrating.

SEASICKNESS PREVENTION

It never fails. Every time we get into a discussion with a new or wouldbe cruising sailor, there comes a moment when a concerned look crosses his or her face and the question is blurted out, "Do you ever get seasick?" I don't think any aspect of sailing causes more worry, and certainly nothing is more demoralizing than being seasick. I know; I am one of the sufferers.

There we were, finally on our way after three and a half years of scheming, planning, and building. I'd sailed lots of times before, but when we set off from San Diego into a confused cross sea, I was so sick that I finally ended up lying on the cabin sole praying for land. "All my dreams ruined," I said to myself. And even more morbid thoughts rushed through my head for over a day. Larry tried joking with me, holding me, teasing me, but nothing helped. Then to my amazement, the second day out my seasickness began to fade away. By the end of the day, I was more than making up for my lack of interest in food. Even more amazing, after three days, I had forgotten that I ever was seasick.

I still get uncomfortable occasionally, and every time it happens I am just as unhappy as the first, but I have learned to minimize the problem. I don't include Larry in the problem because he is one of the outrageously fortunate 10 percent who don't even know what seasickness is. Put him in a boat with bilges full of diesel, odiferous food on the counter, and a vicious sea running and he'll ask where the butter and jam are so he can make a sandwich. But about 90 percent of all people who go to sea do suffer at one time or another. So, an active program of prevention is worth considering.

I'm convinced that 30 to 50 percent of the problem is psychological, and other long-time sailors have supported me in this belief.

Curiously, I never get seasick when we are working delivering other boats, only when Larry and I are together alone sailing *Seraffyn.* When I am being paid to cook on a delivery I've got important responsibilities and don't want to let the crew down, so I guess I'm busier or trying harder. On board *Seraffyn,* I know Larry will take care of any problems, and he handles the boat easily by himself with the aid of our self-steering gear, so I can relax and it doesn't matter. Peter Phillips, who owns fifty-foot *Voyager,* reports the same thing. When he is captain and has a crew on his own boat, he's never seasick. But daysailing as a guest on friends' boats is a different matter. I'm not in any way saying that our seasickness is any less real for being psychological. But by accepting the fact that sometimes it is caused by mental processes, we can more actively fight it.

Doctors are forever coming up with new pills to fight the problem. Unfortunately, they often forget to put the most important instructions on the package. To work at all, a dramamine or any other anti-motion-sickness pill *must* be taken one hour before the motion starts that causes the problem. Once you are sailing out the marina entrance, it is too late. It takes an hour for some pills to dissolve and spread through your body. If you vomit before then, you lose the medicine.

I personally can't recommend any type of antimotion pill because I have given up trying to use them. In the excitement of getting under way I usually forget to take one. Or, if I do take one, it always turns out to be lovely, easy sailing and I have to suffer with the drunk, sleepy feeling the pill leaves. I did try taking a mild tranquilizer (on my doctor's recommendation) an hour before we sailed, and it worked even better than any other pill I'd used. I've asked other sailing friends to try this and they report the same.

Whether you want to use antimotion pills, tranquilizers,

or go without, there are other measures you can take to minimize seasickness.

First: keep your boat very clean. Eliminate any odors you can. It's the odors that do the final trick. A person can be fine until he opens the ice chest and gets a whiff of blue cheese or sour milk. In fact, we've found that people get seasick less easily on a boat with no engine. There are fewer unusual odors to become accustomed to in a nonauxiliary vessel. If you do have an engine, be careful of overfilling the tanks; check any oil leaks and wipe excess oil off the engine itself to eliminate odors.

Ventilate the boat well, and remember that odors you live with day in and day out may not upset you, but they may do the trick for a guest. Don't allow anyone to smoke on board under way if you or one of your guests is prone to seasickness. If you are embarrassed to ask your friends to snub out their cigarettes, put up a sign, "Smoking allowed foreward of the headstay."

Second, if you or your guests have a tendency to get queasy, try living on board at anchor for a few days before you head for sea. There always is a slight motion afloat, and this seems to help you get acclimatized. People who live on board constantly suffer less when they head to sea.

Third, rest well before you set off. I know now that my first real bout of seasickness was brought on by too many farewell parties and an excitement-induced sleepless night before our departure. At sea, get all the rest you can. Your body will cope with weather changes better and mentally you'll be less annoyed if some queasiness does occur.

Fourth, if you happen to be in charge of cooking, prepare enough meals for two or three days *before* you leave port or, if you are on a long passage, when it is calm. I usually make up a pot of stew or spaghetti and sauce or a really thick soup in an eight-quart pot. I mix sandwich fillings and bake fresh bread before each long passage. Then, once we set off, I don't have to put up with the unsettling smells of cooking if it's rough. And if I do get seasick, I don't have to worry, for Larry can turn a fire on under the pot of soup or stew and scoop a bowlful for himself. If you have prepared several meals beforehand and you don't get seasick, you end up with a bit of extra free time at sea to sunbathe or to read a good book.

Fifth, once you are under way in a rough sea, avoid going into either the forepeak or the engine room. The motion is more pronounced in these parts of the boat. Also, if possible avoid using an enclosed toilet. Head areas are rarely ventilated well enough, and the odors multiply when you are in a seaway. Instead use the lee rail, or try a bucket if it's really rough. Even fishermen and seamen on smaller fishing boats prefer not to use a cramped enclosed head.

Sixth, keep warm and active and stay out in the fresh air. Because seasickness is partially psychological in many cases, if you put on your foul-weather gear, get out on deck, and actually join in the sailing of the boat, you won't have as much time to think about the motion. Very few people who sail dinghies get seasick; they are just too busy.

Seventh, if you have a tendency toward seasickness, avoid hot, spicy food. Choose easily digested items such as bread, oatmeal, apple juice, and saltines rather than citrus fruits, lasagna, and bacon.

Eighth, on a very hot, still day, try to keep cool. It's amazing how many people become upset on glassy, calm days when the sails are slatting. Finding some shade, pouring sea water over yourself, or drinking a cool glass of juice will prevent this.

Ninth, if you do become ill, try drinking some sweet fruit juice such as well-chilled apricot or peach nectar. This seems to settle well and provides almost all of the nutrition necessary to keep you from becoming weak or dehydrated.

Tenth, in really bad conditions, if a crew is very seasick, try changing the motion of the boat by easing the sheets a bit and reaching, running, or even heaving-to. We know one tough-looking six-footer who becomes as weak as a baby as soon as the sheets are hauled in hard. He lies in his bunk until the sheets are eased. Then he makes up for lost time—and food. He just can't take the motion of being hard on the wind in anything more than twelve knots or so. But he loves sailing and traveling so much that he is willing to put up with the inconvenience.

Finally, if you have a first-time sailor on board who becomes seasick, don't discourage him or her from sailing. One of our best friends spent years learning about boats and building beautiful dinghies which he sold with an aim of some day having his own yacht. Then he was asked to crew on a forty-foot hot racing machine, and, excitedly, he accepted. In twenty-knot winds he became helpless. The regular crew of the boat teased him, and he never went sailing again. It's rather sad, because he would have made a good sailor with his quick mind and strong frame. But to him sailing wasn't worth the discomfort and ridicule.

I think that is one of the big secrets: you have to *want* to sail and cruise so much that you'll put up with one or two days of discomfort for the reward of new ports and new people.

Normally, few people stay seasick for more than two or three days except in most extreme storm conditions. I did hear of one person who reported she was seasick the whole way across the Atlantic. But it turned out she was suffering not from seasickness but from a problem that can be caused by seasickness. I learned about this when I spoke to Dr. Isola, the port doctor in Gibraltar. He told me that in the past two years he has had to assist in the delivery of nine unplanned babies conceived by cruising people who were using the pill.

As Dr. Isola explained it, an oral contraceptive must stay in your stomach for four to eight hours to spread into your bloodstream effectively. He advises that if you want to be sure of not getting pregnant, use other means of contraception if you have been seasick for more than a day. Pregnancy in its second and third month will cause almost the same symptoms as seasickness, and that was what our friend on her transatlantic voyage was suffering from.

No one enjoys being seasick. But for most of us it is an integral part of going to sea. And the discomfort is quickly forgotten the minute you reach a new port or sail out of a storm into beautiful weather.

Day 15

noon to noon 49 miles, miles to date 1,032

pounding to windward with single reefed main and staysail

Just after noon the wind dropped and sun came out.

Lunch—hard-boiled eggs
tomato pudding
hot chocolate

Dinner—fresh rye bread with butter
salmon loaf with lemon sauce
baked potatoes
sliced tomatoes

TOMATO PUDDING
(An old English side dish)

In a small saucepan put

- 2 large ripe tomatoes cut in chunks
- 1 tbs. butter
- 2 tbs. sugar
- 2 tbs. finely chopped onion
- 1 tsp. oregano

Simmer for 20 minutes, stirring often.
Pour into a small casserole tin.
Top with 1/4″ layer of bread crumbs light sprinkling of salt grated cheddar cheese
Bake at 350° for 20 minutes.

SALMON LOAF

- 1 large can of salmon, drained (mackerel can be used instead)
- 2 eggs
- 2 tbs. lemon juice
- 1 tsp. MSG
- 1/2 cup bread crumbs

Mix well, form into a loaf on a bread sheet or tin.
Bake at 325° for 35 minutes.

LEMON SAUCE

- 1/2 onion, chopped fine
- 2 tbs. butter
- 2 tbs. water
- 1 tbs. lemon
- 1/2 tsp. garlic
- 1/2 tsp. MSG
- 1/2 tsp. salt

Simmer for 10 minutes, stirring occasionally.

Mix 2 tbs. flour into 1/2 cup of milk and pour slowly into the onion mixture, stirring constantly until the sauce becomes very thick.

As soon as the wind died down and my seasickness cleared away (this happens almost immediately), I set some rye bread to rise. The temperature on board is well below seventy degrees, so I warmed the oven for three minutes, then put the dough in to rise. Since I was using the oven to bake bread, I planned a dinner that could all be baked at the same time.

By dinner the old sea was laying down and a light breeze was moving us almost directly toward Canada for the first time in three days.

TIPS ON BAKING BREAD

Bread baking doesn't require very much actual work. In fact, preparing a dough takes eight or ten minutes once you learn the basic tricks. But the rising and baking process requires your presence in the vicinity of your galley for a minimum of two and a half hours. If you are involved with the complications of a job on shore, this may be difficult. But on an offshore passage, bread baking fits the rhythm and time schedule perfectly. You're never more than twenty feet from the galley. There's almost no chore on the boat that can't be interrupted for three or four minutes while you check your rising dough. The motion of a yacht at sea doesn't seem to bother bread dough at all; give it any temperature over 75 degrees and below 110 and it rises merrily away, oblivious to whether you are beating, running, or reaching, whether seas are one foot high or fifteen. If you are heeled and don't have a gimbaled stove, your final loaf might have a tilt, but it will still taste fine, and the homey atmosphere created by the smell of baking drives away going-to-windward blues.

For the uninitiated, bread baking is almost magical. One English crewman on a delivery trip was so fascinated by the process that he insisted on watching me make the dough for each twice-weekly baking. After two weeks he tried his own batch. As soon as he'd set his dough to rise, it was his turn at the wheel. Chris was like a kid waiting for Santa Claus. He opened the engine room inspection hatch ten times an hour and shouted out when the towel on top of his bowl of dough began to take on a rounded shape. His first loaf was slightly browner on one side than it was on the other, but the sandwiches he proudly served at lunchtime tasted great. For the next 4,000 miles I had to fight with him for the right to bake the crew bread.

The ingredients for bread are available worldwide. With a bit of care they will keep quite well, and toward the end of a voyage of more than twenty days, you'll find fresh-baked bread is one of the highlights of your menu.

Dried yeast purchased either in individual packages or in one-pound cans will keep for up to two years. I prefer the cans, and once I open a one-pound can, I store the yeast in a tupperware container. The individual packets of yeast, usually made of some combination of aluminum and plastic, must be stored in a dry place or they will corrode through. Two pounds of yeast last us for about one year of average cruising.

Flour is much more of a problem to keep, especially if you are voyaging in warm waters. Enriched, unbleached flour in five-pound or two-kilo factory-wrapped packages rarely gets weevils, while whole wheat flour usually does. So I've found it pays to buy the enriched flour and bag each five-pound sack in two separate plastic bags, one inside the other. Then, to get the healthy flavor of whole wheat bread, I add granola or wheat germ, which I buy in the cereal section of the market. This usually comes in vacuum-packed jars and never goes weevily. I have kept vacuum-packed jars for up to a year with no problem.

If you are shopping in a foreign country where the only flour available comes from 50- or 100-pound sacks, or if you suspect the flour you are buying has been shipped into the country in large sacks then repackaged locally, try to find large, airtight containers for the flour. Glass one-gallon jars are my first choice. Fill the jars to within two inches of the top. Put in an egg-sized lump of dry ice. Fasten the container top in place so it's not quite airtight. When the dry ice dissipates, seal the container well. Put a tight ring of tape around the lid to form an extra seal. The chemicals in the dry ice will kill any weevil larvae.

If dry ice is not available, five laurel or bay leaves per gallon container of flour are supposed to work as well. I have not personally tested this method, but the sailor who recommended it was experienced.

If you do get weevils, a flour sifter will get rid of most of the ones you can see. If you miss one or two, they will die when you bake your bread. At this point I can hear Larry joking, "Who cares about a few weevils, they just add a bit of protein to your diet." This may sound a bit flippant, but unfortunately weevils are a fact of life in some Mediterranean countries and most tropical ones. The flour you'll buy in places like Sri Lanka, Egypt, Barbados, or Brazil has weevils in it or ready to hatch. They are a nuisance, but once dead, they are not harmful.

On the other hand, weevils do have powerful teeth. Before we left Sri Lanka for Malaysia, we had to buy some local flour from fifty-pound sacks to supplement our supplies. We stored it in two separate tupperware containers under a quarter berth. Two weeks later, in the middle of the Bay of

Bengal, we both started getting sharp bites from something that left a small, red, itchy pimple. A thorough search showed that weevils had eaten right through the tupperware —boring perfectly round one-sixteenth-inch diameter holes in the plastic. They'd also attacked several packages of lasagne noodles. Fly spray killed them easily. But after that I put any suspect flour in glass containers.

When it comes right down to it, baking bread is simpler than storing the ingredients. People in the most primitive countries in the world do it daily on open fires, in stone fireplaces, and on top of old sheets of metal heated by butane torches.

The first thing I learned about most bread recipes printed in American and English cookbooks is that they insist you knead the bread 300 times but don't tell you that all the kneading does is produce a loaf textured like store-bought bread. This just isn't necessary, and in fact most people

Day 15 Lin preparing dough on board a Cruising Cal–39 on a delivery trip.

prefer the coarser, almost cakelike texture of unkneaded bread. So on a day when you'll be around the boat for three hours doing other chores or projects, try this basic recipe. It's the one I use, with a dozen variations.

Use a large salad bowl.
Add 2/3 cup of salt water
1 1/3 cup of fresh water or
2 cups of fresh water
2 tsp. salt

Water should be between 90° and 100°, baby-bath temperature. If you put your bare wrist in it, the water feels comfortable. Too hot and it will kill your yeast; too cool and the yeast will work slower.

Add 2 heaping tsp. dry yeast or 2 packets
Stir until the yeast dissolves.
Add 1/4 cup of either sugar, honey, maple syrup, or brown sugar, plus 5 or 6 cups of flour.

Stir the flour in with a spoon until the mix is too stiff to handle, then start working the last cups of flour in with your hands, adding more flour until the dough stops clinging to your hands. There is no exact measurement on the flour because humidity affects the amount you'll use. It's difficult to work too much flour in, just keep adding until the dough feels smooth and doesn't stick to a clean finger when you press it firmly. It will appear smooth and feel almost satiny at this stage. Mix it with your fingers until it is an even consistency. This usually takes two or three minutes. If you want to knead your bread, go ahead now. But if you are slightly lazy like me, you won't. Form the dough into a ball in the middle of the bowl. Cover the bowl with a clean towel and put it in a warm, dry place to rise. The engine room right after you've been running the generator is great. Or if you are engineless like us, a sunny spot that is out of the wind works well. You need any temperature between 80° and 110° at this stage. If you are in a cool climate, turn your oven on for three minutes. Turn it off and let your dough rise in the oven.

In thirty minutes, check the dough. If it hasn't started growing, it is in too cool a place. If it's starting to get a crust, it's too warm. In forty to forty-five minutes the dough should be about double.

When it has doubled in size either punch it down (yes, hit it with your fist four or five times) and let it rise again to get a smoother-textured loaf. Or, if you have it scheduled for some meal and don't feel like waiting, grease some bread pans or line them with aluminum foil, cut the dough in half, form it into two loaves, and place them in the pans. If you rub your hands with salad oil before you handle the dough, they will stay cleaner. Let the loaves rise again until they are double. Then place them in a cool oven. Turn the heat on to 350° and bake until the loaves are golden brown, or about thirty to thirty-five minutes. Turn the bread pans at least once during the process to assure an even brown color. If your oven doesn't control perfectly, don't worry; the bread may bake faster or slower but it is quite forgiving. To be sure it's done, rap it with a knuckle. If it sounds hollow, it's ready.

Let it cool five or six minutes, then remove it from the pan and rest it on its side or set the loaf on a cake rack so the steam escapes from the bottom.

Don't try to cut the loaf for fifteen minutes at least. It will not only burn your fingers; it will ball up around your knife. This recipe gives you a crusty loaf. The more you knead it, the less crusty it will be.

There are endless variations on this recipe, most of which can be used with the pressure-cooker bread or batter bread recipes that follow.

Substitute 1 cup of wheat germ
or 1 cup of rye flour
or 1 cup of granola
for 1 cup of flour

Add 1 cup of oatmeal
or 3/4 cup of raisins and 2 tsp. cinnamon
or 3/4 cup of chopped onions
or 3/4 cup of grated or chunked cheese
or 2 tsp. garlic powder, 2 tsp. sage, 2 tsp. oregano

Substitute 1 cup of fruit juice for a cup of water.

Instead of making a loaf, make individual rolls, they bake in twelve to fifteen minutes.

Divide the dough into 3 pieces, roll each piece out into a long worm like you did in play school when you made clay pots. Then braid the pieces and let them rise. Just before you bake the braided loaf, brush each lump with the white of an egg. (I use my fingers for this job, rubbing the white lightly over the loaf, it's not too messy.) The egg white will add a nice gloss to the top of the loaf.

For a real treat, take a third of the dough after it has risen once. Put it on an oiled cookie sheet and press it out to form an oval about twelve inches wide, eighteen inches long. Spread a thin layer of butter over the oval with a knife. Sprinkle liberally with brown sugar and raisins, or nuts and chocolate chips. Roll from one side to the other. Roll up the ends and bake to serve at teatime.

You can also fill the same dough with chopped meat, onions, garlic, and green peppers plus seasonings, then bake it.

And finally, this dough makes a good pizza base.

Several people have given me recipes for oven breads that don't need to be formed into loaves. They are quite foolproof because the measurements are exact. The problem with both recipes is that they require not only careful oven control but steady sailing conditions, and in the case of the beer bread, very slow baking.

CELIA VANDERPOOL'S BATTER BREAD

1 package or 1 heaping tsp. dry yeast
1 3/4 cup warm water
2 tbs. shortening
2 tbs. sugar
2 tsp. salt
2 2/3 cup flour

plus one of the following:
1 grated onion
3/4 cup grated cheese
1/4 cup sesame seeds or
2 tsp. cinnamon and
3/4 cup raisins

Dissolve the yeast in water. Add shortening, sugar, salt, and flour. Blend, then beat for 300 strokes. Scrape sides of the bowl. Cover and let rise until double (about 30 minutes). Stir batter down by beating 25 strokes. Spread in a greased loaf pan. Smooth out the top, cover, and let rise again until double. Bake 45 minutes at 375°. Brush top with melted butter and let cool.

Nina Mann from Virginia gave me a recipe that doesn't even need yeast. It makes a heavier loaf that is better with some fruit or nuts to liven it up. The basic recipe is simple.

2 cups self-rising flour
3 tbs. sugar
1 can of beer

Mix well, then bake immediately for one hour in a 350° oven. The recipe needs no salt. The beer must be fresh, any brand will do, and there is no beer flavor left when its finished baking.

Pressure-cooker bread is one of the two solutions left for people who don't have ovens. The other solution is a folding stove-top oven, which may be hard to hold in place in a seaway. This recipe has been thoroughly sea-tested by Jancis Taggert on the thirty-five-foot ketch *Labi Labi* during a voyage from Malaysia to Greece. I've shared one of the first loaves Jancis made. It was good, and nicely browned.

1 1/2 cups lukewarm water or 1 cup fresh water plus
1/2 cup salt water
2 tbs. dried yeast
2 tsp. salt if you don't use salt water
4 cups flour
2 heaping tbs. coarse cornmeal or oatmeal

Combine the water, yeast, salt, and sugar and let stand for 5 minutes. Stir in the flour and let rise in a warm place for about 90 minutes or until double in size. Stir down and let rise again.

Grease the pressure cooker thoroughly and add the cornmeal or oatmeal and shake to coat the cooker evenly. (The meal adds an insulating barrier so the dough can brown.) Pour the dough in and let it rise once more. Then lock the lid on but do not use the pressure regulator valve. Cook over low heat with a flame tamer (asbestos pad) for 40 minutes. Steam will escape through the vent. Do not remove the cover during the baking time.

If you bake more than one loaf and want to store it, wait until the loaf is completely cool. Then wrap it in aluminum foil first, then in a plastic bag. It will keep fine for three to five days.

We have found that fresh-baked bread never seems to get wasted. In fact on deliveries or with crew, I rarely seem to end up with the two-day-old bread I like to use for some of my favorite recipes. Two-or-three-day-old bread makes better french toast. I float three-day-old slices on top of onion or beef soup, top the bread with grated cheese, and bake it.

But my favorite three-day-old bread recipe is English-style bread and butter pudding.

Mix 3 eggs
3/4 cups of milk (1/2 can of evaporated plus 1/4 cup of water)
1/2 cup of sugar
1 tsp. vanilla
1/2 tsp. cinnamon
1/2 tsp. salt
1/2 cup of raisins, sultanas, or chocolate chips

together in a bowl. Add 8 or 10 slices of old bread cut into 1/2″ cubes (3 cups approximately). Toss in with the egg mixture. Add about 15 or 20 small pieces of butter (1/2″ cubes) and toss again. Pour into a well-greased baking pan and bake for 25 minutes at 350° to 375° until the top turns brown.

Let cool completely, cut into squares, and serve as a treat for the night watches.

To preserve bread once you've baked it, or if you purchase from a bakery, paint each loaf all over with a light coating of white vinegar (a clean paint brush or a pastry brush will do the trick). Then double- or triple-wrap the loaf in either plastic wrap or well-sealed plastic bags. The bread will keep mold-free for ten or fourteen days in the tropics, longer in cooler climates. When you unwrap the bread to use it, there will be no hint of the vinegar. (This trick also works on cheeses—the same type of mold must attack both cheese and bread.)

For those times when it's too rough to bake bread, or when the bread supply runs out and you haven't time to bake, I've found several handy substitutes. Baking powder biscuits take only twenty minutes to make. You can use a biscuit mix or

combine 1 cup flour (not sifted)
1 tsp. baking powder
1 tsp. salt
1 tbs. sugar
2 tbs. cooking oil
2 tbs. milk

Mix until a very stiff batter forms. Drop by spoonfuls onto a sheet of aluminum foil or a greased cookie sheet. Bake at 325–400° for twelve or fifteen minutes until the tops turn brown. These are really only good fresh as they get hard as a rock about two hours after they are baked.

Leftover pancakes are a good bread substitute. Larry loves them cold, buttered, and jammed as a late-night snack. Cornbread goes well with meals or as a snack but is best served very fresh.

For treats I like to carry some canned Boston-style brown bread, but this is hard to find outside the United States. Biscuits, or what Americans call crackers or saltines, are available wordwide. They come in large round patties throughout the Far East and South Pacific. They are packed in wonderful metal airtight tins and are usually called cabin biscuits. We use biscuits or saltines for after-dinner cheese or for morning peanut butter and jam, with soup, or crushed as a substitute for bread crumbs in fish cakes and meat loaf. When you are buying biscuits or saltine crackers in countries where they aren't sold in tins, buy small packages so they can be kept individually sealed. The salt on the buiscuits attracts moisture, and after one night an open package will go limp. To revitalize the stale buiscuits, place them on a baking pan and heat in the oven until they are crisp once more.

Day 16

noon to noon 58 miles, miles to date 1,090

fog patches close reaching over a smooth sea

Breakfast—canned mandarin oranges in juice
biscuits and jam
coffee and tea
Lunch—salmon loaf sandwiches with tomato and mayonnaise
hard-boiled eggs
Dinner—spaghetti bolognese
red wine

DURING VEGETABLE INSPECTION TODAY I found that two tomatoes had gotten loose while we were beating the past few days. They were badly bruised. Two others were overripe, so dinner tonight was planned by circumstances.

GALLEY ARRANGEMENTS

The average long-distance cruiser spends less than 15 percent of the hours in any one year at sea. When you've been beating to windward like we have for the past two days, it may seem differently. But to plan the galley of a cruising home only for seagoing is a potential mistake. On the other hand, since the galley on a boat is in a much smaller area than that in a house, and since the amount of foot traffic per square foot must be 100 times that of the average house, traffic planning is extremely important, not only for at sea but for those times spent in the anchorage.

The idea that your galley must be right next to the companionway to be useful in a long-distance cruising boat must be a bit of rebellion against those pre-1940 yachts where the crew all worked forward of the mast. I've sailed on one fifty-year-old, sixty-foot Alden schooner where the galley was next to the foremast, dividing the crew's quarters from the guests (fig. 12A). It was only ten feet from the chain locker, the motion was appalling, the ventilation even worse. A cup of coffee for the helmsman usually arrived cold and half-empty after being carried through forty feet of boat. But fortunately for the cook, if not for the romantics, those days are gone for good.

Putting your galley right next to the companionway also has its disadvantages (fig. 12B). The cook is right in the busiest part of the boat. Unless the boat is very beamy, the cook must dodge anyone coming for a sailbag or going to the WC. If the cook's working counter is next to the companion-

FIGURE 12

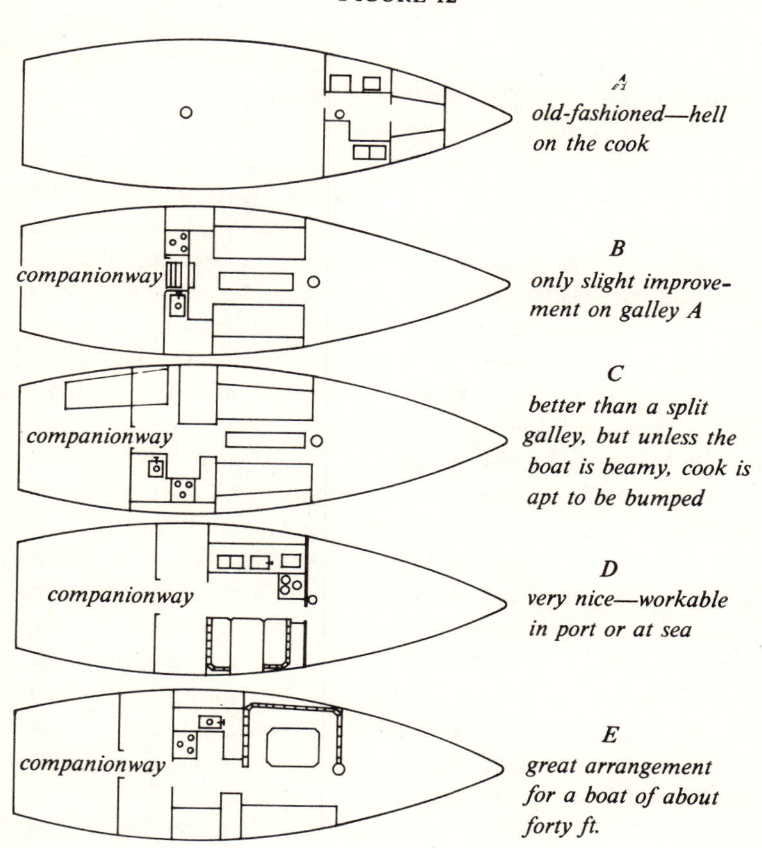

A
old-fashioned—hell on the cook

B
only slight improvement on galley A

C
better than a split galley, but unless the boat is beamy, cook is apt to be bumped

D
very nice—workable in port or at sea

E
great arrangement for a boat of about forty ft.

way, a crewman rushing below stands a chance of putting his foot in his own half-prepared sandwich. Under way, the cook loses the very ventilation he/she needs because the companionway must be shut or spray and gusts of wind will put out the stove. And finally, in most cruising boats the engine is under the forward end of the cockpit, right next to the aft galley. The poor cook who has to dish up a meal in the tropics standing right next to a hot engine has my sympathy.

Although a galley set off to one side of the companionway is a vast improvement (fig. 12C), the most usuable arrangements I've seen are ones where the galley is more toward the middle or forward end of the main cabin (fig. 12D, E). With a large, dorade-type ventilator or opening hatch just above the stove, your cook has the ventilation he needs. He or she is out of the crew's way and in the part of the boat with the best motion. The table on most cruisers is near the mast so the cook can easily reach the table from the amidship's galley. One final improvement on this amidship's galley is an opening portlight right over the sink. Then the cook can enjoy the view or cool off and can get that breath of fresh air that prevents nausea as well.

When I started writing about galley arrangements I spent a day visiting four different cruising boats. All the couples on these boats had cruised for almost a year, and each wife made one statement in common. They all felt the galley sink should be as close as possible to the stove. It really makes sense when you consider cooking at sea. A pot that is hot and boiling over can be quickly transferred into the sink without making a mess. Mugs can be lined up in the sink and soup poured with little lost motion or few spills. If you have to carry a pot of water from the sink on one side of your boat to the stove on the other, there are bound to be mishaps.

If possible, the stove should also be several feet away from the head of any bunks or settees. Sleepy people are often careless about where they put their hands when they are climbing out of the bunk. And, with the inevitable spills on a heavy weather passage, your cook has one fewer worry if there is no one sleeping or sitting just inches from the stove. A dividing bulkhead eighteen inches above stove level will solve the problem if the stove must be near a bunk.

A real must for cooking in a seaway is a back strap for the

cook to lean against while the boat is heeled. This strap should be made of two- or three-inch-wide strong webbed fabric with easy-to-use clips on each end. In a U-shaped galley (fig. 12E) this strap is easy to arrange. It not only gives the cook support but keeps the crew out of the cook's way. On larger boats where the galley may be ten or more feet from the cockpit, I've seen an extension of this strap the length of the main cabin. The cook could carry a cup of coffee directly from the stove to the companionway without having to look for a handhold.

Galley floors deserve much more consideration. It is impossible to avoid splashing a bit of grease on them from everyday cooking even in port. On a long voyage the floors are guaranteed to get wet when your thirsty crew clambers in for a quick cuppa. So, floors must be made of some material that is not only nonskid when dry, but also nonskid when wet and greasy. It should be easy to clean because it will be the most stood-on three square feet of space in your boat. Only one material really meets all of these requirements—bare, edge-grained teak. It is always nonskid. Hot water and detergent and a quick scrub with a plastic pot scrubber will keep it bright. It wears like iron and always looks smart. Iroko, Afromosia, or hard-pitch pine can be substituted if necessary. A fiberglass nonskid patterned surface will get slippery the minute it gets any oil on it. If you don't believe me, spill some diesel or cooking oil on your glass deck and add water, then step on it. Dirt will work into the cracks and scratches after one year's use. Although carpets are nonskid, cheap, and easy to install, and hide rough or shoddy workmanship, they have no place in a galley. Carpets stain easily, pick up odors, and are almost impossible to keep dry, especially at sea. Linoleum isn't nonskid the minute it gets wet. Everyway I look at it, scrubbed teak is the perfect galley floor for the long-distance cruiser.

If you are buying a new boat, building a new interior in yours, or simply looking at improvements you can make, consider your galley arrangements carefully. What works beautifully tied up in a marina can be useless in a rough anchorage or in a seaway. And though you don't spend all of your time at sea, the cook spends almost a quarter of his or her day in the galley, in sea or in port.

Day 17 Galley burns are the most common and dangerous accident at sea.

Day 17

noon to noon 100 miles, miles to date 1,190

closehauled, smooth sea not quite laying our course, gray day

Lunch—chili and beans
bread and butter
cola
Dinner—(picnic-style)
fried canned sausage
bean salad
Larry's favorite seagoing cabbage salad

LARRY'S CABBAGE SALAD

1 cup chopped cabbage
1/4 cup chopped onion
1/8 cup chopped green peppers
1/8 cup raisins (or sultanas)
3 tbs. mayonnaise
2 tbs. lemon juice
1 tbs. sugar

Mix well and let sit for 1 hour before serving.

AFTER TEA THIS AFTERNOON we got out *Ocean Passages for the World* to see if the headwinds we've been having are normal. They are not! But careful reading informed us rain is possible for the next 800 miles or so; after that it's rare. Right now we have forty-five gallons of water left, or 1.4 gallons per 100 miles. Winds should improve, but still we discussed the water situation and reminded ourselves not to waste any. We've had very light drizzles most mornings so have left the rain catcher on the boom just in case. Maybe that is why there's no rain. The minute we take the catcher down the rain will come.

A GOOD STOVE, A GOOD CRUISE

I've never met a crew on any offshore passage that didn't hope for two or three hot meals a day. Cruising, this becomes a fifty-two-week-a-year proposition. If cooking isn't easy and enjoyable, neither is cruising. Good food conveniently prepared is one of the joys of life, and the most important tool the cook uses is the stove.

I'm sold on butane (propane or bottle gas). Why? It lights instantly. Just turn on the safety valve, light a match, and it's burning. No priming, if there's fuel it works. The flame is hot and extremely clean. The stove requires very little maintenance other than a monthly check on the valves and connections. Since you can use either butane or propane in the same bottle, supply is no problem. We have now been in more than thirty countries and have been able to have our tank filled in each.*

Our twenty-pound (ten-kilo) tank keeps us in cooking fuel for an average of three months, including baking our own bread. When we use our gas heater also, it lasts three weeks

---

*Our bottle is the type used for propane in the United States, Canada, and England. It has a reverse thread female fitting. The bottle is rated to 250 pounds per square inch pressure and has a plate stating this. This is far above the safety standards of every country we have visited. The tank has a pressure-release valve, and we carry a transfer tube with the male reverse thread fitting on one end plus hose clamps to secure any local fitting to the other end. By up-ending a full bottle of butane; hoisting it above the level of ours, connecting the two tanks securely, and opening the valves on both tanks plus the pressure-release valve on ours, we can get a full refill from a tank the same size or slightly larger. In England this was especially handy because of their anti–foreign tank law. We just rented an English tank full of butane and did our own transferring on board with all open flames extinguished. So far in the thirty-one countries we've visited, we've had to buy only four different fittings for our transfer tube. They've cost approximately one dollar each.

during an English winter. One tankful costs between three and six dollars depending on the country. Our tank has a level gauge on it which is exceptionally handy, but two smaller tanks work just as well. When one runs out, switch tanks and refill the empty.

The biggest advantage to a butane stove is that only with butane can you get an efficient, clean oven. Is an oven essential? One day we were moored in the estuary behind Punta Arenas, Costa Rica. A glorious fifty-eight-foot, Herreshoff-designed ketch flying a French flag anchored near us, and we were invited for cocktails. We were dazzled by the polished bronzework and traditional teak finish of *Denebola.* We invited her owner to bring her youngsters for tea the next day. I baked fresh cookies for the children. Our very gracious guest said, "I know I am richer than you are, but which one of us is wealthier? You live on a twenty-four-foot yacht, yet you can serve fresh-baked pastries. I serve only things that can be cooked on two burners, and we have a fifty-eight-footer."

She missed the enjoyment of cooking with an oven. So do many other boat wives I meet. Life without baked potatoes, roast beef, or grilled pork chops just wouldn't be the same for us. Tradewind sailing with fresh baked bread ten days from land and casseroles are only possible with an oven. Besides, a diet of fried foods is just what a sailor doesn't need—too much fat and not enough variety. I know stove-top ovens work. But they require steady sailing conditions and time to set up and dismantle. The heat in a folding stove-top oven is just as centralized as in the round-burnered kerosene oven.

Two of the most common reasons we hear for not using butane are: it's not safe, it weighs too much. To the first I can only say, butane can be dangerous, but so can sailing. Both require care, planning, and prudence. A boat stove shouldn't

FIGURE 13

THROUGH-THE-DECK SHUTOFF FOR A BUTANE STOVE

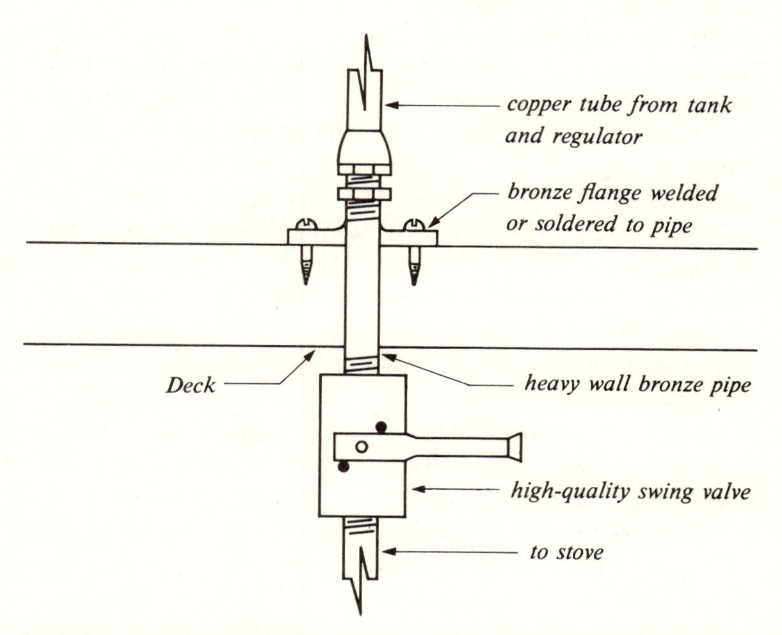

be left unattended. If a pot boils over and you return a few minutes later to find your flame out, you shouldn't relight the stove until you have checked and aired the bilges. A butane stove must be well installed with *the tanks on deck.* There must be a convenient shutoff valve right near the stove, one that shuts the tank off. Connections through the deck should be heavy wall bronze piping. We use a nylon ball swing-type valve. If the handle is at right angles to the piping, the tank is off. It is much quicker and easier to check a swing valve than a gate valve. (See fig. 13.)

We've sailed on boats with solonoid switches to shut off

the butane right at the tank. Although these can be very conveniently installed with the switch right next to the stove and a bright, hard-to-miss indicator light, they have certain disadvantages. The solonoid switch requires constant electricity to start the stove and drains batteries if the stove is used frequently when the engine isn't running. If the ship's electrical supply is out of order, you must by pass the solonoid switch before you can cook. The wiring and switch itself costs ninety-six dollars excluding labor while a direct swing valve can be purchased for about twelve dollars. And finally, to ensure complete safety, your solonoid system should have an explosion-proof switch in the cabin or a gas sniffer and alarm, which add another $150 to your stove costs. If your tank must be several feet from your stove, a swing valve and a mechanical morse cable arrangement would be cheaper and safer than a solonoid switch. (Prices and information courtesy Coastal Propane, Vancouver, British Columbia.)

We repeat: *the tank must be on deck.* So-called waterproof cockpit lockers are not safe. A friend of ours on a well-built Swedish yacht was running from Trinidad to Cartegena, Columbia. His butane tank was in the cockpit locker with two overboard drains near the stern of the boat. After running for four days in heavy wind, Eric went below to start the engine and charge his batteries. His boat contained the explosion, blowing the skylight right through the bottom of his dinghy, burning and partially blinding him. The vapor-proof butane locker drains had been covered by his quarter wake. The tank had developed a leak, and butane, flowing like water, had overflowed the locker, filled the cockpit, and poured over the companionway, filling the bilges. With the tank on deck, butane will run out the scuppers, flowing harmlessly overboard.

We had a small leak in our butane tank. We just asked everyone not to smoke on deck. We used the stove and oil lamps until we were able to repair the damaged tank three months later. Ours is stored in a bottomless deck box forward of the cabin.

And weight? In Sweden we were on board one of the finest finished forty-seven-foot modern cruising yachts we've seen. The owner's wife raved about our butane stove and oven, saying, "Rod Stevens said we couldn't have a butane stove because of the weight." As I toured their floating home I noticed the same designer hadn't complained about the weight of two heads, complete with two wash basins and two magnificent solid teak doors.

What's wrong with kerosene (paraffin), alcohol, diesel, wood, electric, or compressed natural gas? I've used alcohol, kerosene, and electric but not wood or diesel, and I think the disadvantages of wood are obvious for long-distance offshore sailing. I have been told that diesel is great for northern climes but roasts you out of the cabin when you head south. It also means waiting for the first cup of hot coffee in the morning or leaving the stove on all night. I dread electricity because generator failure means no hot food.

Kerosene smells, just enough to make a queasy cook seasick. So does alcohol (methylated spirits). Kerosene and alcohol need priming, and kerosene means two separate fuels to carry. Priming means waiting before you can cook. So the man on watch can't just dash down and warm a cup of coffee quickly. With an alcohol stove the packing glands dry out and must be adjusted frequently or they leak. Both alcohol and kerosene must be pressurized; that requires remembering to pump the tank before your fire goes out, otherwise you have to go through the whole repriming, relighting procedure again. I'm often caught when I'm on a boat with pressurized stove because the fuel in the pressure tank runs out just at the wrong moment. Both fuels must be burning perfectly or they will cause soot. Over a few months your nice white cabin overhead will show this by turning gray or yellow. Overpriming causes fires. I know you can put them out with water, but any fire is a nuisance unless it is the perfect blue glow of a butane fire under a bubbling fish stew.

Each time Larry hears the debate about what fuel to burn, he sits smuggly back and says, "Alcohol is made for drinking, not burning." Considering the cost of methylated spirits as they call it in Europe, I can't help but agree. It's ten dollars a gallon.

Why can't a kerosene or alcohol stove have a good oven? A proper oven needs a fire the whole length of the enclosure (fig. 14). A small, round burner in the center doesn't radiate properly and causes a central hot spot. Using priming cups creates more difficulties. With propane the oven can have a properly shaped burner with a heat-controlling thermostat. Fiberglass inch-and-a-half insulation makes our oven superefficient and produces evenly browned birds and cakes with no burnt bottoms. A grill or broiler under the oven burner gives us space to toast six sandwiches all at once.

After almost forty years of cruising, Eric and Susan Hiscock finally installed a butane stove. Susan's only comment after 8,000 miles of voyaging with her new stove was, "We should have had it twenty-five years ago."

We do carry a single-burner Primus kerosene stove. We use it as a backup in case we run short of propane and also carry it with us if we go ashore for a camping trip. In extremely hot climates, the kerosene-burning primus can be set in the cockpit so the cabin isn't overheated. In boats larger than *Seraffyn,* primus stoves in a sea swing mounted on a bulkhead can be quite handy for slow-cooking soups and stews.

Compressed natural gas may some day be the answer to the one worry about butane. CNG, lighter than air, rises and floats out the companionway instead of settling in your bilges. It burns just as well as butane, and in fact any stove

FIGURE 14

PLAN VIEW OF A PROPER OVEN FIRE FOR EVEN HEATING

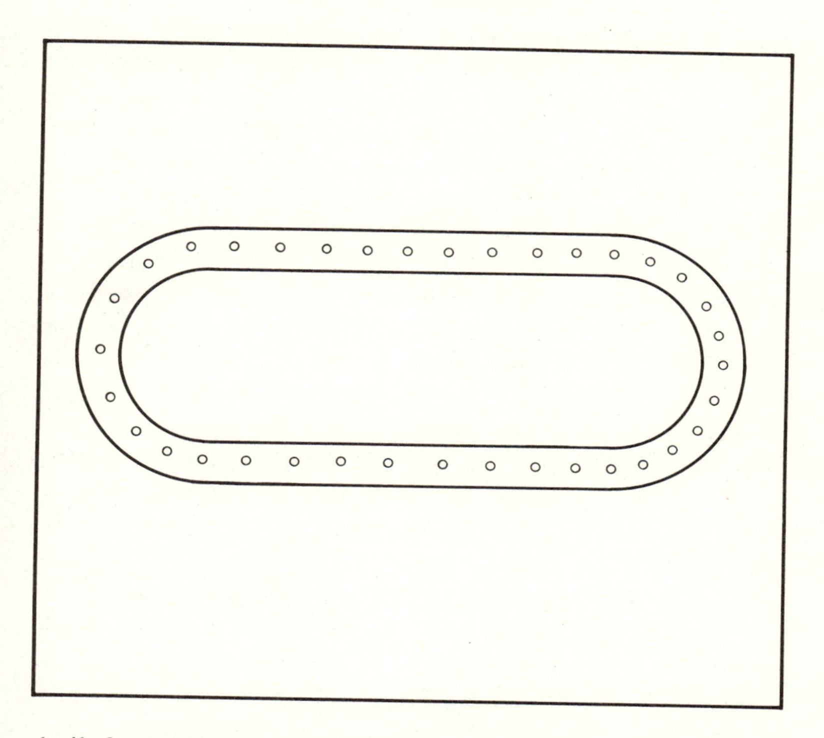

built for CNG can be used with butane. Unfortunately, CNG is only available in the United States and at this stage is extremely bulky. To get the same amount of cooking power as a five-gallon butane tank provides, you would need to carry twenty-two gallons of CNG. But the gas systems people say they are working on these problems right now.*

If you are worried about the space for a stove that has an

*Gas Systems, Inc., 5361 Production Dr., Dept. S, Huntington Beach, Calif. 92649 oven, consider not gimbaling it. Except for boats designed and used for long-distance ocean racing, races where the boat may be on the same tack, bashing to windward for days at a time, gimbaled stoves are a waste of space, an extra expense, and potentially dangerous.

I'm sure no one will argue about the extra space required to properly gimbal a stove. The extra expense involved is the gimbaling brackets, flexible piping, and most necessary of all, a proper lock to use on the stove when it is being used in port.

Burns are the number-one hazard at sea, and gimbaled stoves can be the cause of dangerous burns in two different ways. First, the stove is free to swing. A person accidentally losing balance and falling against it in a seaway can cause a pot to tip off. This happened to a friend of mine during a transpacific race several years ago. She was wearing her oilskin pants. The boat lurched, she bumped the stove and spilled the contents of a boiling pot of coffee inside her pants. She had to be flown off by helicopter for treatment of third-degree burns. Cruising people don't have the support of a Trans-Pac race committee and escort vessels, so a burn like this could prove fatal. Even in port this free swinging can cause burns. A friend was tied to a mooring in Avalon harbor at Catalina. She had a pot of boiling water on top of the stove ready for the corn on the cob she was preparing. She bent over and opened the oven door, which changed the center of gravity of the stove. It tilted forward, the water on the stove top poured over, and she received third-degree burns over most of her forearm. The same thing happened during the 1979 Newport Beach to Cabo-San Lucas race. Help couldn't be found for two days, and the unfortunate crew on *Maverick* had extensive scarring.

The second danger of a gimbaled stove is that few are provided with quick-to-use, individual clamps for each burner. A pot is set on and expected to stay in place. A sudden lurch, a change of tack, and the free pot slides across the stove, bumps the rail, and pours on the cook or cabin sole. Larry really noticed this when he sailed in the 1974 round-Britain two-man race. He was on a thirty-footer with a gimbaled stove and sea rail. Yet when they were beating out to the Shetland Islands, he had to tie their teapot down with marline or it flew off the stove, adding one more bit of racket to keep the man off-watch awake. If you must have a gimbaled stove, please have good seagoing pot clamps (fig. 15), a solid three-inch-high sea rail, and a warning for each new crewman—don't grab the stove for support! And consider gimbaling the stove athwartships so it is bulkhead mounted. I've never seen this tried, but it would be far safer.

I've a passion for commercial boats, and I've never been on board one that was fitted with a gimbaled stove. I had the dubious but very interesting privilege of being cook on a 100-ton Costa Rican shrimp trawler for a month. I fed our crew of six with little difficulty by using oversized pots clamped to a three-inch-high sea rail on a solidly attached stove. A shrimp boat may not heel like a sailboat, but it sure can roll.

On *Seraffyn* we have bolted our oversized cooker amidships to the aft side of our forward bulkhead. We've a three-inch-high solid bronze sea rail with great, easy-to-use clamps. We've twice been on our beam ends, once because of an unexpected williwaw and the second time because of a hurricane. Both times our high-profile, six-cup coffee percolator has stayed put.

What do I do when we are beating to windward? Luckily *Seraffyn* is a beamy boat and doesn't immediately assume a thirty-degree heel. About fifteen to twenty degrees is right. More than that and it's time to shorten down. So, deeper pots solve the problem. Since we rarely race *Seraffyn* long distances, I can usually get Larry to shorten down when it's

FIGURE 15

Plan and Side View of a Good Set of Pot Clamps

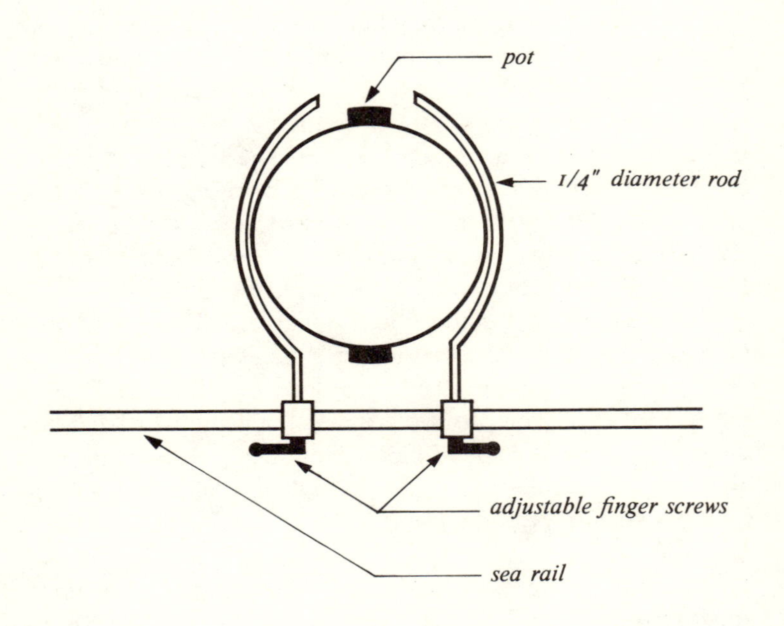

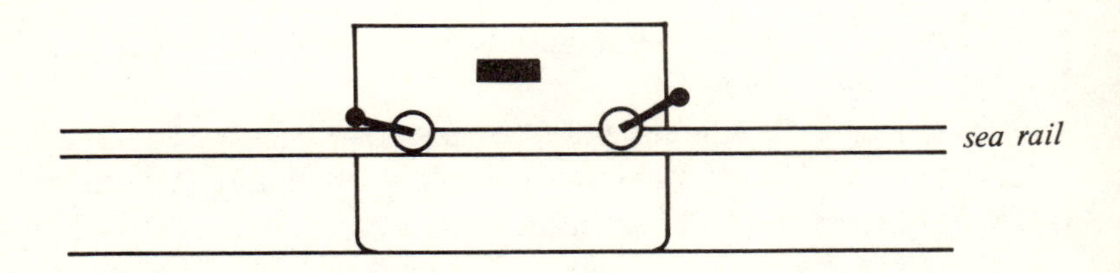

mealtime. During an ocean passage, five minutes lost means little. Living on board means about 80 or 85 percent of our cooking is done in port. That leaves only 15 percent to be done at sea, and odds are half of that should be with fair winds and calm seas. (Odds have been against us at times, I will admit.)

One special advantage of having a thwartships-mounted, nongimbaled stove, i.e., the cook is facing either fore or aft when using the stove, is that if the liquid in a pot does overflow or overboil, it usually spills either to port or to starboard, not toward the cook.

People often tease us, "Did you build the boat around the stove?" No, we didn't, it just happened to fit in the space the designer allowed. But if it hadn't, we would have figured a way to make this a home. Because that's what having a butane stove with an oven and proper grill means to me—the difference between living on board and just camping out.

Day 18 Onions, eaten daily, not only give the cook a good chance to shed some tears but add vitamins to canned foods.

Day 18

noon to noon 73 miles, miles to date 1,263

hazy, wind fresh from SE
sheets eased just a bit

Lunch—tuna fish salad sandwiches
cabbage, carrot, and bean salad
Dinner—Larry's Heavy Weather Hash

HEAVY WEATHER HASH

Dice and boil 3 potatoes until almost soft enough to eat.
Put in large frying pan with
2 tbs. cooking oil
1 onion, diced
10 garlic cloves, diced
Sauté for 5 minutes, then add 1 can of corned beef and cover.
Simmer slowly for 5 minutes more.
Add tomato cut into chunks
Cover—remove from heat and serve 4 minutes later.

WE HAD A FINE MIST ALL NIGHT, and this morning we were surprised to find that our water catcher had added over a gallon of fresh water to our supply.

Right now we are making five knots but slamming into a leftover head sea. The boat is heeled about twenty degrees. Chopping onions and getting them safely from cutting board to pot is taking a lot of patience. It's so tempting to ask Larry to shorten sail. But we'd lose almost a knot of speed if he does. We've had so little fast sailing this trip, and Canada is such a long way ahead. Besides, I know the wind is starting to ease.

Just after I wrote this Larry noticed me getting impatient

with something I was trying to cut. "Come on, sit down and have a drink," he insisted. "So what if dinner is a bit late tonight." An hour later the motion seemed easier, or my patience a bit stronger, and the last of my dinner preparations went along much better.

HEALTH AND THE COOK

For the past few days Larry has been complaining about a sore tooth. My first thoughts were of vitamin deficiency. But last night a small abcess formed at the base of the offending tooth. Out came the medical chest and our medical guide book, *Being Your Own Wilderness Doctor* (Stackpole Books, Harrisburg, Pa.). We started Larry on the recommended course of antibiotics. This morning there is a definite improvement. But I still don't rule out a possible vitamin deficiency. This is a real problem on board cruising boats, not only those making long passages such as we are, but also on board those visiting unusual ports of call. It seems our bodies adjust to the vitamins we eat during our normal shore life, and when our diets vary drastically, be it because we are using mainly processed and canned goods, or eating tropical fruits and vegetables instead of apples and pears, then vitamin deficiencies can crop up. The symptoms and results can be drastic.

Peter Tangvald was crossing the Atlantic on his thirty-foot *Dorothea* several years ago when he started having tremendous pains around his heart. He was unable to leave his bunk for several days while *Dorothea* steered herself through storm and calm. When he landed in the Caribbean islands, his pains disappeared almost immediately. The same thing happened again during his forty-day passage across the Indian Ocean. He assumed it was a heart attack or some problem connected to the rheumatic fever he'd had as a child. On reaching France he went into the hospital to find that in both instances he had been suffering from beriberi, a vitamin-deficiency disease. We spent a week moored alongside Peter and his wife, Lydia, in Manila last spring. He told us that before he'd met Lydia, his complete at-sea diet came from cans. "Vitamins," Peter commented, "I thought they were something for hypochondriacs to worry about." But now Lydia plans offshore meals that include whole-grain breads, wild rice, and as much fresh food as possible plus vitamin supplements. Peter, who is now fifty-six, has the energy and vitality of a thirty-five-year-old.

I know we may sound like health-food nuts, but we have both been surprised to find that problems we developed at sea were caused by vitamin deficiency. I arrived in Florida after two years in the tropics with small ulcers on my gums and bleeding around the edges of my teeth every time I brushed them. When I went to the local dentist for a routine check-up, he informed me that I was suffering from the first stages of scurvy. I'm not keen on tropical fruits so had missed out on the necessary quantity of vitamin C.

During our Baltic cruise Larry developed pains that were diagnosed as kidney stones at first. A Polish doctor finally told us he was suffering from vitamin B12 deficiency. An overnight miracle cure brought on by one injection of B12 convinced us. Larry had been avoiding bread, noodles, and potatoes to try and keep his weight down. We'd been unwilling to pay the price for fresh meat in Scandinavia and had been using our canned meats. Grains, potatoes, and meat are the main sources of vitamin B12.

We still do not go running to the health-food store for our provisions. But we do take a multiple vitamin tablet every other day at sea, one that contains thiamine (B12) A and C plus magnesium. We add wheat germ or other natural grains to the bread we bake and carry fortified orange juice concentrates to provide extra vitamin C.

On deliveries we provide vitamin tablets for the crew. So

far no one has objected to taking them. So far we've never had a serious health problem among our crews.

Vitamin tablets are easy to store. We purchase them in glass bottles of 200 at a time and keep them out of the light in a cool place. They have a shelf life of one year if they are kept perfectly dry.

In the tropics or in extremely hot summer weather there is an additional health concern for the cook—salt deficiency. When people sweat profusely, their body uses more salt than normal. If this isn't replaced, headaches, severe muscle cramps, and irritability may follow. The miracle cure here is one teaspoon of salt swilled down in a small glass of water. The headaches will often disappear in ten to fifteen minutes. Prevention is the better course. During our voyage down the Red Sea, I developed cramps that were beyond the limit of most pains I'd had before. Both of my legs were affected, and I was unable to leave the bunk to stand watches for thirty hours. We'd had ten days of 110° weather before the cramps developed, and I am not naturally a heavy salt user. Clouds covered the sky the day my cramps developed, and as the cooler weather cut down perspiration, the cramps slowly went away. But their weakening effects made walking difficult once we reached Aden three days later. When we spoke to a doctor there, he immediately pointed out salt deficiency. Many people prefer to carry salt tablets in the tropics, but our doctor has assured us that table salt works faster. Salty treats such as popcorn, peanuts, or potato chips help prevent the problem.

Slightly off the subject but of great importance, since a many of my readers will be women: don't wear nylon panties or nylon bathing suits in the tropics. They will help cause or aggravate cystitis, which is extremely painful and irritating. Nylon does not absorb perspiration and creates the hot, damp atmosphere next to your skin and private parts that will allow bacteria to incubate. Men should also avoid wearing nylon trunks and shirts for the same reason. Cotton is cooler and healthier.

Skin cancer is a real concern for fair-skinned people who take up cruising. Those with light eyes are particularly susceptible. A sunhat and good sun-screen lotions are the best preventitives. Preparations that contain 5 percent PABA are recommended by every doctor I have spoken with.

Dental care is one real cruising problem. American and Canadian dentists are the best in the world. Therefore, have your teeth checked and cared for before you leave home. A good program of flossing is worthwhile—but bring a good supply of floss with you. It's hard to find once you're under way.

The cruising life is normally an extremely healthy one if dietary problems are avoided. Contagious diseases such as people working in crowded offices and schools normally contact just don't happen at sea. Colds are rare, injuries less likely than on shore, and tension-caused ailments seldom exist. But boredom on long passages can be a problem, and this is where the cook can contribute tremendously to the health of the crew. A smash-up meal when the ship is slatting, becalmed in a fog for the fourth day; a steamy, hot mug of rich, creamy chocolate when the crew is wet and cold from a sail change; a surprise cake to break up the sameness of a tradewind passage—all contribute to mental stimulation and therefore to the health of the crew.

It may seem like the cook is being burdened with a lot of jobs; medic, psychologist, dietician, purser, bottle washer—but if you are at sea with only two or three on board, many jobs come your way that never occurred to you before. But in return, everything you do will be appreciated, and you'll rarely be bored.

Day 19

noon to noon 104 miles, miles to date 1,367

Same fog and gray but fresh wind, close reaching over a lumpy sea. By dinnertime the wind drew aft, and we eased sheets until we were beam reaching.

Lunch—scrambled eggs
leftover corned beef hash
Teatime—cheese and biscuits
last chocolate candy bar
Dinner—Chinese-style gingered chicken
mee (Chinese style rice noodles)
white wine
camembert cheese

GINGERED CHICKEN

1 cup large chunks of cabbage
1/2 cup onion chunks
1 green pepper cut in chunks
1/4 cup sliced cucumber with rind left on
1 tbs. chopped fresh ginger
10 chopped garlic cloves
1/2 tsp. MSG
2 tbs. cooking oil

Sauté all together until cabbage and onions start to lose their opaqueness.

Add 1 can of chicken meat with natural juice, heat until sauce starts to boil.

Thicken with 1 tbs. cornstarch dissolved in 1 tbs. soy sauce, stirring constantly until all vegetables are coated. Serve over rice noodles.

WE ARE MOVING FASTER THAN HULL SPEED. The sea is a bit lumpy but starting to even out as the wind holds steady from the south. There's a light drizzle, and in the past two hours we've caught about four gallons of fresh water. If it drizzles all night, we could fill our tanks. Then all we'd need is a sunny day so I could splurge and wash my hair completely in fresh water.

Day 20

noon to noon 151 miles, miles to date 1,581

foggy, running wing and wing with the lapper on the pole, smooth sea

Lunch—crab bisque with mussels (packaged bisque mix and canned mussels)
liver paté sandwiches with tomatoes
Dinner—baked potatoes
pumpkin squash with honey sauce
pork ragout

SQUASH WITH HONEY SAUCE

Cut 1 small acorn, butternut, or pumpkin squash in half and scoop out the seeds. In the scooped-out center put

1 tbs. butter
3 tbs. honey
1 tbs. brown sugar
1 shake of cinnamon
1 tsp. lemon juice

Place in a baking dish with aluminum foil crumpled around the squash to hold it upright. Bake for 40 minutes at 350 °. Warn the crew to eat carefully as this squash stays very hot inside.

PORK RAGOUT

2 small cans of stewed pork (Chinese Great Wall brand)
1 sliced onion
3 sliced carrots
3/4 cup red wine
1/4 cup gravy mix
1 tsp. sweet basil

Toss together in a casserole pan and bake covered for 30 minutes.

STORAGE ARRANGEMENTS

We are moving beautifully, but as we come over the top of some waves the motion is enough to make things in the oven scoot from side to side. A spare bread tin holds the pots in place; a nest of crumbled aluminum foil keeps squash and potatoes from rolling around.

The rain increased this morning, and we filled our water tanks completely. We now have as much fresh water on board as when we left Yokohama, and there are only 3,000 miles left to go. The rain continued after our tanks were full. The seas were quite calm, so I decided to collect some extra water in my big cooking pots and spare buckets and give both us and the boat a cleanup and wipedown.

As usual I started by first inspecting our stores lockers. *Seraffyn* has four main food storage lockers, one under each quarter berth, which hold about ten cases of food each, and a larger one under the head of the forward bunk, plus one smaller locker under one settee which I use for all of our eggs and daily supplies (rice, flour, sugar, and so on). Larry has the opposite settee locker for tool storage, and I often have to fight him when he tries to encroach on my stores lockers with things like a new transformer-converter for his electric drill.

I don't use any kind of stores list. Instead, in the two quarter-berth lockers which are subdivided naturally by the boat's frames, I have certain areas for categories of stores. Starting from aft on the port side I fill the locker with condiments (vinegar, catsup, spices, mustard, cornstarch, bread crumbs). Forward of that goes noodles, then there is a section for canned tomato products, then canned and packaged vegetables, then fruits, then milk products, and finally treats (cake mixes, candy, dried fruits).

On the starboard side from aft to forward: packaged beverages (tea, coffee, cocoa), soups, beans, main-course items, toiletries, flashlight batteries.

When I stock up, I put six of each item in the quarter-berth lockers. The rest, along with the large supply of rice, sugar, and flour, go in the big forward bunk locker.

Once every week I try to check the quarter-berth lockers, making sure no packages are split, and if any cans are showing signs of rust I try to use them as soon as possible. I note what items are in short supply and "go shopping" in the big bin forward.

I prefer to plan my meals the same way once we run out of fresh food. I look over the cans and packages in the locker until something catches my eye.

Many people prefer a stores list, and with a larger boat and larger crew for extended cruising it would probably be a good idea. When a boat has twenty-five or thirty possible storage lockers for items to be hiding in, many will be forgotten. If you do use a stores list, one person only should be in charge of taking items from lockers and crossing them off the list. And a systematic program has to be arranged to make sure each storage locker is checked every two weeks at least. It doesn't take more than that for a slow drip from condensation to create havoc with a case of packaged noodles or for a rusty can to stain the paint work.

One final warning if you use a stores list. Don't start preparing a meal until you have all your ingredients out of their various lockers. Zillah, who worked as cook on the magnificent charter schooner *Carina,* told of one near-disaster when she planned an elaborate cordon bleu dinner for the discerning pair of charterers who were paying $3,000 a week for their cruise. Because of sixty-foot *Carina*'s multitude of lockers and exotic supply of stores, a stores book is used religiously. Unfortunately, when it came time to put the wine-filled casserole in the oven topped with a special cheese, Zillah checked her book to find the cheese was in the locker under the charterers' bunk. The charterer was in her bunk sound asleep. Dinner was two hours late that evening, the time fortunately filled by an unusually good sunset and prolonged cocktail hour.

On most cruising boats this wouldn't be a problem, but you might plan a meal only to find the one can you need has already been used and not crossed off the list, or it has been ruined by rust.

We don't prepare our cans in any way before we store them on board *Seraffyn* or when we are delivering boats. On deliveries the cans are rarely on board more than three or five weeks and don't have time to rust. There usually are more than sufficient lockers so that we don't have to worry about them getting into the bilges and losing their labels. On *Seraffyn,* which has a wooden hull with no leaks and no condensation, we rarely find more than one or two cans during any year that have to be tossed overboard. And that's usually because I forgot to check one corner of the locker for too long. To further help keep our cans from rusting, we wash each locker with fresh water three times a year.

If, on the other hand, your boat has fiberglass or metal storage lockers, rust and soggy labels could be a problem. The first solution is to line your lockers with plastic open weave matting, which will insulate the cans from the hull. If this is not enough and your cans start to show signs of rust (not just slight discoloration but real rust), then for the next trip line the cans up with the labels secured tightly, and spray can and label with spray varnish or lacquer before storing them away. This is extremely time-consuming, but if you are laying on stores for six or eight months and your boat is a damp one, it could prevent a lot of wastage. I do not believe in removing labels—not only does this take time but it means that all the cans look alike and a quick survey of your can locker won't tell you where your deficiencies are.

I would avoid storing cans of any sort in the bilge unless your bilges are so large that the cans can be stored right in the cases. There is nothing more unappetizing for the cook than having to reach into a dusty, greasy bilge and sort through wet cans. If you must store individual cans in the bilge because of lack of space, then it is best to remove the labels from the cans, mark the tops, and varnish each can before you set sail.

Canned goods are safe to use for up to one and a half years if they show no signs of rusting through. If any individual cans get puffy or bulging ends, discard them. But if every can in your locker gets puffed ends within the space of a few days, decide if there has been a large temperature increase in the sea water. If there has been, the canned food is safe and the puffing caused only by internal expansion. We learned this when we sailed out of the seventy-two-degree waters of the Mediterranean into the eighty-eight-degree waters of the Red Sea. Every can in the below-the-waterline lockers puffed up within two days. We used them anyway with no ill results. Three weeks later in the seventy-eight-degree Indian Ocean, they deflated to normal size and shape.

Day 21 Going to windward, you need three extra hands.

Day 21

noon to noon 128 miles, miles to date 1,709

foggy and rough, running under just staysail
late afternoon wind dropped and set full sail

Lunch—leftover crab bisque
leftover pork ragout
instant mashed potatoes
Dinner—tossed cabbage salad with Thousand Island Dressing
mashed potato salad
garlic and onion omelet

MASHED POTATO SALAD

2 cups leftover mashed potatoes
1/4 cup chopped onions
1/4 cup chopped green peppers
1/4 cup leftover green peas (optional)
1 tsp. dill weed
2 tsp. MSG
1 tsp. sugar
4 tbs. mayonnaise
Mix well and then let stand for at least 2 hours in a cold place.

COOKING IN ROUGH WEATHER

On days like today, a successful meal is anything that's hot and stays on the plate until it gets eaten. This is when I'd really like a gimbaled eating box like the old Cal 40s had. Their table had enough room over it for a long tray that had holes for drinks, a section for condiments, and room for one bowl for each crewman. (See fig. 16.)

Some boats have gimbaled dining tables, but this is space-consuming and doesn't work well in practice. A gimbaled table has all of the drawbacks of a gimbaled stove. If a person leans on it at the wrong time, everything comes sliding off. If the table starts swinging when someone walks past, it can give them a wack, especially if it is properly ballasted with

FIGURE 16

Gimbaled Condiment and Cup Tray

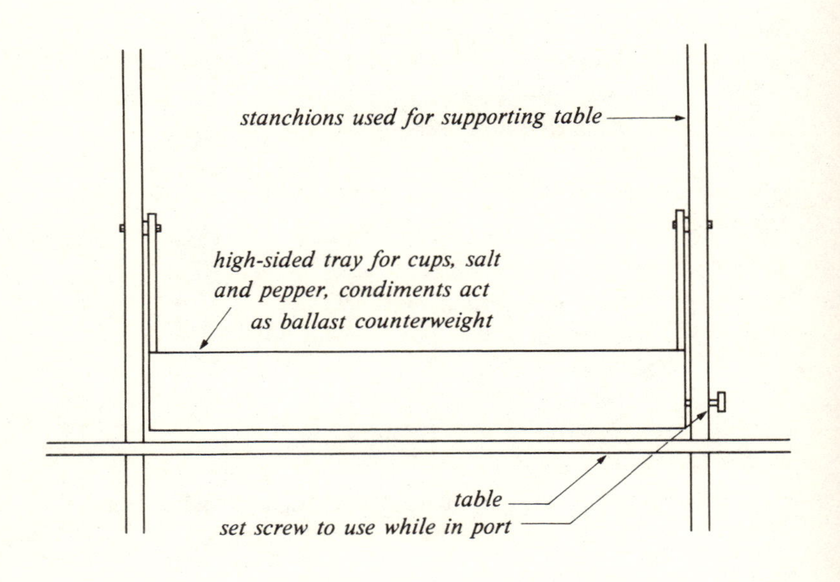

100 pounds of lead. A table that tilts to different angles and bolts in place would be a good solution if you were going to be on the same tack for a long time. But in running conditions like these you need something to hold things in place not only for heeling but for the surging as you run off the top of a wave.

Annabelle and Gordon Yates have a good cup and plate holding tray on their Great Dane 28, which they've cruised from Denmark to San Francisco. It clamps onto the tabletop and has compartments for glasses, plates, bowls, condiments, and silver. If the same could be incorporated with holders right in the galley, the cook could load the tray there, then bring it ready to the table.

As it is right now, even with a damp towel rolled up on

the table, the salt rolls just out of reach when you want it. Your coffee can't be poured until you are finished with your main course or it will spill.

Weather like we had this morning is the ultimate test of a sea cook. The crew is dying for hot, spicy food; the cook, if he or she is prone to seasickness at all, isn't feeling too inventive. If the weather was really bad, the crew wouldn't expect so much; but as long as we can hold canvas and sail on our course, it's hard to go on to storm rations. Luckily most of our cruising is in fair weather.

Day 22

noon to noon 115 miles, miles to date 1,814

fresh wind, running wing and wing over a lumpy sea, very cold and light drizzle

by evening—force 7, reefed main and staysail

Lunch—pancakes and maple syrup
canned mixed fruit salad
Dinner—the old standby, tuna fish casserole
cranberry sauce
white wine

TUNA FISH CASSEROLE

2 cups cooked macaroni noodles (or twist noodles)
1 can solid tuna fish (drained)
1 can cream of mushroom soup (condensed)
1/2 cup milk

Mix all together breaking tuna into large chunks.
Put in a casserole, top with grated cheese, and bake 25 minutes at 375°. Serve with cranberry sauce or chutney.

ONE OF THE MAIN REASONS I decided to make tuna casserole was to use the oven and warm the boat up. It is less than fifty degrees on deck. With the oven going, it's cozy down here. I think Larry liked my choice of meals tonight because it was pretty rough by the time we ate. His comment: "This tuna casserole is good rough-weather eating; sticks to your plate and to your ribs."

INSTANT FOODS

Instant foods definitely have a place on board during ocean passages, even though they are often more expensive than the uncombined ingredients. For the pancakes I served today I used a Singaporian variety of Bisquick. If I'd had to make the pancakes from scratch I'm not sure I would have. Other instant items I've found indispensable at sea include instant mashed potatoes. These can be used several ways, and with only a dash of garlic powder, evaporated milk, and some MSG, they taste better than fresh potatoes. Instant mashed potatoes can be used to thicken fish cakes, as a topping for a meat pie, or as a thickener for a vegetable soup. Though fresh water is needed to prepare instant mashed potatoes, it's little more than that required to boil up regular potatoes. I buy instant potatoes in two-pound cans, then store them for up to a year in a plastic two-quart fruit juice pitcher with a tight-fitting cap. I don't consider them a substitute for fresh potatoes when I'm planning a stores list.

I discovered instant noodles in the Orient. They are now available in the United States in supermarkets and discount stores. These packages of rice noodles contain just enough to serve two people for spaghetti or other noodle dishes. Unlike regular noodles, they require only three minutes to cook. For heavy weather they are great. I still carry a good selection of regular noodles as their texture is definitely different.

Minute rice—I wish I had some on board right now. Minute rice isn't as tasty as brown rice that has been boiled for twenty-five or thirty minutes, but on days when the sea is frolicsome it is worth its weight in gold.

Gravy Mix (Bisto)—We carry three or four eight-ounce packages of the English gravy mix, Bisto. This is now available in the foreign food section of many markets. It has far better flavor than the average individual packages of gravy mix. I use it not only to make gravies quickly but to thicken stews and soups and to add flavor to the gravy from canned meat. It is best to add the gravy-making powder to a bit of liquid, then pour it slowly into the heating pot. I often use wine instead of water for this. Be sure and store Bisto inside a sealed plastic bag, or open the cardboard package and empty it into a glass container, as the salt in the mix will attract moisture and ruin both packaging and contents.

Freeze-dried peas and beans—Surprise brand from England are excellent; we buy twenty-four two serving packages at a time.

Freeze-dried and dehydrated soups—Although current research has shown that these soups contain fewer vitamins than do canned soups, I carry a variety of packages on board. By adding a few vegetables or a can of meat, a packaged soup can become a complete meal. Instant onion soup makes a great gravy if it is mixed with one cup of water and brought to a boil then simmered ten minutes.

Packaged cakes and cookie mixes are invaluable. I keep an assortment at hand because the hassle of getting out measuring cups, spoons, beater, flour, milk to make a cake in a seaway on a small boat usually means I don't. I choose a variety of mixes that need only eggs and water added. On long voyages I store these mixes in plastic bags since the packages are not too water-resistant.

Instant puddings—My favorites are cream caramel (flan) and instant butterscotch pudding. These require milk, and we've found that powdered milk doesn't work well, but evaporated canned milk mixed one part water to two parts milk is good.

I have never tried instant meals of any sort; they always seemed too expensive. But if they are within your budget, I'd try some out on shore beforehand.

Day 23

noon to noon 118 miles, miles to date 1932

almost no wind, seas calm

It's cloudy and cold, but Larry was able to get a sight through a break in the clouds.

Lunch—tomato soup (canned)
Greek salad
camembert cheese and biscuits
Tea time—lemon pudding cake
Lapsang souchong tea
Dinner—leftover tuna casserole
surprise peas and butter
whole wheat bread

LEMON PUDDING CAKE

Prepare 1 package of lemon pie filling. Put into the bottom of a greased bread-baking tin. Then prepare one small package of white cake mix and pour on top. Bake 20 minutes at 350° or until cake is done. Let cool 15 minutes, then serve in bowls.

WE USED OUR LAST TOMATO TODAY. Not bad considering none of them were as green as they could have been. Altogether in twenty-three days we used up thirty-five large tomatoes.

One of the cabbages rotted from the inside out. First time that has ever happened. But I'd been forewarned; the cabbages were picked in the height of the Japanese rainy season from a field that was probably three inches deep in rainwater. We now have only one large cabbage left but lots of potatoes and onions.

Since we had a lovely calm after several days of boisterous weather, on went the oven. I set bread to rise. We had a scrubdown in the oven-warmed galley. Larry came up with a good idea. He took the galley table out of its sliders, placed it between the two settees, used two of the quarter-berth cushions and two bunk boards and made a nice square bed. We took our big blanket and lay together in the warm, cozy cabin. Outside it was less than fifty degrees Fahrenheit; the forward double bunk was covered with vegetables, but Larry's little square bed was a delightful place to spend part of our afternoon.

Luck stayed with us today. A fresh wind came up late in the day, and by dinnertime we were bouncing into a leftover slop; but I'd had time to bake bread and finish our lemon cake before that happened.

MILK

How I longed for sour cream after two years of cruising in Mexico and Central America. Larry dreamed of a glass of real ice cold milk as we roasted our way down the Red Sea. And I didn't have any whole milk to bake a double devil's food birthday cake as we approached Costa Rica.

When you head offshore, milk products do become a problem. There is little powdered milk available in Mexico, Central America, or any African states. Fresh whole milk will not keep on board a cruising boat for more than a week, and canned evaporated milk just doesn't taste quite right in puddings.

Fortunately for cruisers, there is a product called sterilized or long-life milk, available in cans in the United States under the Dairygold label. In all Commonwealth countries long-life milk comes in cardboard cartons of various shapes and sizes. This milk will last up to six months in its sealed containers and tastes quite good well-chilled. For cooking or baking only the most discriminating can tell the difference. Only one warning: always open the cardboard containers of long-life milk in the sink, then transfer the contents to a pitcher with a tight-sealing top. Otherwise you'll get messy spills and the milk will spoil quickly. Once opened, this milk must be stored in an icebox, or below seventy degrees.

Powdered milk has a definite place on board. Unless you drink it daily, stay away from large-sized containers. The milk powder will stay usable for as long as it is kept perfectly dry, so small containers will assure better flavor and fewer lumps. I use powdered milk for things like pancakes and baking. Other cruising friends report that powdered milk makes excellent yogurt. (See recipe in *Joy of Cooking.*) Stock up on powdered milk in the United States or Commonwealth countries for best quality.

Canned evaporated milk is available worldwide—in fact, most foreign babies are raised on it. We have a Mexican friend whose mother ran out of names after her seventh child and named him for the milk he drank, Carnation. For baking or drinks I add one-third water to two-thirds evaporated milk. The flavor is a bit different, but many friends claim to prefer it in hot chocolate or clam chowder. Once again, transfer evaporated milk into a glass or plastic container once it is opened. An evaporated milk spill in your icebox will cause a real stink.

Two very useful milk products we carry are condensed sweetened milk and Nestle's double cream. The first is a very common canned milk mixed with sugar. Eaten right out of the can it's delicious; mixed into hot chocolate it's great. A book of recipes is available from the producer which will really add to your dessert list. This milk product is available almost worldwide.

Nestle's double cream (on the can it's simply called cream) is available in Commonwealth countries and on the specialty shelf in U.S. markets. The six-ounce can contains cream sc thick it is hard to stir. I use it mixed with a bit of brandy and powdered sugar for topping cakes and fruit. It blends into eggs to make wonderful omelets. Add a teaspoon of vinegar, let it stand two hours, and it substitutes well for sour cream in dips and stroganoffs.

Before each ocean passage I plan on buying twelve liters of long-life milk, twelve small cans of evaporated milk, two pounds of milk powder, six cans of condensed sweetened milk, and four cans of double cream. That usually lasts the two of us three months. We do not drink milk more than twice a week. So if you are a family of milk drinkers, I'd add a case or two of long-life milk. You'll rarely be able to buy fresh milk except in a few developed nations and large seaports.

Day 24 After a while you feel like you are leaving a trail of trash behind you as you sail.

Day 24

noon to noon 20 miles, miles to date 1,952

cold, force 7 headwind, can head for the Aleutians or Hawaii but not Canada

by dinnertime, hove to

Lunch—peanut butter and jam sandwiches
lemon pudding cake
raisins and nuts
Dinner—hove to and served
chicken and rice

CHICKEN AND RICE

1 can Chinese brand braised chicken
1/2 cup leftover peas
1 onion, sliced
8 garlics, crushed
2 tbs. gravy mix

Simmer together for 10 minutes, then serve over a bed of rice.

I DON'T KNOW IF THIS REALLY TASTED as good as we thought it did; but hove to, cold and depressed, it sure hit the spot.

The cook is feeling lower than a snake's belly. I hate beating, especially when there's more than 2,500 miles to beat if this wind doesn't change! The pilot charts promised me a run!

TRASH

After twenty-four days at sea you feel like you are sailing on forever, leaving a trail of cans, bottles, and boxes to mark your path. I find myself feeling guilty about this. Cans, organic garbage, paper, and bottles all will sink or be eaten if they are tipped overboard individually at sea. But plastic is always a problem. One solution is to put any plastic bags inside bottles or jars you are jettisoning, then fill the jars completely with water so that jar and plastic sink to the bottom. The other is to carry plastic items until you reach shore where they can be buried.

When you are cruising into big ports in foreign countries, you will often find that all your concern about garbage is wasted. We paid a small Mexican boy twenty-five cents to dispose of our garbage when we landed in La Paz, Mexico. One hour later we watched with shock as he poured the bags of garbage right into the bay. The next day we tried to locate a garbage can and were told by several local residents, "Throw it in the bay." That was ten years ago. Last week (April 1979) when we delivered a Cal-39 to Mazatlan, Mexico, we found the same thing happening. It's the same in most parts of the Orient, the South Seas islands, and almost every African country. I have no answer for this, but I am glad to see that North Americans are so careful about their waste. We've been away ten years, and almost every harbor we've visited since we returned is definitely cleaner now than it was in 1968.

Day 25 No matter what type of salt shaker you choose, a few spoonfuls of rice will keep the salt pouring.

Day 25

noon to noon 3 miles, miles to date 1,955

set sail again just before lunch winds force 6, sheets eased a bit

*seas lumpy
heavy fog*

Lunch—tuna salad
rice salad
bread and butter
Dinner—mock party ham
baked potatoes
baked squash with honey sauce

MOCK PARTY HAM

1 can of Spam sliced into 1/2″-thick slices. Arrange in a baking pan, decorate with maraschino cherry halves and pineapple chunks. Top with a mixture made of

1/4 cup honey
2 tbs. Dijon mustard

Baste twice during baking.

BEING HOVE TO SURE BEAT BASHING into those headseas, but our three-mile noon to noon is hard to take.

Now we are moving again, it feel's great. On the other hand, this heavy fog is a bit spooky. We know there is shipping out here somewhere, but what is the use of keeping a careful watch? Fortunately, we have an exceptionally good radar reflector, a thirty-five-foot-long roll of aluminum foil crumpled inside our hollow wooden spar.

OUTFITTING A GALLEY

Larry and I were married three weeks before we launched and moved on board *Seraffyn.* We had no guests at our wedding, and as a gift Larry handed me $200 and said, "Outfit *Seraffyn*'s galley with things you'll enjoy using every day. She's going to be your home for quite a while."

In 1968 $200 went a long way. I bought a set of Revere Ware stainless steel, copper-bottomed pots, a set of English ironstone dishes, and tupperware plastic containers. They were the best I could find at the time. We've since added to that basic inventory. But I'd still start out the same.

Ironstone dishware is heavy and rather expensive. It will break if handled too roughly, but it has the appearance of nice china and can be heated so food served on it stays warm. I'd choose it every time over any kind of plastic dishes I've seen. In fact, to me plastic dishes, plastic mugs, and plastic bowls mean camping out. If a boat is to be your home, nice dinnerware counts. After all, you are going to be using it three times a day all year round.

Ironstone coffee mugs work great for soups at sea. Since they are heavy, the mugs have less tendency to slide about than plastic or metal mugs do. Try to find ones with large handles so that men on board can put two or three fingers through for a real secure grip.

For cold drinks at anchor or on calm days at sea, we've recently discovered pewter. Though eight large-sized wine glasses cost nearly seventy dollars in Malaysia, where they are made, we know they'll last a lifetime. They don't impart any flavor to drinks; they keep cold drinks colder and they look quite elegant. Unlike silver or other metals they require no polishing. We used to buy cheap wine glasses, but when someone accidentally bumped into one that was sitting on deck and broke it, festivities ground to a stop while we searched for bits of broken glass with a flashlight.

For rough days at sea we have recently acquired a set of stainless steel serving bowls with flat bottoms. They are about eight inches across with two-inch-high sides. We use these in place of dinner plates for any dish that has a tendency to slide or overflow (spaghetti bolognese, beef stew).

In the spring of 1979 we delivered a new Cal 39 to its Mexican owners. There were twelve place settings of Malamine Yachting Tableware on board plus the brochure for these bowls, cups, and dishes, which claimed that the soft plastic ring embedded in the bottom of each item would "prevent sliding even at heeling angles up to 25 degrees."

After an 1,100-mile voyage that included some strong winds, I was impressed. Cups didn't slide around the cockpit. Serving bowls could be left on the table as we sailed, and, best of all, nothing rattled in the dish storage racks. My only complaint is that like all melamine, the dinner plates started showing scratches from the serrated table knives after eight or nine uses. Perfection would be something like unbreakable Corningware dishes with Yachting tableware nonskid rings. But since they don't exist, I plan to order a set of the soup bowls and serving bowls for our next boat.*

Although a high-carbon steel carving knife holds a better edge, we've finally given up and purchased a set of stainless steel knives for bread, fish cleaning, and carving. With a steel handy, sharpening is not too much of a problem. But stainless steel or not, these knives are still subject to rust and pitting if they aren't cleaned frequently or wiped with cooking oil when they are stored away for more than a week. A light coating of cooking oil or butter rubbed on the sharpening steel will keep that from rusting and make it last ten years at least. One warning: do not sharpen knives on deck, the tiny steel shavings will show up as rust stains on your paint work.

Plastic storage containers are essential on a boat, and there is only one brand we've had complete success with, Tupperware. It is one of the most heat-resistant plastics I've used, (it will melt if exposed to direct flames). It doesn't get brittle or crack with age or saltwater contact. It doesn't stain from common boat compounds or chemicals such as kerosene, motor oil, or bleach. It keeps its airtight seal. I may sound

---

*I have since acquired a set of yachting tableware bowls. We used them on our voyage south along the Oregon-Washington coast in October. They stayed right in place on *Seraffyn*'s varnished table, even during a 35-knot beam-reaching wind.

like the tupperware lady, but I'm speaking after ten years of using the same set of tupperware to store not only dry goods but glues, nuts, bolts, and the assorted garbage that lives in the damp area of our bilges. We've used other brands, some highly recommended such as Stewarts, made in England, or Alladin. Both tended to grow brittle and crack after being exposed to salt water for two or three years. It's worth the nuisance of searching out the tupperware lady when you are outfitting your boat.

Because of *Seraffyn*'s small size, my selection of cooking ware is somewhat limited. The two most important seagoing pots live in the oven—an eight-quart soup pot that is eight inches deep, and a four-quart soup pot, also eight inches deep, both Revere Ware. Lobster, crabs, a bucket full of clams—all have taxed the size of the biggest pot. But in a seaway these extra-deep pots shine. Even the sloppiest wave can't slurp a soup or stew over their sides if I fill them only halfway.

Along with a regular saucepan, a small double boiler, and small frying pan, we have a ten-inch-wide cast-aluminum skillet. This is a substitute for the cast-iron skillet I'd prefer. Only cast iron makes perfect pancakes or perfect fried steaks. But the salt air turns cast iron into a mass of rust unless it is oiled and kept oily constantly. Storage space for an oily cast-iron pot is a problem I haven't solved. So the cast-aluminum frying pan does the best it can, which isn't too bad; and it certainly is lighter.

Two stainless steel bread tins, four small stainless steel casserole tins (large soup bowl size), three graduated salad bowls (four, eight, and eleven inches wide), and an oven-sized grilling tray complete the inventory. In actuality we've never been short of a pan to cook in, but if we had space I'd like certain other items, foremost being a set of Corningware-style casseroles for oven-to-table serving in port.

Second would be a pressure cooker. Until recently I've

been off the idea of a pressure cooker, especially since one blew a hole through my family's ceiling when I was five years old. But after seeing the new safety models available, on which the top is placed inside a rim on the pot then clamped up into position, I've started reconsidering. In Trieste, Italy, at the 1976 world half-ton regatta, I was asked to prepare ready-to-serve meals for two different crews of five men each for the four-day offshore race. Local sailors loaned me three pressure cookers, and after hard-boiling three dozen eggs using only ten minutes' worth of butane, boiling up five pounds of potatoes in ten minutes, and preparing three pounds of wild rice in eight minutes, I was on my way to being convinced.

In Manila I met Linda Balser on board forty-nine-foot *Styx* and saw all of the meat she had canned for her voyaging. The results were far superior to any commercially canned products I've tasted. She'd put up hamburger, beef chunks, pork chops, lamb bits—all with no spices or gravy so that she could use them any way she saw fit. Now I know that as soon as we have a larger boat I'm getting a pressure cooker and canning outfit—especially when I think of the places like Malta where pork costs sixty cents a pound, or Sri Lanka where fillet of beef cost thirty-two cents a pound. But, of course, to take advantage of these bargains requires a set of canning jars, the space to store them, and the pressure cooker.

A pressure cooker must be used with special care on board a yacht both because your galley is so small, and because cruising cooks often wear a lot less clothes in the galley than normal cooks do. A good friend of ours was badly burned when she removed the top from her pressure cooker a bit too soon. She was wearing a bikini and the steam burned her midriff in a three-inch-wide patch. If you use a pressure cooker on board, be sure it is fully cooled before opening.

Don't overfill it in a seaway as there is even more likelihood of clogging the steam-escape valve than on shore. Place a towel over the top as you are opening the pressure cooker so any steam is directed away from you.

One indispensable gadget for foreign cruising is a meat grinder. Much foreign beef is too tough for use as steaks, and few butchers have grinding machines. The new home-style plastic-bodied grinders with clamps cost only eight or ten dollars and will be used more than you think. Big ugly clams run once through the grinder can be made into delicious clamcakes. Bits and pieces of leftover meat run twice through the grinder become the beginnings of delicious paté; all of your meat leftovers run once through become the base for a good meat loaf.

A stainless steel cheese grater, stainless steel tongs and spatula, some wooden spoons and salad servers, and a good teakettle complete my galley equipment. I have opted for stainless steel everywhere I could after trying other metals with no success. A copper teakettle looks beautiful on top of a polished stove top until the kettle is three weeks old. Copper starts to tarnish within a day at sea. If you really enjoy polishing yours, great! But watch the inside of your copper kettle; it will start to lose its tinning after three or four years of use. Enameled aluminum looks excellent for a boat because it is colorful, easy to clean, and light. But with the rough and tumble of making passages, it will start to chip. I always worry that the chips of enamel will get into the food I am preparing.

Invest in good galley gear; don't buy anything that serves only one purpose. Start out with the smallest selection you can live with so that as you travel and see treasures that will add to your galley pleasure you'll still have the space to store them.

Day 26

noon to noon 129 miles, miles to date 2,084

foggy, not so cold, beam reach, setting more sail

Lunch—rice salad
leftover Spam
hard-boiled eggs
Dinner—carrot and cucumber salad
mackerel cakes
lemon slices
canned sweet corn
white wine

CARROT AND CUCUMBER SALAD

1 cup thin-sliced carrots
1/2 cup thin-sliced cucumbers
2 tbs. olive oil
2 tbs. vinegar
2 tsp. sugar
1/2 tsp. dill
1/2 tsp. MSG

Mix and let sit for hour.

MACKEREL CAKES

1 small can mackerel, well drained
1 egg
1/3 cup chopped onion
6 garlic cloves, minced
3/4 cup mashed potatoes (very stiff)

Mix well together; if mixture is wet-looking, add 1/4 cup dry instant potato mix. Drop in large spoonfuls into hot, greased frying pan and pat down into 3/4″-thick patties; fry until crispy brown on both sides.

STOVE-TOP FOOD PRESERVATION

Since the above recipe made more mackerel cakes than we could eat at one sitting, I cooked up the extras and left them sitting in the pan to be heated up tomorrow. Leftovers on an offshore passage can be a nuisance. We usually let them sit on the stove top and use them up in the next day's cooking. If I put them into plastic containers and store them in the icebox, which now has no ice but is cool enough to keep things for two or three days, I would probably forget about them. But highly visible, sitting on the corners of the stove top, leftovers make perfect snacks or the basis for the next day's meal plan.

This trick came from the captain of the Costa Rican shrimp trawler we worked on for a month. I had been hired as cook and Larry as navigator for some offshore lobster exploration work. Johnson, a British Honduran who was captain, had previously worked as cook on trawlers, so we had some great impromptu cooking contests. Since most of the crew were Costa Ricans, I had to learn some of the local dishes. Johnson showed me how to boil up two gallons of pinto beans and spice them so the crew could then mix them in with some of the two gallons of rice I'd boiled to make the local favorite Gallo-pinto. When I started to package the leftover rice and beans to store them in the ice room, he stopped me. "Don't waste your time. Leave everything on the stove top; after everyone is finished eating for the day, cover each pot, bring it to a full boil for two minutes, then shut the fire off and don't open the pot until you need it tomorrow. It will keep good for seven days if you heat it every day." I followed his advice and found it to be correct. As long as there are no tomatoes in your soup, stew, or beans, they will keep for over a week if brought to a full boil each day. This is handy when you want to make up a big soup or stew for the first few days at sea. Not only does it save icebox room; it means only one pot to wash, once. The contents of the stove-top simmer pot seem to taste better day by day. In the case of the beans, Johnson taught me to add some new flavor each day. The first day the beans were boiled up with just salt and garlic. The second day I added chopped onions; the third, chunks of sausage; the fourth, bits of fish and crab we'd had for dinner. Only on the day when I knew the pot would be almost finished did I add tomato chunks and loads of oregano. The crew loved it.

The trip we took with Johnson was in Costa Rican waters where the temperature never dropped below eighty degrees, yet things did last for six and seven days at a time this way. Up here where the temperatures range around fifty to sixty degrees, I wouldn't be afraid to keep most stove-top dishes for up to ten days. The signs that things have gone bad are obvious: little air bubbles form around the edge of the pan and the pan smells sour.

Day 27 The first time we caught a fish was on our way down the Red Sea. Larry felt like a king.

Day 27

noon to noon 102 miles, miles to date 2,186

Sun is out, but it's foggy and damp. We're beam reaching; seas are regular; we're moving fast.

Lunch—packaged oxtail soup
mashed potato salad
mackerel cakes
Teatime—We are celebrating being at the halfway mark on our Pacific chart by sharing a whole bottle of red wine,
camembert cheese,
cheddar cheese,
biscuits.
Dinner—chicken curry
rice

CHICKEN CURRY

1 chopped onion
1/3 cup raisins
10 chopped garlic cloves
1 tbs. olive oil

Sauté above until onions are transparent.

Add 1-1/2 tsp. curry powder
1 can chicken in supreme sauce or 1 can chicken meat and 1 can of white sauce

Simmer slowly for 4 or 5 minutes and serve over rice or noodles.

CATCHING FISH

Larry has doubled his fishing efforts. We now are towing two fish lines, one from our leeward quarter and one from the end of the vanged-out boom.

During the first four years of our cruise, we never dragged a fish line, though we did carry one on board. I guess we had all the fish we wanted to eat from those we caught skin diving or bought fresh from fishermen. Besides, every time I thought of pulling a leaping, bucking live fish on board and slaughtering him on our beautiful teak decks, I pictured blood and guts everywhere, scales in the sleeping bags, and a stink that would linger for days. During the first years of our cruise, we rarely made voyages longer than eight or ten days so didn't have a great need to supplement our menu with fresh fish.

Then in the Mediterranean we started dragging a meat line, 200 feet of line with a leader and various lures, led to a shock cord that had a tin can with a couple of nuts and bolts in it which was supposed to act as an alarm if we caught a fish. Well, we dragged that line for six or seven thousand miles with no luck other than one massive tangleup with the taffrail log. On the other hand, it was fun to yank on the shock-cord alarm, then sit back and watch the mad scramble Larry made trying to get out of his bunk to reel in the fish that wasn't there.

We asked every fisherman we could about tackle, lures, and so on. One would say, "Not moving fast enough." The other would say, "You're moving too fast." Or, "Too long of line," or "too short" or "too big a hook," "too small, wrong color, wrong lure for the fish in our sea." We tried each new idea with no success.

We read stories of other sailors reaping a harvest of flying fish off their decks each morning in the tradewinds. The ones that landed on *Seraffyn* were usually two inches long, and they never landed in pairs; we were lucky to have one in a week. When we finally caught an eight-incher, we fried it and disappointedly dumped it overboard when we found it bony and strong flavored.

Then in Rhodes harbor, Greece, we were tied up next to

two Australian yachts that had come through the Red Sea. The youngsters on both boats raved about the fishing they'd had. Larry spent two mornings teaching Simon, the sixteen-year-old son of Ross and Margaret Irvine on *Girl Morgan,* how to splice wire. Before we set sail, Simon came over with a gift, his own secret fishing lure and the promise that even *we* could catch fish with his tackle.

In the middle of August we finally got a tow from Port Said through the Suez Canal. We had only four hours to catch the tow; Canal paperwork filled all of it. The bureaucratic hassles involved with stopping at Port Suez on the far end seemed worse than sailing without fresh stores. So we set off down the Red Sea with plenty of canned provisions but only four days worth of fresh meat on thirty pounds of ice. Six days later we pulled out Simon's lure, an extremely simple affair, two ounces of lead with a one-inch, three-prong hook covered by a skirt of dark-pink-colored plastic cut from a shopping bag, and secured around the bullet-shaped lead with a fine piece of string. We put it overboard on the end of 200 feet of 100-pound test, green monofilament line just after lunch. We were running wing and wing at close to five knots while we had a cool drink before sunset. I had just suggested that we reel in the line so it wouldn't foul up in the taffrail log at night when the tin can alarm went off only inches from my head. Larry rushed over and grabbed the fishing line. "We've really caught one!!!" he shouted. Then as he began pulling in the line hand over hand he shouted out a string of orders so quickly that I am still not sure I heard all of them. "Quick Lin, drop the genoa. Slow her down or we'll lose the fish. Unclutch the windvane. Pull in the log. Go get something to kill the fish with; it's a big one. Grab a bucket of water to soak the deck. Get a drop board in place so it doesn't jump down the companion way. God, it's a big one." I did manage to douse the genoa to slow our speed; I got a bucket of water and sloshed the deck so fish blood wouldn't soak into the bare wood, and I got the drop board in place. When Larry pulled that three-and-a-half-foot-long glowing silver kingfish into the cockpit, I was so excited that I let out a scream. Then I remembered he needed something to kill the twenty-pound fish with before it leaped overboard. I brought the anchor winch handle back to the cockpit and hid behind the dinghy so that I didn't have to watch the murder scene. That was definitely some of the best fish we've ever tasted. We each had a one-pound fillet sautéed in butter and garlic with tartar sauce. The rest was used up within two days.

During the rest of our voyage down the Red Sea we caught a fish every time we dragged our line. Just before dusk seemed to be the favorite time, and five to six knots did seem to be the best speed. Our favorite fish was the kingfish, a fine-nosed, flat-bodied fish. Our least favorite was the larger, red-fleshed tuna we caught; they were too dry. The small tuna were delicious sautéed only for a minute on each side in olive oil and lemon juice. All the tuna made good cold salads.

A month later, crossing the Indian Ocean, we had a strange fishing adventure. We had been drifting for a week caught in the intertropical convergence zone where the only wind came in tiny squalls spaced about an hour apart. These squalls would last only five or ten minutes and swing round the clock. We'd already been at sea for sixteen days and only covered 800 miles, so the miserable twenty-eight-mile-a-day averages we were now recording plus constant sail trimming were getting more than a bit boring. Then we noticed a large fish using the shade of our hull for shelter. Each time we'd spurt ahead on a squall, *Seraffyn*'s bow would scare up a flying fish. The big fish under our transom would take off at unbelievable speed. Then two or three hours later we'd see the flicker of his tail under our transom again. This went on for four days. We tried everything we could think of to catch him: lures, casting, Larry even tried shooting at him with the spear gun. The fourth afternoon, when we were absolutely becalmed, Larry said, "I'll climb down very quietly from the bowsprit, you hand me my spear gun, and I'll try and get that devil." Larry barely had time to take the gun from me before that curious fish swam right at him. The fish was so close to Larry's face mask that Larry had to backpaddle to get a shot. The spear took that fish right in the center. I was reluctant to take the jerking and bleeding fish, spear, and gun from Larry, especially when he warned me, "You drop that fish or spear gun, you'd better dive in after it." Fortunately, Larry climbed on board quickly to take charge, and when the dust settled, we saw we'd caught a sixteen- or eighteen-pound mahi mahi (dolphin fish, dorado), one of the sweetest-tasting fishes there are. To this day we know of no one else who has ever caught this deepwater fish on a spear gun.

One problem with trolling for fish at sea is that you usually catch fish that weigh fifteen or twenty pounds. This seems to be more fish than the average crew can eat. But there are ways of preserving the flesh so that it can be used for up to two weeks without formal canning. When we catch a large fish we fillet it, removing all bones by cutting the fillets down the center. Then we take about three pounds of the filleted fish for each of us and fry it lightly in butter or oil and lemon juice. I remove all of the meat other than what we plan to eat right at that meal from the pan and finish cooking our dinner. Then I return the partially cooked fish to the pan, cover the pan, and let it sit until the next day. We usually use another third of the fish for lunch the next day. Reheating the remaining fish for a minute on each side will make it last yet another day even in the tropics. I find Larry enjoys two meals of sautéed fillets with a sauce, then a meal of spiced fish cakes.

If we have more fish that we can use in this way, I sterilize several jars by dipping each jar and its lid into a pot of boiling salt water for two minutes (peanut butter or jam jars are best because of their wide mouths). I let the jar cool off under a clean towel, then put in large chunks of the uncooked filleted fish until the jar is three-quarters filled. I add three or four garlic cloves, a piece of carrot if it's still available, and several peppercorns, then fill the jar completely with a mixture of half-olive oil or salad oil and half-vinegar or lemon juice. Then I put a sterilized one-inch square block of wood or the cork from a wine bottle on top of the fish to keep it below the level of the marinade at all times. We then stand the well-sealed jars in our bilges, where they have lasted for up to ten days even in the Arabian Sea, where we had water temperatures of up to eighty-five degrees. The marinade cooks the fish, so that when it is time to use it, I drain the marinade off, chop up some onions, tomatoes, and green peppers, and mix them well to make a lovely salad. Or add the fish and a few tablespoons full of the marinade to some precooked rice and heat thoroughly for a main course.

We have never been tempted to try drying the extra fish because during our stay in Costa Rica we often caught the aroma of the fishing boats hung with drying cod, which was the major cash industry. I know I couldn't live with that smell on board a boat as small as *Seraffyn.* But if you have a larger boat or a less keen sense of smell, you could fillet any extra fish, rub it well with coarse ground salt, then lay it to dry on sheets of newspaper. Cover the fish with a waterproof covering at night to keep the dew from settling. Turn the fish twice a day for three days. When it is stiff as a bone, store it away in a dry container. Reconstitute the dried fish by soaking it for three hours in fresh water, changing the water at least two times. Fried in olive oil, this is the national dish of Portugal. Good fish jerky can be made by soaking boned fillets of any white fish in soy sauce for twenty-four hours, then drying them by hanging the fillets from a line. The

Japanese variation on this is to use half-soy sauce, half-sake, plus a pinch of ginger.

We once asked a marine biologist how to decide if fish we caught were poisonous. His answer was, "If it looks like a fish should look and isn't ugly, eat it. If it is a barracuda and weights less than four pounds, eat it." We've followed his advice and had no problem, nor have we heard of anyone else getting even an upset stomach from fresh, caught-on-board fish. Deep-sea fish are almost all safe as most poisonous fish get so by eating reef life.

One of our very favorite fish recipes came from that voyage down the Red Sea. I had some spaghetti bolognese sauce left over when we were coming through the Straits of Perim. In fact, I was planning on using that for dinner when we caught an eight-pound kingfish. I sliced an onion and arranged the rings all over the bottom of my deep skillet. I set three large fillets of kingfish on top and added a quarter cup of fresh water, then covered the pot and steamed the fish for about eight minutes, just until it started to flake apart easily. I poured the bolognese sauce on top and steamed it for two minutes more. We ate that with the last bottle of Italian sparkling wine we had to celebrate clearing the Red Sea! I don't know if it was as spectacular tasting as I remember, but then with food it's often the mood of the moment that counts most.

Now in the North Pacific our luck is back to normal, even though the Japanese fishermen we met presented us with five or six different lures, absolutely guaranteed to work. But Larry is the sort that will keep on dragging what I call his "optimist line" because there is nothing so good as a fresh-caught mahi mahi, unless it's a freshly caught kingfish!

Day 28

noon to noon 143 miles, miles to date 2,329

no fog, smoother sea, all sail set to a light southerly

Lunch—dressed-up pork and beans
hot dogs (canned)
sweet pickle chips
Teatime—fresh buttered popcorn
Dinner—country-style French onion soup
roast pumpkin squash with honey sauce
camembert cheese and biscuits
red wine

DRESSED-UP PORK AND BEANS

can of beans
1 tbs. Dijon mustard
3 tbs. catsup
1 tbs. sugar
Heat well, serve topped with chopped onions.

COUNTRY-STYLE FRENCH ONION SOUP

Slice 3 large onions into a deep saucepan
Sauté in 3 tbs. butter until transparent.
Add 10 chopped garlic cloves
1 tsp. MSG
1/2 cup red wine
water just to cover the onions
salt to taste
Bring to a boil and simmer 10 minutes.
Mix gravy mix with a bit of water and add to the onion soup until it is as thick as cream. Pour the soup into a casserole (in our case I used a bread-baking tin). Top with pieces of stale bread. Top with grated cheese (I used processed cheddar cheese, fresh is better). Sprinkle heavily with parmesan cheese. Bake in a hot over for 25 to 30 minutes, until the cheese browns lightly and the soup forms a dark film. Let cool 10 minutes before serving, or everyone gets burned tongues.

ON CATCHING A SEAGULL

Pandemonium at 0700 today. A seagull dove on the fishing lure, got hooked by the wing, tried to take off but only managed to water ski along with his wings flapping wildly. Larry heard the birds squawking at the same time the fish alarm went off. He rushed on deck and reeled the wildly flapping bird in. "Lin, get up," he yelled. I opened the companionway cover to see a tangle of fish line, a subdued, bleeding bird, and a white-faced Larry. Fortunately, the hook had not gone into the bird; it had only hooked behind its wing, causing a small flesh wound. While Larry held the bird somewhat quiet, I cut the leader, disentangled the hook, and unwrapped the fishing line from around the frightened bird; then Larry tossed him into the air. After one indignant cry, the bird spread his wings and flew off. My only thought was, "Thank God we didn't catch the nine-foot-wingspan albatross that has been following us for the past ten days." Subduing him would have been a struggle.

Larry put a larger lead sinker on the fish line before resetting it. I hope it stays below the gull's diving range now.

This afternoon the fog cleared and the decks dried off for the first time in sixteen days. We opened up the whole boat, and I was able to take a careful inventory of stores. It seems the only items I'm a bit short on are saltine biscuits (crackers) and cooking oil. It seems a shame to use olive oil for frying, but that's what it will have to be before the end of the voyage. We've got several cans of butter left also. The variety in our can lockers is not as great as when we started, but that's to be expected.

We are past the halfway mark, closer to Canada than to Japan. There is a fair wind and a lovely sea. So thoughts of actually reaching our goal occupy my mind. A big juicy hamburger, fresh strawberries, cherries, a beefsteak; guess we would never appreciate them so much if we didn't have to do without sometimes.

Day 29

noon to noon 128 miles, miles to date 2,457

light fog, watery sun shining through, but it's not warm

seas regular, moving very fast on a close reach with all sail set

Lunch—clam chowder
scrambled eggs
leftover beans
Dinner—spaghetti bolognese
red wine

CLAM CHOWDER

3 potatoes cut in small chunks

half salt water, half fresh water to cover potatoes
Boil until potatoes are tender
In a separate pan, sauté 1 small onion cut in small pieces in 3 tbs. butter.
Pour in with potatoes.
Add 1 small can of clams in their juice
1/2 can evaporated milk
1 tsp. MSG
1 tsp. garlic
Heat until the milk starts to simmer. Add salt if necessary. If you have bacon or sausage, add small cooked chunks with the onions.

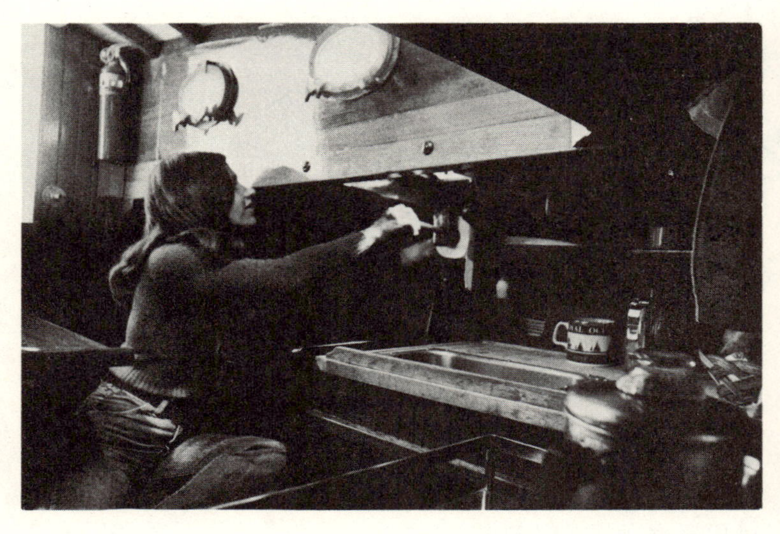

I don't know how Columbus got across the Atlantic without paper towels.

FIGURE 17

SIMPLE INSTALLATION FOR A PAPER-TOWEL HOLDER

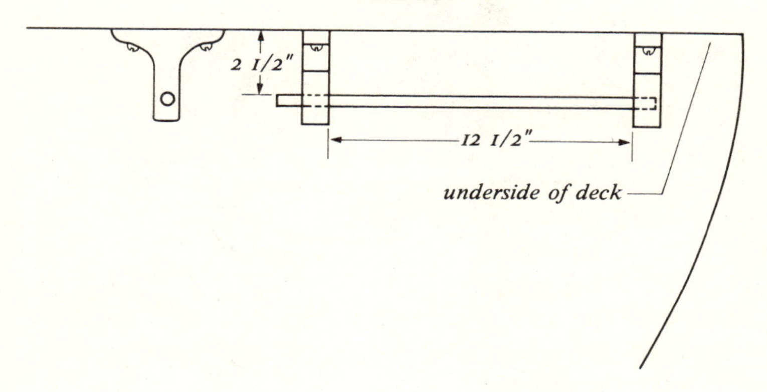

PAPER TOWELS

I don't know how Columbus crossed the Atlantic without paper towels. I know our boat seems to be fueled by them. We use at least a roll a week. So Larry has installed a paper towel rack to the underside of the deck, above the sink and a good distance from the stove. Since paper towel sizes are different in almost every country, a standard holder doesn't work. The simplest solution is two pieces of wood fasted to the underside of the deck 12 1/2" apart with holes drilled for a half-inch wood rod to slip through (fig. 17). This has fit every size paper towel we've run into.

Annabelle Yates on board *Amobel* has found that by cutting each roll of paper towels in half she saves a tremendous amount. I know I have grabbed a whole paper towel for a job where half would have worked just as well.

Day 30 We finally caught a fish today.

Day 30

noon to noon 122 miles, miles to date 2,579

foggy—cold, no sun close reaching on a fresh breeze by evening almost closehauled

Lunch—fried tuna steaks
tartar sauce
cabbage, raisin, and onion salad
Tea—hot chocolate and raisins
Dinner—chili and beans
tuna steak bits
bread and butter

TARTAR SAUCE

1/3 cup mayonnaise
2 tbs. sweet pickle relish
1 tsp. lemon juice
1/2 tsp. MSG

WE CAUGHT A FISH TODAY! It's the first one since we left the Indian Ocean. I sure was glad because Larry has been trying so hard, and early this morning something big took half his fishing tackle. He repaired the tackle, set it, and only minutes later a fifteen- or eighteen-pound tuna grabbed one of the three plastic squid covered three-prong hooks.

I must admit that I was disappointed to have caught a tuna because the ones we'd had in the Red Sea were strong flavored and dry no matter how we cooked them. But there must be some difference in the type of tuna, or it might be something to do with water temperature (Red Sea eighty-five degrees, North Pacific sixty degrees). This tuna tasted absolutely great. The uncooked flesh was a lot lighter colored, and the cooked steaks were almost pure white.

We ate an amazing amount of tuna for lunch and were both looking forward to another steak for dinner. It's been a long time since we had fresh meat of any kind.

Larry filleted off about ten or twelve pounds of meat. I'm not worried about keeping the portion we didn't eat; it's only about forty-five degrees out in the cockpit right now.

ON COOKING FOR A CREW

During our first delivery job together, there was another woman on board. She was the wife of the owner. We'd been hired because the owner had a heart condition and wanted the insurance of extra crew on board for the 1,200-mile offshore passage. At the wife's suggestion, we took turns in the galley. One day she did all of the work—cooking, serving, and cleaning; the next day was my turn. Never again. Though we didn't have any open disagreements, both of us grew to hate the arrangement. I'd inadvertently use up the exact piece of meat she'd planned on for her dinner. She'd use up the leftovers from my previous day's work, so I had to replan my next day's menu. I didn't clean up the galley the way she preferred. She moved the can of such and such so I couldn't find it. Just like in a house, two chefs can't use the same kitchen constantly. And on a yacht during a long passage, the problem of keeping track of stores and menu ideas for three weeks ahead makes two cooks even worse.

In Malaysia we met Peter Thuell, who had retired from his job as manager of a local tin mine, outfitted his thirty-five-foot ketch for a voyage "home" to England, then advertised for three crew to make the voyage with him. Three experienced onshore sailors joined him, two young men and a girl. Peter had never made any passage longer than two or three days and asked our opinion on how to arrange galley duties. "Put one person completely in charge of the galley. Have that person keep track of stores, water, and making sure the galley stays in order. Have each crewman help the cook all of one day, washing dishes, serving, peeling carrots," I suggested. Larry agreed, and Peter, who was locally well known for his ability to get along with people, felt our reasons made sense.

You should have heard the furor in the tiny Perak Yacht Club bar that night. Both of the young men challenged me. "Peter told Jancis she's in charge of the galley! That's not fair. What if she gets seasick? What if I don't like the way she cooks? I like to cook, too. Why should we do all the dishes and dirty work!"

It was almost five months later when we were in Brunei

that we read a long letter telling the end of the story. "Food was great on the trip," wrote Bob, one of the young men. "Jancis took charge of the galley and turned out great food except for the few days when she was seasick. But that didn't matter because all of us were too seasick to eat anyway. Each of us men took turns making breakfast so we got to indulge our cooking instincts. Boy, the competition to create the most exciting breakfasts sure got good results. Jancis cleaned the breakfast dishes, we guys did the rest. All of us tried our hand quite successfully at bread baking. Jancis did a great job of keeping track of stores. Only small problem, ran short of nibbles toward the middle of the Red Sea. All of us gained weight too."

This problem of nibbles is most acute when there is a crew of hungry young sailors on board. It's amazing how important snacks become for night watches. Fresh popcorn, individual candy bars, peanuts, sausage slices, dried fruit or trail mix, potato chips, fruits, cheese, cookies, cake, or pie—anything that can be snacked on with no cooking, no dishes, will evaporate. On deliveries or whenever we sail with crew, we've found it best to have a snack box easily available to the man going on watch. I put anything in the box that is available for that particular day without cutting into our stores. But if a snack item is a particularly favorite sweet that can disappear into an unconsciously greedy sailor's stomach, leaving the rest of the crew feeling left out, it's best for the cook to give out rations direct to each person. I say this because of one incident that occurred when we had two extra crewmen on a long delivery. All of us loved a particular English toffee I'd come across in Gibraltar. I'd bought an eight-pound sack, and it grew shorter by inches each day. So we decided six toffees per man per day was a fair amount. Three days later I handed out rations. Jim was asleep when I did so. I gave Ken his six and six to be handed to Jim when watches were changed. The next afternoon at cocktail time Jim asked, "Why didn't we get any toffees yesterday, run out already?" Seems Ken put all twelve in his pocket and steered happily through the night popping candies, forgetting only half were his. Fortunately, both men had a good sense of humor. A court-of-inquiry decision to punish Ken was: no toffees for one night, double ration to Jim, one extra for the rest of the crew, except the cook who was personally to hand each crewman his ration in the future. This may sound a trifling matter but, at sea, trifling matters can create ego-bruising blowups.

The snack box or fair rationing of snack items is important because it makes clear to the crew what foods are off-limits. I've had an uninformed crew eat a one-pound chunk of cheddar cheese as a snack, thereby ruining a ham and cheese casserole I'd planned for the evening. I was at fault because I hadn't told him to ask first, nor had I explained what foods were off-limits. This was his first long passage and he was used to rummaging through the refrigerator at home.

The same crewman taught me another important lesson. We'd picked him up during a three-day stop at Antigua. One of our original delivery crew had asked if he could jump ship because he'd fallen in love. He helped locate the crewman for us the evening before we set sail for the last 2,000 miles of the voyage. Two days out I discovered our new crewman didn't like candy, didn't like pancakes, waffles, french toast, or doughnuts. He didn't like cakes, in fact, didn't like anything sweet. Providing enough nonsweet breakfasts and snacks for him severely taxed our stores. Since then I've been careful to find out if any potential crew has special dietary tastes. Some interesting new ideas have come up from these few minutes with the crew before each voyage, and a quick trip to the local market has made the crew that one bit happier at sea.

Though it's important to find out generally what particular crewmen do or don't like to eat, I find it best to avoid saying, "I'm going to cook such and such today; does that sound good to you?" Invariably one or the other crewman will say, "I don't really feel like . . ." or "Can't we have such and such instead." And if that doesn't happen, the weather will deteriorate and it will be impossible to cook what you planned, so the crew ends up disappointed. Take it from me, keep your cooking plans to yourself. Keep the crew in suspense until you put dinner on the table. It's much more fun to be surprised.

One final secret when you are cooking for a crew was given to me by a well-respected charter cook. "Save the best meals you can for the last four days of the voyage." Crewmen, like everyone else, have short memories. They'll soon forget that fabulous stew and salad with fresh bread and cream caramel pudding you served on day sixteen of a thirty-day voyage. But serve that the night before you get into port and they'll leave the boat saying, 'What a cook; made the whole trip more fun.' "

As for the expense of feeding extra crew, on deliveries we pay for all expenses and have found that food costs us between three and four cents per crewman per nautical mile (based on an average for Europe, U.S., and Caribbean prices from 1975 to 1979). If the crew on your boat is sharing expenses, this would be a reasonable amount to charge for food and beverage based on the type of menus in this book plus snacks, but not including wine, liquor, and beer.

With regard to liquor and crews, we have found that it is best to let the crew know how you feel about drinking on board before you leave port. In our case, on deliveries we provide two beer a day per crew for warm-weather passages and liquor for one cocktail at night plus wine for occasional dinners. We invite the crew to bring along extra if they wish to be able to treat the rest of the crew to a drink.

It is definitely harder to cook for a crew than for a husband-and-wife cruising team. I'd say that each extra crewman adds one hour a day to the cook's workload. Shopping for the extra food adds time before your voyage. Most cooks feel obligated to cook slightly fancier meals when there are extra crewmen on board. I know I would never suggest cook's night off when we are on a delivery. That's one of the reasons couples seem to make the most lasting cruising and voyaging teams.

Day 31

noon to noon 91 miles, miles to date 2,670

raining, heavy wind, right down to reefed staysail and double-reefed main, closehauled

Lunch—tomato soup (canned)
cheese
liver paté (canned)
biscuits

Dinner—tuna fish steaks with a choice of tartar sauce or bolognese sauce
mashed potatoes
sweet corn (canned)
white wine

PERFECT TUNA

A bit too rough for fancy cooking. But the tuna is keeping well since the temperature outside is about fifty degrees today. Larry feels our tuna was absolutely perfectly cooked and suggested I tell my secret. I only followed the instructions of an Italian fisherman. I selected pieces of meat from near the belly of the fish, cut them across the grain in half-inch-thick slices and put them into a pan with an eighth-inch of hot olive oil for 1 1/2 minutes, then turned the slices over to cook for one minute—no more, only until the meat was white right through.

We had an especially lovely evening. It's been eighteen days since this cold, foggy weather set in. Today's progress wasn't great. Every four or five days we seem to run into a gale. But by dinnertime the seas were calmer, and we had already unreefed the staysail and shaken one reef out of the main. Dinner was delicious—nothing like fresh fish eaten at sea with a nice bottle of Liebfraumilch. Then over our meal Larry started telling me about some stories he was reading. He got the book out of his bunk and asked if I'd like to hear one by Jack London. The chill in our cabin seemed to diminish as the seventy-below Yukon winter foiled London's character in his attempts to light a fire. The story drew to its close as we finished the bottle of dinner wine. I turned our oven on to warm us a bit while Larry lit the oil lamps and I did the dishes. One of those special moments drove away the discomforts of a long ocean voyage. Then Larry climbed into the quarter-berth and I sat down to my special private hour, pen in hand, heart at home and peaceful.

Day 32 Feeding two shifts of eight hungry racing sailors takes a special kind of cook.

Day 32

noon to noon 100 miles, miles to date 2,770

fog trying to lift

closehauled, occasional glimpses of the sun

Lunch—fresh tunafish and egg salad
sweet corn
sweet pickle chips
Dinner—pork stew with onions, potatoes and red wine

FRESH TUNA AND EGG SALAD

Steam small chunks of fish until just white, let cool, then break into flakes.

Mix 1 cup fish
2 hard-boiled eggs, cut in bits
1/4 cup chopped onions
1/4 cup mayonnaise
1/2 tsp. MSG
2 cloves garlic, pressed
Salt and pepper

Let stand for 1 hour.

AS I WAS SITTING BELOW DURING my first watch this evening, I began thinking of all the different types of cooking positions on board sailing yachts. I've cooked on delivery trips, voyages, harbor hops. I've even cooked on a shrimp trawler for a month. I've prepared the food for day races and long-distance races up to three or four days long. But I've never cooked on a charter boat or on a long-distance race.

Charter-boat cooks are often more highly paid than the captains. And well they should be, since most people who are paying $300 to $400 a day expect exceptional cooking. I remember reading through some of the menu plans from *Carina,* the sixty-foot schooner skippered by Ian Staniland out of Malta. Eggs Benedict for breakfast, sweet rolls (freshly baked) for coffee time, chef's salad, sautéed sanddabs for lunch, a fruit platter for teatime, six different hors d'oeuvres for cocktail time, Guinea hen cordon bleu with scalloped potatoes and buttered baby carrots for dinner. It's meals like these that help get *Carina* her 65 percent return-business average. With charters scheduled only a day apart, the cook really has a rough time keeping his or her stores up. I know that some charter cooks I've met were basket cases after a fifteen-week season. But, charter cooks do usually have one advantage over offshore cooks: they can run off and buy refills once or twice during the week when the boat is in a port with shops.

Race cooks, on the other hand, have the hardest cooking job afloat. I've seen some of the problems they have when we were on the race committee for the Long Beach to La Paz race and the Acapulco race.

COOKING FOR A LONG-DISTANCE RACING CREW

Being cook on a long-distance racing sailboat must be the hardest job afloat. Since the whole purpose of the voyage is to win—to push the boat and its crew to the limit—the cook is under tremendous pressures. No one considers shortening sail to give the galley crew a break. The cook has to be able to rush out in case there is an all hands on deck emergency. He/she has two shifts to feed, three times a day plus snacks. Galley facilities may be limited. I've never cooked on any race that lasted over three days, so this winter I interviewed six different long-distance racers and cooks, trying to find the hints that made these sailors a welcome addition on board. Sandy Mackenzie represents the maxiracers, since he has worked as cook on seventy-two-foot *Windward Passage* during seven Transpac races. Jim Hollywood on his ultralight displacement Santa Cruz 30 just finished the 1,000-mile Long

Beach to Cabo San Lucas race. He represents the small end of the offshore ocean racing fleet. In between are four more cooks on boats from thirty-five to sixty-seven feet; each had suggestions that could help you be more prepared if you choose to cook or provision for a long-distance offshore race.

Sandy MacKenzie's full-time hobby is joining maxirace boats for each of the major ocean races. He started when he crewed for Bob Johnson on board *Zia,* a seventy-five-foot ketch, back in the late 1950s. Someone on board had to cook a meal; he volunteered. Bob Johnson liked the meal, Sandy enjoyed cooking; the position stuck. Since that time he has been cook on seventy-three-foot *Ticonderoga,* seventy-three-foot *Windward Passage,* sixty-five-foot *Robon,* and, lately, seventy-nine-foot *Kialoa.* His list of races includes seven Transpacs, Los Angeles to Tahiti six times, SORC seven times, Transatlantic once, Sydney-Hobart twice, Hong Kong to Manila, plus several others. Sandy is blue-eyed, trim, and fortyish. He wouldn't go to sea if he couldn't go as cook: "I like racing, but I don't like being out in the weather when I can be dry and warm next to the galley stove," he says. He takes care of all the provisioning, all the cooking, and usually all of the cleaning up during races. He stands no watches but says he "could be available in case of emergencies."

On *Windward Passage,* which carries a crew of fifteen to eighteen men, Sandy has no limit on his food budget but figures on about $2,300 to $2,500 for the average Transpac. The owner covers this. Although Sandy writes out a general meal plan for various races, these are only to be used as a shopping guide. At sea it's open the freezer and see what interests the cook. His plans keep these basic facts in mind: racing crews eat more; most of the crew on *Windward Passage* are thirty-year-old businessmen straight from offices who may be prone to seasickness or have a tendency to overweight; storage space is no problem as far as food supplies go nor is weight, and finally, the freezer on this boat carries twenty cubic feet of food and will work 90 to 95 percent of the time.

Sandy does almost all of his shopping right at the local supermarket, looking for one that has a good butcher and specialty section. Occasionally he'll buy a prepared meal from a specialty restaurant such as the chicken prepared by the Rusty Pelican in Newport Beach, California. This prerace shopping now only takes Sandy about two days in an American port. But when he joins in a place like Hong Kong, he likes at least three days to shop and get readjusted before a race.

At least 90 percent of the food eaten on *Windward Passage* and *Kialoa* is prepared right at sea. Sandy is definitely a meat-and-potatoes sort of cook—fancy sauces and elaborate casseroles are reserved for the rare races that last more than ten days. His typical menus include:

breakfast—juice, sausage, cereal, eggs, toast, coffee
lunch—soup, sandwiches, sometimes grilled sandwiches
dinner—roast, salad, potatoes baked or mashed, vegetables, cookies, beverage
beverages—Tang (the main standby), Coke, 7-up, Gatorade, lemonade, beer, tea, or coffee. (There is no hard liquor on board *Windward Passage* during races.)

Sandy says that his menu plans rarely change with the weather. When it's particularly rough, he may substitute scrambled eggs for easy-over. But he did mention one particularly rough Sydney-Hobart race when hot soup was all anyone wanted.

Frozen, large-sized packages of vegetables are a dinner

mainstay—broccoli, beans, mixed vegetables. One crate of fresh oranges and apples, another of lettuce are stored in the lazzerette. As things are used up in the refrigerator, Sandy brings lettuce in from the lazzerette to extend its life. English muffins come out far better than toast for a large crew, and almost everyone prefers trail mix to candy bars. It seems that most of the crew hope to lose a few pounds and come back lean, mean, and tanned with a few scars to prove they've been out ocean racing. A box full of candy is hard for them to resist.

Sandy goes light on desserts, choosing Sara Lee frozen cakes and pastries for long races, strawberry short cake for short ones. Leftovers are never a problem; they just don't happen.

Sandy had a lot to say about stoves. First and foremost was, "I hate alcohol stoves, bottled gas is the only way to go." Both *Windward Passage* and *Kialoa* have large butane four-burner stoves with ovens and broilers. But *Kialoa*'s stove has two ovens. "It's great," says Sandy, "I can cook two separate twelve-pound roasts and feed a hot one to each shift of nine men." Gimbaling a stove as large as this is a problem. Sandy feels that most gimbaled stoves swing too easily: "They need lots of lead on the bottom." But life with gimbaled stoves has proven less than rosy for Sandy. In the 1972 Bermuda race, *Windward Passage*'s stove came right out of its gimballs. Later, for the Sydney–Hobart race, the crew added a fifty-pound chunk of lead to the bottom of the stove to slow its motion down. Unfortunately, no one thought to check the stove at its most extreme angles before the race. When they hit the rough stuff, the lead lump caused the stove to hang up on a bilge stringer. "I had to watch it every minute. If the stove stuck, everything on top came flying off the next time we surged over a wave!" From that experience and many others Sandy warned, "Never stand in front of your stove during heavy weather. No matter how good the gimbaling, no matter how high the rails, someone could bump into you, you bump the stove, a pot tips, and you've got a nasty burn."

Although freezers are a necessity on a race boat with crews as large as *Windward Passage*'s, they are no less prone to failure than on smaller boats. Just before the Transatlantic race, the generator started giving trouble. Mechanics worked through the night trying to find the problem. Just as the boat reached the starting line, the mechanics got off. Fortunately, Sandy had decided to lay in a supply of canned food, just in case. Unfortunately, five days later when the electricity quit, he found the crew hated meat pies. "I tried making casseroles, adding spices, but there's no way around it, the results were awful," Sandy told me, adding, "With the electricity out nothing worked. Good thing the stove was butane and we found a box of candles on board."

The storage areas on both *Kialoa* and *Windward Passage* are quite open, so Sandy keeps no stores list. But one comparison he made bears repeating. "WP has all the cooking things in holes under the counter. I think that's a lot safer than *Kialoa* where everything is in racks above the stove." He found two very special pieces of galley equipment on *Kialoa.* First was a five-foot-long gimbaled serving shelf right in the galley between the stove and table. The shelf is a perfect place to serve out nine bowls of soup or plates full of sandwiches. His second favorite was a large rectangular griddle with two-inch-high sides especially fabricated out of quarter-inch-thick aluminum to cover completely the front half of the stove and two burners. Wooden caps on its ends act as handles. "I can fry up eight or ten steaks at the same time that way. No worry about hot fat overflowing or steaks sliding off."

For pots and pans Sandy prefers Farberware or Revere-ware with stainless steel sides. Solid plastic mixing bowls and tupperware bowls with covers are on his list, along with throwaway foil pans for roasts. One other special item he carries to feed large racing crews are teflon-lined muffin tins. "I break an egg in each hole, bake them in the oven twenty-four at a time. They come out just like poached eggs—perfect for eggs benedict."

On *Windward Passage* all dishes and cups are good quality throwaway plastic, so there is very little galley clean-up. On *Kialoa* dishes are heavy-duty plastic, which the crew helps wash. Sandy said he does all the galley work on WP. "These guys have sailed together for years. They've never been asked to help in the galley. They probably wouldn't like it. *Kialoa's* crew has always been expected to chip in, so there's no questions, no complaints."

Sandy plans on a half-hour for each meal for each watch. "That's all the time they seem to want." His meal schedule is:

breakfast	0630	first watch
	0700	second watch
lunch	1230	first watch
	1300	second watch
dinner	1830	first watch
	1900	second watch

Seasickness worries Sandy a bit, because if he got sick it would mean slowing up the team effort. But he says seasickness is rarely a problem on *Windward Passage,* possibly because pierhead jumpers are discouraged. All of the crew is supposed to be on board two days before a race, to get acclimated and help with last-minute preparations and decisions.

Sandy has tried cooking on cruising boats. He says it's

easy. You can eat when you want; the crew pitches in to make their own sandwiches. But there is none of the excitement or thrill of being involved in big league offshore racing. And that's why Sandy cooks.

Big boat offshore racing has traditionally been a world closed to women. In the 1955 Transpac, Helen Henrickson was the only woman registered as crew on any boat over thirty-eight feet in length. She only joined sixty-seven-foot *Nam Sang*'s crew when absolutely no one else could be found to cook. I've met some of the men who sailed with Helen on that race, and their comments ranged from "good job" to "great!" But Helen said she'd never again volunteer to cook on a large racer. "It's just too much work, too much responsibility."

During that race *Nam Sang* carried eleven crew. Helen planned each day's meals, precooking a large ham, a turkey, and a sirloin roast, then stored the precut meat in the refrigerator. *Nam Sang* only had a small deep freeze, which was used for about fifty pounds of meat. Greens were stored in the hard dinghy, which sat upright amidships. Burlap bags covered the vegetables, and each day the cook wet the bags down to keep things fresh. All other stores were canned or packaged.

Helen definitely feels today's racing cook has a better selection of canned goods available. She had only bacon, pork sausage, ham, or fish to choose from. Helen now sails extensively on her own thirty-six-footer and finds modern freeze-dried products a boon she could have used on *Nam Sang.*

One thing Helen told me was especially interesting in light of today's racing rules and concepts of super-fast sailing machines. The 1955 Transpac rules required every boat to carry a minimum of thirty days' stores, including half a gallon of fresh water per man per day. The 1979 rules only required twenty days' provisions and one quart of water per man per day. When I commented that today's races took less time, Helen answered, "We finished on *Nam Sang* in eleven days two hours, and *Morningstar,* who beat us, finished in only nine days." I remembered this as I listened to the results of the 1979 Transpac. The first boat to finish, an ULDC, came in after sixteen days, others finished after twenty days. Theoretically, their provisions could have run out.

Pat Walker joined sixty-one-foot *Sorcery* as a cook because "that's the only way I could go! If I had my druthers I'd be a watch keeper or deck hand. The cook has a lot more work, not much more recognition but its about the only position available for women on offshore racing boats today."

Pat is a redheaded, elegant forty-year-old who'd look more at home at a board meeting or cocktail party than on the foredeck of a sailing yacht. She's often seen bound for a night on the town in exotic foreign ports, dressed in the long, slinky evening gown and mink coat she carries as standard equipment along with her wet weather gear and sea boots. Pat has spent most of her adult life working on boats ranging from thirty-six-feet overall to ships the size of *Star of the Pacific,* 138 feet on deck. The sheer magnitude of the cook's job on this three-masted schooner would have daunted any less determined person. Its electric restaurant-style range had two ovens, each large enough for a forty-five-pound turkey. Food was stored in a walk-in freezer with a separate icemaker. Baking meant nine pies at a time; lunch called for menus including sixty grilled cheese sandwiches. Yet Pat told me that cooking for nineteen people on board *Star of the Pacific* was far easier than taking care of thirteen men on board *Sorcery,* even when the boat was between races. The main reason for this was that she had two galley helpers on the 138-foot schooner and the "best of everything" in the galley. On *Sorcery* the cook did everything on her own, including washing up, and dinnerware consisted of seven sets of plates, which had to be washed between each change of watches.

Pat joined *Sorcery* in Puerto Vallarta after the 1977 Marina del Rey to Puerto Vallarta race. The cook on that race quit and returned home, so Pat took over for the voyage to Hawaii, Hong Kong, and Okinawa. During this time the boat joined various day races and one long-distance race. Pat left after several months from Okinawa, and *Sorcery* continued on to Japan.

Cooks who join a race boat in a foreign port have special problems. Pat found that the previous cook had supplied many of his own pots, pans, and spices, and of course had taken them home with him. "Next time I join a boat in a foreign port," Pat said, "I'll bring my own spices, my favorite knife, a decent frying pan, and measuring spoons." She really missed American supermarkets and such foods as English muffins and prepackaged breads. She shopped at public markets and substituted local foods like tortillas and chilis. With only four days to provision the boat, Pat was glad to have the help of some crewmen who ran after last-minute items such as bread and perishable vegetables. The owner put no limit on the budget and supplied liquor until there was a fiasco on the Okinawa race. The owner bought forty cases of beer. Halfway through the ten-day race, the beer ran out. From then on, the owner declared, each man brings his own beer.

Pat says she is always pessimistic compared with the skipper when it comes to carrying emergency supplies. "I add a week to his estimate and buy extra rice, flour, and powdered milk, just in case."

According to Pat, it's a good idea to make a meal plan of

the main courses for any race that will last more than one week. It helps avoid repetition and guides your storage plan. She tends toward mixed dishes rather than roasts in her planning. "Roasts large enough for thirteen people take up a lot of space in the freezer and mean leaving the oven on for three or four hours. In hot climates that's no good." Although Pat asks the owner his preferences before planning her menus, she says its a disaster to ask the crew. She wasn't laughing when she told me, "If you find a vegetarian on board, throw him over the first day out."

Racing crews eat more than cruising crews. They never miss a meal and are burning up more calories. The cruising man might sleep through a few breakfasts or skip a meal to keep his weight down. So Pat buys about 25 percent more food for races.

Before leaving port, Pat tries to cook up at least a large coffeecake and as many main meals as possible. She uses throwaway aluminum pans for things like lasagne and casseroles, and the morning before races she makes up a big pile of sandwiches.

At sea she plans a hot breakfast every other day. For lunch ready-made sandwiches impress the crew much more than "build your own." But Pat claims its easier to make a good hot meal than to create good sandwiches.

Real baking such as lemon meringue pies is rare on a race. Coffeecakes in disposable pans fill the gap. Pat keeps a goody drawer with candy bars, raisins, and fruit for the crew. The stores lockers are off-limits.

Sorcery, like most class-A racers, has good cooking facilities. Stores go under bunks. There is a large pantry, and bread goes in with the sails. The freezer has a list of its contents taped to the top so that items can be found quickly to cut down cold loss. Pat commented that *Sorcery*'s stove had some burners that couldn't be used because of the position of the sea rails. *Sorcery* carries two big thermos jugs in permanent holders, one for ice water, one for hot. Pat gave these special mention.

Meal schedules were planned to fit watch changes. On short races this was quite flexible, but on longer ones it was up at 0530 for the cook, first breakfast at 0730, second at 0800. Pat found breakfast the worst meal of the day. "You can't let the eggs sit, no one wants cold toast."

As cook on *Sorcery,* Pat did not stand watches but did work twelve hours a day, including occasionally helping to bag sails. On short races where food could be prepared ahead, she was able to join the crew on deck more. She did get the only bunk on board other than the owner's that didn't have to be shared.

According to Pat, there is no problem finding crew for class-A boats. On most the sailing master is often the only person who always stays with the boat; cooks can change as often as every race. The attitude of the owner influences not only the life of the cook but also the spirit of the crew. If the owner expects the crew to help the cook, they will. If the owner appreciates his crew, isn't too tightfisted, and provides a good cook, a team is likely to form that stays together through race after race.

Women definitely have a harder time on board racing boats. They have to work twice as hard to prove themselves, Pat says. But she adds, "Any girl who has free time, is a decent cook, and good-natured, can get a spot quite easily, especially in a foreign port." She warns, "Try to choose a boat with disposable dishes and try a short race first."

One crewman just to handle the cooking may be an ideal way to race, but on boats under fifty feet it's just not practical. Besides, the cooking facilities on smaller offshore racers are rarely conducive to the type of menus maxirace crews expect. So for long-distance offshore races on boats thirty to fifty feet, most of the food preparation is usually done beforehand by wives or crewmembers. Comprehensive menu plans seem to be standard, and often provisions weight is a major consideration.

Ed Greeff has now crewed and skippered in more than twenty Bermuda races. His wife, Betty, takes charge of menu planning but rarely joins the crew for the race, as she prefers the cruising that comes afterward. Since 1968 the Greeffs have owned and raced forty-seven-foot *Puffin* II, a Sparkman Stephens yawl.

The galley facilities on *Puffin* are planned with cruising in mind—an alcohol stove with an oven and a refrigeration unit but no deep freeze. The alcohol stove is a bit of a problem because the flame can't be easily regulated. It tends to overcook food, especially the portions being kept warm for the second watch. The only solution Betty has found is to carry three flame tamers (asbestos pads to set between the pot and flame).

Food storage is a problem on long-distance races with *Puffin*'s full complement of nine crew. But Betty claims racing crews tend to eat less than cruising crews because they are more prone to seasickness. This surprised me at first because of what I'd heard from the maxirace cooks, but as I spoke with other smaller class racers it became clear that seasickness is a problem that plagues class-C and D racers (fifty feet and under) and the people who cook on them.

Betty plans her complete menu (see fig. 18), then uses it as a guide for her shopping. Since fresh meat can only be kept for three days, canned meats form the main courses for the bulk of any race longer than seven days. *Puffin* has room to store fresh fruit and vegetables for ten days, and Betty plans on two pieces of fresh fruit per day per person. But no other

FIGURE 18

Meal plans for the crew of *Puffin II,* Bermuda race, 1974

FRIDAY	*SATURDAY*	*SUNDAY*	*MONDAY*	*TUESDAY*	*WEDNESDAY*
Lunch	*Breakfast*	*Breakfast*	*Breakfast*	*Breakfast*	USE UP ALL LEFTOVERS!
ham & swiss on rye fresh fruit- cookies or donuts	orange juice cornflakes or oatmeal coffee or tea eggs & bacon toast & coffee ring	orange juice cornflakes or oatmeal coffee or tea eggs & sausages toast-corn toasties	grapefruit juice or Tang cornflakes or oatmeal chipped beef & eggs toast & coffee (use up corn toasties)	juice French toast (syrup) bacon coffee & tea	
Dinner	*Lunch*	*Lunch*	*Lunch*	*Lunch*	
roast chicken rice frozen peas & onions peaches—cake	leftover chicken lettuce & tomatoes pumpernickel fruit & cookies or donuts	soup cold cuts & cheese & tunafish sandwiches with lettuce fruit & cookies	soup roast beef sand-wiches with lettuce & tomatoes fruit & cookies	soup ham sandwiches on pumpernickel fruit & cookies	
	Dinner	*Dinner*	*Dinner*	*Dinner*	
	hamburgers—onion soup mix frozen string beans potatoes—canned boiled, or baked pears—cake	roast beef mashed potatoes carrots cherries & cake	ham with pineapple macaroni & cheese bean salad applesauce & gingerbread	roast beef hash zucchini with corn & tomatoes peaches & cake or cookies	

snacking is allowed during the day; it throws the menu plan off. For night watches there is peanut butter, jam and crackers, nuts, and candy.

The Greeffs have found their crew prefers concentrated fruit-juice drinks to colas and carbonated beverages. Concentrates also take up less room. One cocktail before dinner is standard.

Lack of storage space is the thread that ran through our whole conversation with the Greeffs. A boat built to cruise six in comfort just doesn't have the room for elaborate stores for nine racing sailors.

But Betty and Ed stressed that during a race, hot, dependable food counts more than fancy cooking. It's the party after the finish line that's the real goal!

Bill Lapworth, designer of Cal boats and an active ocean racer, told me, "Most people racing on thirty-five- to forty-footers get lots of peanut butter and jam." In many cases this may be true. One Cal 40 crew that was preparing for the 1979 Transpac wanted to remove the stove and table to save weight. Trail mix and freeze-dried meals were planned to lighten the boat further. This may have been a satisfactory solution, but for team morale and good health I was far more impressed with the menu plans used by Doc Holiday on board his Ericson 35 during two successful Long Beach to La Paz races. In 1969 *Aquarius* took first in class. In 1975 she finished first in the Ocean Racing Fleet. Other *Aquarius* wins include the Puerto Vallarte race, Whitney series, and Ensenada race twice overall.

Betty Holiday takes charge of the provisioning for offshore races but does not join the crew. She explained, "On *Aquarius* we had a total of six crew including the skipper. The crew shared in the food preparation in that I would have the wife of married men prepare one main evening meal, usually a meat dish or casserole. All meals were cooked in advance and put in aluminum disposable pans, wrapped with foil, then frozen. The watches were three men on, three off, so the food packages were servings for three. The single fellows contributed hors d'oeuvres for happy hour or canned meats, which were used the last days of the race when the ice was gone. You must remember ours was a small boat, and all the crew knew each other very well and all were friends. We tried to have the best food possible with excellent French or domestic wine with every evening meal. The crew were all experienced deep-water sailors most with boats of their own. They were taking time from their companies and professions to race on *Aquarius* and win. So food-wise I really tried to keep them happy.

"Liquor was limited to one cocktail of their choice at happy hour, plus the wine with dinner. Food was heated in the oven. Everything was precooked, and roasts were presliced, so if there was a malfunction of the stove the crew could at least eat the food cold. They went strictly by the menu, so no decisions had to be made. They decided among themselves who would cook.

"Dry storage was a problem on the Ericson because she didn't have a bilge. In a knockdown even a few quarts of water from the bilge would wet the storage lockers as high as the dish racks. So all the under-the-bunk storage compartments would be a little damp.

"Our icebox was very small but efficient. We carried seventy-five pounds of ice and put the frozen food on top, arranged efficiently according to the menu plan, plainly labeled. Every morning the menu was checked and the frozen evening meal taken out and allowed to thaw so a minimum time was needed for heating.

"Each canned meal was stored with all its ingredients together in a plastic bag labeled with the appropriate day.

Doc and Betty Holiday with the trophies won racing their Ericson 35 Aquarius.

Alternate days' meal packs were put on opposite sides of the boat so the weight would be distributed evenly as the meals were used up. Any food which was not eaten and could spoil was discarded as there was no room to store leftovers.

"Paper plates were used for all meals, plastic glasses for cocktails and wine. Each crew had his own labeled ceramic cup which he kept clean or dirty himself. We used regular silverware because storage for plastic sets for three meals a day for ten days takes a lot of room. There were a few sets of plasticware on board, so if the weather was rough everything could be discarded. No styrofoam was used for obvious litter reasons.

"We had a sketch of the boat [see fig. 19] showing storage areas which corresponded to the menu plan so the crew knew

FIGURE 19

AQUARIUS STORAGE PLAN

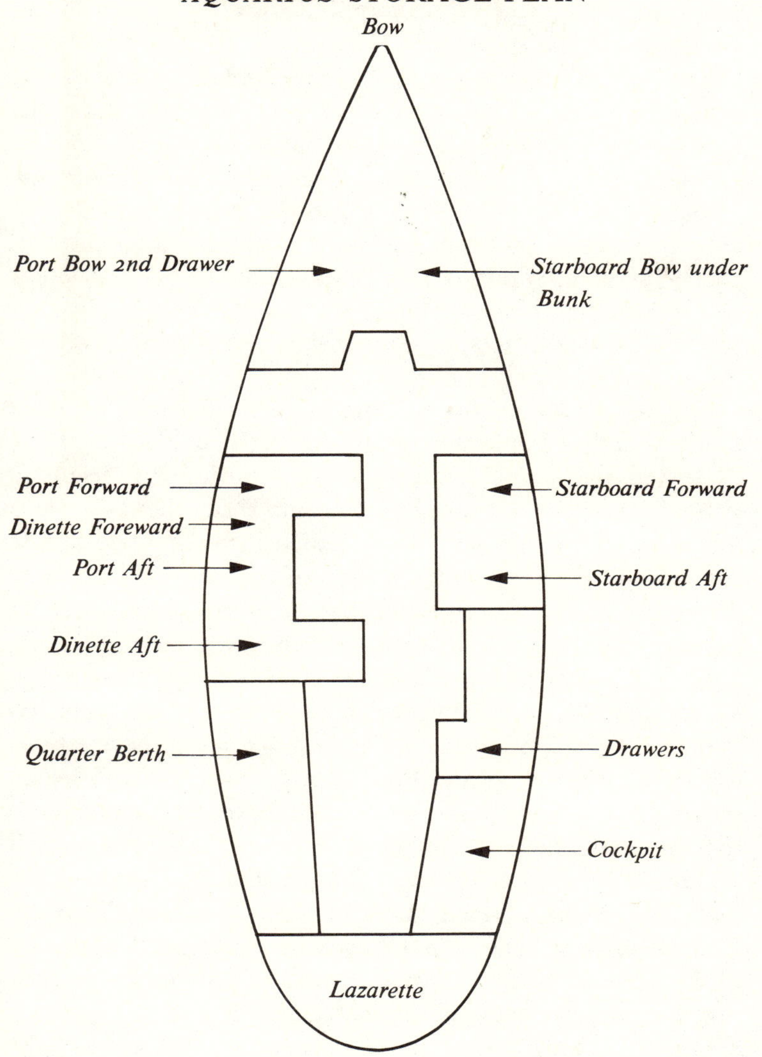

where to look for everything they needed. Ice was at a premium and was used only for cocktails. The race rules specified the amount of liquid required for each crew and not a drop more was carried."

The Holidays use the same basic meal plan for every long-distance race. As Betty said, "It works, everyone likes the food, and who cares if two weeks out of every year you get the same menu." The captain is expected to prepare the fanciest meal. Doc chooses cornish game hens stuffed with cheese and ham, which he freezes then seals inside a dry-ice-packed styrofoam chest. This is served at the halfway point of the race. Another crewman always provides a Chinese-style meal which he spices up by putting his own original fortunes inside each cookie.

For night watches there is the usual goody drawer plus a thermos full of hot water to cut down the use of the stove. Betty has had some serious doubts regarding the use of a gimbaled stove at sea during a race and the tendency toward meals sealed in bags which are heated in boiling water. She feels a pot of boiling water on top of the stove is extremely dangerous during a race. Betty told me of two separate recent cases of cooks being badly burned. One woman was boiling corn on the cob on top of the stove. She opened the oven to check her casserole, and the open door changed the gimbaled stove's center of gravity. The boiling water and corn tipped onto the cook's arm and lower body, causing third-degree burns. In the second case, a crewman bumped the cook and the cook bumped the stove, upsetting a pot of spaghetti noodles and again causing third-degree burns. So on *Aquarius* all meals are heated in foil-wrapped pans in the oven. Betty also commented that meals in a bag pack have one other disadvantage: if the bag springs a leak while it is boiling, a complete meal can be waterlogged.

On *Aquarius* cooking may be secondary, since all of the

crew is needed to sail the boat. But cocktail hour and dinner-time are the event of the day.

Jim Hollywood had raced extensively with the Holidays on board *Aquarius.* So when he took his own Santa Cruz 30 on the 1,000-mile Cabo San Lucas race, Jim choose to follow a proven example for his food. There was no built-in ice chest on the super-light displacement *Mas Rapido,* so Jim bought two cheap styrofoam iceboxes. One he packed with regular ice. The second he used for the meals planned for the last part of the race. These were prefrozen, then placed on top of dry ice. The chest was then sealed with two layers of duck tape and stored under the sail bags. Five days later when the chest was opened, the meals were still frozen.

Mas Rapido had only a two-burner stove and sea swing, so casseroles had to be heated carefully in their throwaway foil pans. The most successful meal of the race, one the whole crew raved about, was burritos. Jim simply fried up some ground beef, set out flour tortillas, grated cheese, salsa, and chopped onions. Each crew made their own burrito and ate it on top of a napkin without messing up any plates.

Whatever size boat you are racing on, the cook's job is mainly one of organization beforehand. Good food helps the crew work harder. It also improves the morale and creates a team that works together to win races. I'll never forget reports that came from the first Round the World race. Chay Blyth on eighty-foot *Great Britian II* raved about how tough his paratrooper crew was. They could race on C rations and curry eaten with the one spoon carried for each man. But the Mexican entry, *Sayula,* a sixty-five-footer, won that race, and her crew raved about prime rib dinners, fine wines, and frozen strawberry desserts in the middle of the stormy southern sea.

Menu Plan for *Aquarius*

Day	Menu	Location
Saturday	Bring your own brown-bag lunch	
	Supper	
	Pot roast and vegetables	in oven
	Sourdough garlic bread	
	Lettuce, tomato, and avocado salad	lazarette
	salad dressing and croutons	galley locker
	red wine	
	cake—Hickory Farm, your choice	
Sunday	Breakfast	
	juice	
	scrambled eggs, 1 doz.	quarter berth
	can mushrooms	
	package chopped ham and grated cheese	icebox
	salsa (put a couple spoonfuls over each serving)	
	banana bread	port bow
	Lunch	
	poor boy sandwiches (heat in oven and add a package of 1000 islands dressing after heating)	icebox
	carrot and celery sticks (already cleaned)	lazarette
	fruit	
	soup optional	dinette aft

Supper

	sweet and sour pork	meat in icebox
	2 cans sweet-sour sauce*	
	can mandarin oranges*	std. aft, heat these together with meat in large pan
	rice—follow directions on box	dinette aft
	lettuce, avocado, and crouton salad	lazarette
	salad dressing	
	French rolls	port bow
	fortune and almond cookies	dinette fwd.
	rosé wine	std. aft

Monday Breakfast

juice	port fwd.
hash brown potatoes	dinette aft
fried eggs	quarter berth
or	
instant hot cereal	dinette aft
or	
granola	
milk for cereal	icebox
beverage	
date bread	port bow

	Lunch	
	meat loaf sandwiches (may be fried)	icebox
	small loaf white bread	port bow
	pickles, relish, catsup, etc.	galley
	chips and cookies	dinette fwd.
	Supper	
	prime rib (put in foil and heat in oven)	icebox
	cans white potatoes with butter and parsley (heat in same pan with meat)	stbd. aft.
	whole green beans (cold with mayonnaise on top)	marked Monday supper
	sliced tomatoes and avocados	lazarette
	biscuits and honey	stbd. aft
	chocolate pudding	stbd. aft
	red wine	dinette fwd.
Tuesday	Breakfast	
	juice	pt. fwd.
	eggs benedict	quarter berth
	ham	quarter berth
	English muffins	port bow

	Lunch	
	chili	std. fwd.
	crackers	dinette fwd.
	carrots and celery	lazarette
	cookies (your choice)	dinette
	Supper	
	roast pork (put in foil pan, add gravy and heat)	icebox
	2 boxes instant mashed potatoes	std. fwd.
	asparagus tips (cold)	stbd. fwd.
	sliced tomatoes	lazarette
	mushroom gravy	icebox
	biscuits and honey—2 packages	icebox
	rosé wine	
	date bars	dinette fwd.
Wednesday	**Breakfast**	
	juice	
	French toast (3 eggs and powdered milk)	prt. fwd.
	2 cans corned beef	
	syrup and jelly	
	Lunch	
	hot dogs	icebox
	buns	port bow
	pickles, relish, peppers	galley
	shoestring potatoes	port aft
	soup, optional	dinette aft

	Supper	
	shrimp cocktail (serve in plastic glasses with chopped lettuce and avocado)	icebox
	cocktail sauce	
	6 chicken cordon bleu	icebox
	drumstick rice	
	canned peaches	std. fwd.
	biscuits and honey	icebox
	lettuce, artichoke, tomatoes, and avocados	lazarette
	dressing	
	white wine	
	fruitcake	

(Place chickens in foil pan, keep them wrapped so the cheese sauce won't run out. Heat up a can of chicken gravy if you wish, but I don't think it is necessary.)

Thursday	Breakfast	
	juice	
	hotcakes (use 2 eggs)	quarter berth
	spam	
	eggs (fried)	
	syrup or jelly	galley
	Lunch	
	fried cheese sandwiches	icebox and port bow

	pickles and olives	galley
	fruit or cookies	
	Supper	
	spaghetti and meat sauce (spaghetti and sauce are together already)	icebox in milk carton
	Add can tomato sauce	stbd. fwd.
	sourdough garlic bread (use garlic salt from galley with butter)	port bow
	Parmesan cheese	
	Lettuce, tomato, and avocado salad	lazarette
	salad dressing	
	red wine	stbd. fwd.
	Hickory Farm cake	stbd. fwd.
Friday	**Breakfast**	
	juice	
	scrambled eggs with mushroom	
	link sausages	
	salsa	
	apricot bread	port bow
	Lunch	
	tuna fish sandwiches	
	small jar mayonnaise	
	pickles, peppers, chips	stbd. fwd.
	Supper	
	canned corned beef	
	German potato salad	

	onions (heat)	port fwd.
	canned brown bread	
	cabbage salad	lazarette
	dressing	
	butterscotch pudding	
	cookies	
	red wine	
Saturday	Breakfast	
	juice	
	pancakes (3 eggs, powdered milk)	
	canned ham	
	fried eggs	
	Lunch	
	dried salmon	
	cheese spread	
	canned sardines	
	pickles	
	Rye Crisp	stbd. fwd.
	Dinner	
	canned turkey and gravy	prt. aft
	cranberry sauce	
	instant mashed potatoes	
	green beans	
	canned brown bread	
	cabbage salad	lazarette
	fruitcake	
	wine	
Sunday	Breakfast	
	Tang	
	canned hash	

eggs
dried orange toast

Lunch

tuna salad sandwiches
bread or crackers

Dinner

canned beef
potato pancakes
cabbage salad — dinette aft
cookies
wine

Emergency Meals Behind Dinette

Monday — Breakfast

Tang
cereal
beverage

Lunch

soup
open-faced cheese spread sandwiches
candy
Kool-Aid

Supper

roast beef
gravy
potato pancakes
three-bean salad

candy
beverage

Tuesday Breakfast

Tang
hotcakes
coffee

Lunch

tuna sandwiches
Kool-Aid

Supper

Lipton's beef stroganoff
garlic bread
candy
beverage

Wednesday Breakfast

Tang
hash and egg
beverage

Lunch

soup
crackers

Supper

macaroni chili
canned brown bread

Thursday Breakfast

Tang
cereal

Lunch

soup
sardine and crackers

Supper

Lipton's chicken casserole
three-bean salad

Friday

Breakfast

hotcakes
coffee

Lunch

tuna sandwiches
beverage

Supper

dried chipped beef
instant mashed potatoes
candy
coffee

Saturday

Breakfast

cereal
coffee

Lunch

soup

Supper

Lipton's stroganoff with tuna
beverage

Day 33

noon to noon 73 miles, miles to date 2,834

light ESE winds, foggy, not so cold

closehauled, very calm sea in spite of large swell from SW

Lunch—potluck soup
camembert cheese
biscuits
Tea—blueberry cream pie
Dinner—surprise peas
oven-browned potatoes
grilled Spam slices

POTLUCK SOUP

To leftover pork stew (about 1 cup, mostly gravy)
Add 2 1/2 cups water
1 package dried cream of mushroom soup
1/2 chopped onion
Bring to a boil, stirring constantly.
Cover and let simmer 8 minutes.
Add 1 cup cooked tuna chunks
1/4 cup red wine
Simmer 2 minutes more.

BLUEBERRY CREAM PIE

Graham cracker crust—21 graham crackers broken up into small crumbs.
1/4 cup sugar
1/4 cup melted butter
Mix well, then press into a pie tin (I used my small frying pan).
Pour in 1 can of pie filling (blueberry, cherry, or whatever).
Bake in 350° oven for 15 minutes to thicken and set crust.
Let cool completely and top with mixture of
1 6-ounce can of Nestle's cream
2 tbs. sugar
1 tbs. rum

OVEN-BROWNED POTATOES

Wash and cut potatoes into large chunks skin on, boil until they are tender but don't fall apart. Drain and place on a cookie sheet or baking pan. Dot liberally with butter, sprinkle with garlic powder, salt, pepper, and MSG.
Place under the grill and cook until browned, turning the potatoes occasionally.

ON SINKS AND COUNTERS

Larry offered to do the cooking and dishes today as a birthday treat for me. It was a good chance for him to see how the galley works. Since he is in charge of research and development, he'll possibly have more sympathy for some of my requests. I must admit that my day is slightly emptier without the cooking.

The sink drain plugged up today—sure sign the seawater temperature is dropping below seventy degrees. Seems that any cooking oil or grease from canned meats coagulates at that temperature and forms a clot in the sink drain right at the waterline level. The cure? A pot full of boiling salt water in the sink, then Larry squeezes on the sink drain hose—it always works. That's one good reason for having clear, flexible drain hoses. You can see the clog and massage it along its way to the sea. Prevention: don't pour grease in the sink; pour used coffee grounds down the drain once a day. They seem to absorb any floating grease and flush it away.

Our sink doesn't drain when we are hard on the starboard tack. That is one of the problems on small boats or those with deep keels and moderate freeboard. The way to get around this is to have the sink as near to the centerline of the boat as possible, but even this may not solve the problem.

Even if your sink is above the waterline when the boat is level, it may submerge when you are heeled well over. It is imperative that you have a convenient shutoff valve for the drain. Kelly, a friend of ours who was new to cruising boats, had a real catastrophe when he set off on his new thirty-foot racer-cruiser. He was hard on a starboard tack enjoying the exhilaration of a fresh breeze in the Solent. Since he was single handing, he didn't go below until an hour later when he wanted a cup of coffee. His boat was filling with salt water. As it went over each wave, a geyser of salt water would shoot up through the sink drain. He came about on the other tack, pumped the forty or fifty gallons of salt water out of the bilges and cabin. Then he found the shutoff valve. The only problem was that the salt water had been spraying over his new gas stove. Four days later all of the parts on the stove were beginning to rust and corrode, and within six weeks Kelly found he had to buy a new stove.

If I had the space I would definitely have double sinks on a boat. They give you that secure spot to put the dirty dishes while you wash and rinse the others. One double sink available for the vegetables you plan to rinse or chop up, one for dishes you are using to cook with means fewer things roll off the counter and onto the floor. Fiddles around the edge of the sink counter are never high enough to catch a whole cabbage or a large jar of mayonnaise.

While I am speaking about sinks and counters, I'd like to say that there is really only one material for both that works perfectly and lasts year in, year out. That is stainless steel. If you are fortunate enough to be able to get a fully molded one-piece sink and counter unit, you'll find it's easy to keep clean and rot-proof; you can cut on it without worrying, and it will polish up beautifully even ten years after you install it. I know stainless steel is nowhere near as handsome to look at as our laminated maple drain board was. But that maple did have to be scrubbed and bleached every week. It got scratched if I was the least bit careless with my chopping knife. It rotted near the corner where the water gathered next to the sink, and it delaminated so that two years ago we had to replace it (which took four days work and cost forty-five dollars in materials). We used laminated ash this time, and it is more rot-resistant and again looks very handsome and white. But I know next time I'd like stainless steel, with a big, beautiful, but easily replaceable maple cutting board sitting on top.

Formica is a very poor choice for cutting board or counter surfaces. It marks easily after it is six months old. Since it is rarely applied with resourcinal glues, the plywood base under it usually starts to rot within a year or two, especially where any water faucets come through.

Fiberglass is slightly better in that it doesn't rot or delaminate, but it nicks quite easily when you are chopping vegetables. After a year a fiberglass sink will lose its gloss and start to show scratches and stains.

To relieve the starkness of a stainless steel counter top, I would still use teak fiddles like we have on *Seraffyn*'s ash counter. They are 1 1/4" high and we leave them bare, so that to keep the fiddles nice looking we need only scrub them once a month with a pot scrubber. Galley fiddles should be at least 1 1/4" high to catch plates and bowls. But making them any higher creates too much of a barrier for the cook.

Maple cutting boards or, in fact, any wooden chopping board you use should have small rubber feet underneath. These feet keep the board from roaming around if there is any dampness on the counter top. They also elevate the board and let air circulate underneath it so that no mold, fungus, or insects start to grow on its bottom. I always remember Larry's story of one voyage he made to Honolulu on an eighty-five-foot schooner. The cook was terrible. He kept the galley somewhat tidy, but his cooking was worse than uninspired. After two weeks at sea the crew demoted the cook and took turns doing his job. On Larry's day, he decided to clean up the galley a bit extra. He moved the big cutting board from its position on the counter top and found the whole surface covered with maggots. Small, rubber, screw-in feet would have prevented this by allowing more air circulation.

To keep the wooden cutting board or drainboard on our boat looking good, I scrub once a week with bleach. I use straight bleach, let it sit for five minutes, then add some cleansing powder such as Ajax and scrub with a Golden Fleece or plastic Scotch Bright pad. If it is sunny outside, I put the cutting board out to dry and further bleach itself out. Pure lemon juice will work almost as well if you are out of bleach.

One further item on sinks and cleaning: never carry Brillo pads on board. They will rust almost instantly if exposed to salt air. The little metal strands will break off and create rust spots on any white paint you have. Our choice for pot scrubbers are either the Golden Fleece or plastic Scotch Bright type pads, available everywhere. They are useful far beyond their service in the galley. Scotch Bright makes a perfect scrubber for cleaning your boat's bottom when you are skin diving. It cleans teak decks and trim beautifully without digging out the soft summer grain as bristle brushes do. Scotch Bright can be used as a filter over the end of your bilge pump hose. It can also be used as an insulating barrier or rattle quieter when cans, dishes, or pots start rolling in a seaway.

Meanwhile, back to the North Pacific. With Larry's usual luck, it was so calm at dinnertime that he was able to set the table with our pewter wine goblets, a Japanese linen tablecloth, his version of fancy folded napkins and silverware. It was a lovely treat to sit back and play the guitar while Larry washed and wiped up after dinner.

Day 34

noon to noon 87 miles, miles to date 2,930

foggy, closehauled, fresh breeze

Lunch—onion and garlic omelet
fried chopped ham
blueberry pie
Dinner—chicken-tomato casserole

CASSEROLE

Grease bread tin, then add
1 layer cooked noodles (long macaroni)

1 layer canned tomatoes
1 layer sliced onions
sprinkle of oregano
Repeat.
Top with chunks of canned chicken meat and the juice.
Sprinkle on a 1/4″ layer of bread crumbs.
Add a light layer of grated Parmesan cheese.
Bake for 35 minutes at about 375°.

COOKING AT A TILT IS ALWAYS FRUSTRATING, especially with the pitching motion a small boat has going to windward. Today was no exception. That is why I scratched the idea of baking fresh bread when the wind got up a bit. Seems like I made a good choice, because by dinnertime the wind started to back, and now at 2030 we are on a fast beam reach for the first time in two weeks. If this keeps up, tomorrow I'll enjoy a baking spree.

PIPE LIGHTERS

One small item I've not mentioned else where in this book is our much-appreciated set of Ronson pipe lighters, a farewell gift from my mom. We've got three—one for each cabin, one for the galley, and one for the rigging kit. We never have to search for a place to put out a match. They always light right away. The long tongue of flame reaches in under a big stewpot to light the burner. Unlike flint-operated stove lighters, the flame from a pipe lighter is visible so I know where I stand. Ronson brand lighters are by far the best bet. Every country we've been in has someone who cleans and rebuilds these rugged lighters. Two of ours are now ten years old.

Both have been serviced once in England at a cost of two dollars each. The butane refills and flints are easily available and worldwide. Besides lighting the stove and oil lamps, they work great for burning the ends of lines and sail thread when Larry is doing any rigging or sail work.

Day 35

noon to noon 131 miles, miles to date 3,061

cold—drizzling, fresh S wind, beam reaching over a growing swell

Lunch—leftover casserole reheated by adding a few tablespoonfuls of water and covering with aluminum foil, than warming on the top burner

Dinner—fresh hot whole wheat bread
butter and honey
baked salmon loaf with onion sauce
baked potatoes
steamed cabbage

By noon we were screaming along at 5 3/4 knots. The barometer had fallen by three millibars in two hours, occasional rain squalls swept by, and white caps crowned half of the waves. So I decided it would be wise to prepare for a blow. I set bread to rise and planned a fish loaf so I'd have leftovers for tomorrow in case it grew real rough. But by dinnertime the barometer started rising slowly, the seas grew steadier, and our speed dropped to 5 1/2 knots with one reef in the mainsail and the lapper set.

Dinner was a great success. The hot oven warmed the boat up wonderfully and also dried out Larry's boots so we could patch them.

ON PRESERVING BUTTER

Canned butter is definitely the easiest way to solve the butter dilemma, but it is not easy to find in the United States. There is one brand that you can often order called Dairygold. It comes in one-pound cans and, according to the manufacturer, requires refrigeration. We have found that it lasts well without refrigeration for up to three months if stored in the lowest part of the boat. This butter is delicious and tastes just like fresh but has a bit more salt in it, which we both like. In the Far East you can often buy canned Australian or New Zealand butter, which is also good.

On the other hand, preserving your own butter may be the easiest way to go, and it's definitely cheaper. In Malta, where excellent butter costs only about seventy-five cents a pound, we bought fifteen pounds of butter in quarter-pound cubes. I sterilized old peanut butter jars by immersing them completely in boiling water for two minutes, then lifting them out with sterile tongs and placing them on a clean surface to cool under the covering of a clean towel. I boiled a quart of fresh water and added about five tablespoons of salt, then let this mixture cool. After putting in two cubes of the butter, I filled each jar to overflowing with the cooled saltwater mixture; then Larry screwed the tops on as tight as he could. We stored these away right with our canned supplies. The butter kept for up to five months even though we were in places like the Red Sea where water temperatures were close to ninety degrees. When we opened each jar of butter, we rinsed it once with fresh water. The butter tasted the same as it had the day it had been put up.

Margarine purchased in individual plastic tubs is a good substitute for butter. We've kept the unopened containers for up to four months with no spoilage.

Day 36

noon to noon 131 miles, miles to date 3,197

force 7 beam reach, intermittent rain, fog

Lunch—salmon loaf sandwiches topped with sweet pickles
tomato soup
Dinner—sloppy sea soup

SLOPPY SEA SOUP

1 can whole tomatoes
1 onion in chunks
1 can kidney beans
1 tsp. oregano

2 tbs. sugar
1 tsp. garlic powder
1 tsp. chili powder

Put all in a deep saucepan and bring to a boil, then simmer for 5 minutes.

Add 1 large can (1 pound) stewing beef or stewing pork—heat until boiling. Serve with bread and butter.

I DON'T THINK THIS SOUP IS AS GOOD as the raves it draws. I just think anything hot and spicy you serve on a day like today will seem like ambrosia.

Today is one of those times when I remember the gentleman at the yacht club bar in England who said, "I can't understand you chaps who go out of sight of land for weeks at a time and don't wash and all that rot."

We seem to be leaping from wave top to wave top. It's damp as hell, and in the cabin we need two sweaters to keep warm. The stove is festooned with socks hanging to dry. If you stick your head outside you are likely to get a faceful of spray. Slicing a piece of bread is almost an acrobatic feat. Thank God I prepared something yesterday when I saw the barometer taking a plunge.

But to look at the bright side, we've got lots of butane left, so we can heat the cabin using the oven. The stove doesn't need priming, so it's easy to heat a cup of coffee. The boat doesn't leak, and there is a dry sleeping bag to cuddle into. And foremost, we're flying toward our destination. At this rate we could be there in ten days. So my thoughts are turning to some of the delights waiting for us there: a hot bath in a deep tub; thick, tender rare steaks; hot fudge sundaes.

CLOTHES FOR THE OFFSHORE SAILOR

When you begin cruising, you'll have to revise the way you think about clothes completely. Since the adventure that lies ahead of you may last three months, six months, a year, or even longer, your offshore wardrobe must be adaptable enough to carry you through changes of season, changes of climate, and changes of life-style. You'll need clothes to suit deserted island anchorages, exotic cities, and the open sea. Although everyday dress styles become free-form among sailors, certain basic facts should help make your cruising life more comfortable, more sociable, and safer.

The most important item in your sailing wardrobe is good wet-weather gear. Invest in the best you can find—it will last five to ten years under average cruising conditions. Get wet gear that is easy to take on and off. For eight years I had an over-the-head, parka-type jacket and pants with a draw-string top. Since they were a nuisance to get on and off, I usually dashed out on deck without them, praying I'd miss any flying dollop of spray. But seven out of ten times I'd end up with damp pant legs. Other times I'd stay below rather than struggle into my gear—and I'd miss the sight of a lovely cloud formation or porpoise playing at our bow. Two years age we bought convenient zip-front jackets and suspender pants. The difference is almost magical. Rainy days are more fun; flying spray is a challenge instead of a threat.

Our new wet gear has a soft, flexible, clothlike outer surface. unlike plastic-coated gear, such as some Norwegian-made jackets we had, the moisture doesn't seem to ball up and stick, so the outer surface dries more quickly, and storage is less of a problem. The gear is designed to feel flexible and nonbinding. This is extremely important, since just wearing wet-weather gear cuts down your efficiency.

Imperative design features for any foul-weather gear you choose are comfortable, adjustable, Velcro storm cuffs and adjusters around the ankles, plus suspenders. The cuffs and ankle adjusters keep rushing water from sneaking under your gear; suspenders (and a fly with a zip for men) make a visit to the head less traumatic. Our gear is made by Atlantis. Other manufacturers we have heard good reports on from ocean-racing sailors are Henry Lloyd and Storm Force. We can't give a final recommendation on these brands as we haven't tested them for ruggedness in all conditions. These three brands are all expensive, but manufacturers offer to alter them to your correct arm and leg lengths. They also give good guarantees, so should be offering better-quality items. We have tried buying fishermen-style gear to save money. Unfortunately, the less expensive gear only worked well in heavy rain, not heavy spray, or under the special stresses of hauling up sails, trimming sheets, or working on the foredeck in a gale.

When you are fitting wet gear, forget appearances. Buy it loose. Try the gear on with a tee-shirt, a light sweater, and a bulky sweater. Then reach up and pretend you are pulling a halyard with all your strength. Wray your arms across your chest and try to touch your shoulder blades. If the jacket feels snug across the back, get one size larger. (I remember how unhappy Larry was when the shoulder ripped out of his new size 44 wet jacket right in the middle of the North Sea in November. He normally buys a size 42 windbreaker. The jacket fit in the shop, but one extra sweater was too much. Now he buys a size 46 jacket, though he weighs less than 180 pounds.) Alter your pant legs so they are just below your ankle bone, arms almost to the top of your thumb. That way movement won't work them above your boots or let your sweater poke out and get wet.

Don Street once told us that he likes having two different

types of foul-weather gear: lightweight nylon that is like a waterproofed windbreaker, and normal, heavy-duty gear. He claims people don't mind getting into lighweight gear for a possibly damp row ashore or a walk into town. The lightweight gear can be crammed into the bottom of a shopping bag or knapsack on days when it might rain before you get back to the boat. Because it is so light and nonbinding, people don't mind keeping it on for light spray and sprinkle days at sea. Then when the real heavy rain or spray comes along, Don puts his second pair of heavy-duty gear right on over the first. I'm thinking of trying his idea on our new boat, where we'll have more storage space.

Your sea boots should be roomy enough to hold your feet, a pair of cotton socks, and a second pair of wool ones and still pull off easily. There may come a day when you end up overboard and have to swim to a life ring or climb up the side of your plunging boat. That's when it will be essential that you get those boots off fast, since their water-logged weight could be the difference between life and death. Larry and I disagree as to which boots we like best, but we do agree on two basic design features. First, boots should be as tall as possible, almost to your knees. Second, the soles should be a solid, closed pattern with tight slits cut in so they don't pick up stones easily but still give good traction on a wet deck. There is nothing more frustrating to the owner of a nice yacht then the scratches he finds on his deck after crew men come straight from the gravel parking lot on a rainy day. The best soles we've found are on Topsider boots; the worst for this offense are soles with an open pattern of spaces with small round knobs in each center.

I vastly prefer very flexible topped, soft-lined, lightweight boots like the ones Romika makes. Larry loves the stiff fisherman-style boots made by Sperry (they weigh almost three pounds per boot.) Mine last about two years, his last eight years.

Foul-weather-gear storage should be close to the companion way, easy to reach, and well ventilated so the gear dries out. Well-rounded hooks near the engine compartment are the best idea. We've come to accept the fact that all wet gear, no matter how carefully aired and stored, will eventually develop mildew spots. Mildew doesn't seem to damage anything but the gear's appearance. We do try to wash the gear in fresh water two or three times a year while we are cruising. This gets the salt out of the inside so the gear dries more quickly at sea and feels less clammy.

Before each passage we inspect our foul-weather gear and boots, then patch any tears or leaks. Contact cement and thin cotton patches work better than anything else we've tried, since they form a very flexible patch. First we sand around the hole with 150-grit paper, then we apply a thin layer of cement to both the cotton patch and the boot or jacket. We let this sit for twenty minutes, then put the patch in place and coat the area with more contact cement.

A good pair of deck shoes is a must on racing boats and a real plus on offshore cruisers, even in warm climates. Even if your boat has teak decks, there will be times when you'll need the traction of nonskid shoes, especially after heavy spray has had time to dry partially and create a salt crust that can be as slippery as ball bearings with bare feet. I've spoken with the skippers of several offshore racing boats who require their crew to wear leather deck shoes on watch. They protect toes from accidental collisons with cleats or deck-mounted winches and prevent a lot of blood and curses. Again, try to buy nonskid soles that don't pick up pebbles.

Cold-weather clothes are a must even if your plans today are to cruise only in the tropics. When we arrived in Rhodes,

Greece, we met two Australian families on two separate boats who sailed up the Red Sea after extended cruises around the great Barrier Reef, Indonesia, and across the Indian Ocean. Both the crew of *Shikama* and *Girl Morgan* told us, "The Red Sea wasn't bad until we got to the last 300-mile stretch. Then it got cold. We couldn't believe it could get so cold only twenty-six degrees north of the equator. We'd thrown away most of our heavy clothes since we hadn't needed them for over a year." They were both sailing up the Red Sea in March, and the temperatures they were talking about were in the low fifties with twenty- to twenty-five-knot headwinds. That's cold—especially if you've been in the tropics for a while. We keep at least two complete changes of warm clothes on board for tropical sailing and five for northern climates.

I had a lot of trouble keeping warm at sea until I met Marsha Rasmussen, a ski instructor at Alta, Utah. We were guests in her home, and before she let me out for my first day on the slopes, she vetoed all of the clothes I'd brought with me and redressed me from her own wardrobe. "Forget synthetics except for your outer layers," was her advice, "Dress in several light layers so you can strip off easily if your exertions make you warm." Cotton long johns don't take much room on a boat, nor do two or three pair of soft cotton gloves—a pair of workman's waterproof gloves to fit over a pair of cotton ones. Two cotton long-sleeved tee shirts, two sweatshirts, and two good wool sweaters, plus tight-weave jeans and a sailing jacket, should keep you comfortable down to forty-degree sailing weather. Your wet weather gear makes an excellent extra layer for those frosty windy days. A ski toque and soft nylon scarf around your neck will cut out stray gusts for night-time sailing. With Marsha's recommendations I found we not only had good gear for cold sailing nights but were prepared when our cruising adventures introduced us to people who invited us up to their mountain homes for a bit of skiing.

These invitations make cruising in foreign lands a special adventure. So, in spite of the desire to go native and reduce your wardrobe to shorts and bikinis, I'd recommend every cruising person keep some special dress-up clothes on board. Margret Irvine, a delightful Australian artist we met in Greece, cursed her sailing friends back home who'd told her not to take any fancy dresses along on her two-year cruise. She'd been invited to share an evening at the local formal dining and dancing spot, but her family's cruising budget couldn't stretch to buy some new shoes, a dress, and a sport jacket for her husband. So they missed a lovely party. Since you'll be meeting new people in new places each time your dressy clothes are called into use, one or two sets will be sufficient. Larry carries a dark blue corduroy blazer jacket which passes for "jacket and tie" evenings in British yacht clubs or casinos. I carry some permanent-press nylon long dresses and a velvet suit.

For everyday tropical crusing life, try to stick to cotton as much as possible. Although it is slightly harder to care for, it is cooler and helps prevent rashes, since unlike nylon, cotton absorbs perspiration and allows your skin to breathe. Loose, white long-sleeved shirts are more comfortable for hot days, and they keep the sun off your skin. Lots of cruising people have learned these facts the hard way. I've seen cruising wives busily sewing cotton flour sacks into long-sleeve shirts once they tied up in the tropical heat of Panama or Columbia.

Carry some shirts or shifts that can be used for quick coverups when you leave your boat for a row ashore. It's amazing how respecting local dress customs will improve your cruising life. In sleepy Andraitz, Mallorca, only twenty-eight miles away from the resort capital of Palma, thirty yachts lay tied to the stone quay. The locals didn't object to seeing girls in bikinis and men in swim trunks as the crews worked or lounged on deck in the sun. But the café owners only forty feet away wouldn't serve any sailor who came in and sat at their shoreside tables without shoes or shirts.

Local custom almost worldwide seems to accept Bermuda shorts for men, day or evening. I've found loose skirts or sarongs acceptable and cooler to wear ashore in the deep tropics. I've also found I get pinched or nudged less in Italy or the North African countries if I wear skirts instead of short shorts.

Dress to protect your skin from the sun if cruising is your long-term plan. Although a golden tan is beautiful to look at, an hour a day will maintain a tan, and that hour is enough sun exposure for people born in higher latitudes. Skin cancer and brown spots will develop after three or four years of tropical cruising if you don't wear a sunhat. I know of one woman who was allergic to the sun and still enjoyed cruising by putting a sun curtain around the brim of her sunhat. Loose cotton shirts can be worn for days spent in the water skin-diving or swimming.

Although going barefoot feels wonderful, it's a dangerous pleasure in tropical climates. Not only is there the chance of stepping out of your dinghy onto a sting ray or black sea urchin hidden in the sand, but staph-type infections thrive in the dust of tropical villages. The slightest nick on a toe, an open blister, and you can pick up infections that will turn into boils that can ruin a month of your cruise. Soft leather sandals or tennis shoes are a must. Plastic flip-flops are handy for quick forays ashore, but should be worn with caution. A sailing friend lost his wife in Telok Anson, Malaysia, when she was carrying a load of croceries across the deck of one yacht on to her own which was tied alongside. As she stepped over the lifeline of the first yacht, her damp, sweaty foot slipped off the rubber sole of her flip-flops, she tripped, and her head hit the toe rail of her own boat. She broke her neck and died instantly.

Clothes kept on a boat do require extra care. They must be aired three or four times a year. If they are in a hanging locker, they must be tied down before each passage, or the motion can cause hangers to wear holes through the shoulders of your favorite jacket. I have had no success at all storing clothes in plastic bags for long periods. They seem to mildew more than those left open and folded on shelves. For special items, like my leather jacket and Larry's sport coat, we've found a cotton cover keeps dust and salt off without allowing mildew to form. One rule I have learned the hard way: don't store clothes you've worn on a hot day back with your clean clothes. The sweat on them will start a mildew infestation. Leather shoes will grow mildew during long passages if they aren't used because they have bacteria on them from your feet. A scrub with a toothbrush dipped in half-clorine bleach, half-water will remove the mildew and slow its subsequent growth.

Choosing the clothes for your sailing life may seem like a problem, but once you solve it, it's out of the way for years. Because of the simplicity of your life, the occasional purchase of some particularly interesting local blouse or shirt will perk up your whole wardrobe. Because you are always meeting new people instead of spending each day at the same office, school, or store, your wardrobe will *always* seem larger than it is. I know that the blouse I got in Greece, the sarong skirt from Sri Lanka, and the leather shoes I had custom made in Malaysia (cost eight dollars) got me many sincere compliments at a party in Japan.

Take the time to consider all of your cruising wardrobe from wet-weather gear to sailing shoes to cold-weather clothes before you leave the United States, England, or Australia. Yacht clothing is hard to find anywhere else. In those places where there is a marine store that imports sailing gear, it will cost almost double. Cottons and wools are the same; they may cost three times as much in the South Pacific Islands. Just as proper food promotes a healthy, happier crew, the right clothes can add to your health, safety, and pleasure as you sail toward new experiences.

Day 37

noon to noon 100 miles, miles to date 3,297

hove to—storm winds in evening set sea anchor to keep the boat riding at a 45-degree angle to the rising storm

Lunch—leftover soup
camembert cheese
bread and butter
Dinner—tuna fish and
baked beans eaten straight out of the can
swilled down with a rum and water

COOK MISERABLE. WWV Honolulu reports this storm has a gale radius of 600 miles and storm-force winds within a 300-mile radius. We are less than 200 miles from its center. There is another storm forming in the North China sea; I hope we can get to Canada before that one hits us, too!

Day 38

noon to noon 11 miles, miles to date 3,308

Laying to a sea anchor, but wind is a bit lighter. Caught some glimpses of the sun for our first fix in six days. That's why we made eleven miles when we weren't moving. In late afternoon set staysail and reefed main, beam reaching over a big swell.

Lunch—chicken curry with raisins and onions
noodles
Dinner—country-style potato salad
last cabbage salad
hot dogs

COUNTRY-STYLE POTATO SALAD

Boil 4 potatoes cut into cubes with their skins left on until the potatoes are fork-tender.

Add 1/4 cup mayonnaise
1 tbs. dijon mustard
1 tsp. worcestershire sauce
1 onion, diced
1 tsp. sugar
1 tsp. garlic powder
1 tsp. MSG
Salt and pepper to taste

Let stand for at least hour before serving.

A HOT CUP OF CHOCOLATE SEEMED to compensate for my absence during the wet, cold job of pulling the sea anchor in. Radio reports state that both large storm systems that have been chasing us seem to be dissipating and heading northeast, away from us. It's good to be under way again, and it's actually easier to cook since the boat's motion is more regular than when we were hove to.

The rattling of pots and pans during that storm has convinced me: the next boat is going to have individual holes for each pot, lined with felt so that they can't ping against their neighbors. Searching out the pot that is rattling, stuffing rags and potholders around it, then climbing back into the bunk, only to have a new solo start up somewhere—it drives you crazy.

SALT

Larry is at it again, pounding the salt shaker on the table, trying to clear up the holes so he can get some salt on his meat. Even with our closing-top tupperware salt shaker quarter-filled with white rice, we still have trouble getting salt to pour, especially if I have used the shaker to flavor something that was steaming away on the stove top. There are several solutions, most of which I try at one time or the other, but during the recent bad weather I've gotten lazy.

First, keep a separate salt shaker for cooking—then the one for table use doesn't get opened as often. Second, when you are filling the shakers from your main salt container, place a thin layer of salt on a flat dish and bake it in the oven for ten or twelve minutes. Then pour the super-dry salt in the shaker with a fresh supply of rice. This way the rice only has to absorb moisture let in while the shaker is in use. Third, buy only salt that comes in half-pound plastic containers or smaller and keep the container inside a sealed plastic bag. Fourth, buy a rock salt grinder for table use.

We have been testing a salt grinder with nylon cutters (made by Maddison in England) for the past three months and so far I'm absolutely sold. Rain or shine we get just the right amount of salt on our salad.

Day 39

noon to noon 100 miles, miles to date 3,408

No fog! Cloudy, dead run with 12- to 15-foot seas reefed main and staysail on the whisker pole.

Lunch—leftover potato salad
hard-boiled eggs
pickled beet salad
Dinner—spaghetti bolognese
red wine

PICKLED BEET SALAD

1 can sliced beets, well drained
1/4 onion, sliced thin

3 garlic cloves, sliced thin
1 tbs. olive oil
2 tbs. vinegar
1 tsp. sugar

Mix well and let sit 4 or 5 hours before serving.

IT WAS UNDER CIRCUMSTANCES JUST LIKE this that I chipped my tailbone in *Seraffyn*'s galley. We'd been in a gale —hove to for a night in the North Sea off England. The

Peeling eggs for lunch during a calm, sunny day at sea.

winds abated and filled in from astern, so we started running. All seemed great—the motion was much better than it had been. So I was caught off-guard and just wasn't holding on when a cross sea from the previous day's gale made *Seraffyn* lurch. I flew only three feet before hitting the edge of the ice chest. The damage was painful but not serious. I still have to sit on hard chairs, since tailbones don't heal. Lesson learned—wear a galley harness or hold on even after a storm!

Day 40

noon to noon 111 miles, miles to date 3,519—Less than 1,000 miles to go!

dead run—lumpy sea drizzle and gray sky

Lunch—chili and beans
Teatime—hot buttered rum
cheese and biscuits
Dinner—silver dollar pancakes
maple syrup
canned hunters' sausages
long-life milk

HOT BUTTERED RUM

1 inch dark or gold rum in a coffee mug
2 level tsp. sugar
1 tsp. lemon juice
1 shake of cinnamon

Fill with hot water; put a dab of butter on top and stir lightly.

FREEING THE GALLEY SLAVE

The term "galley slave," used in yachting circles, has the same connotations as the term "mother-in-law" when used by comedians. It is an overworked, generally untrue bad joke.

Sure, cooking on an ocean passage is hard work. But being part of any adventure is hard work. And that's the reason most of us sail small boats across oceans. It still is and always will be an adventure, fraught with the unseen, the uncontrollable.

The best-prepared ocean voyagers can't control the weather. A voyage planned for about twenty days can take fifty because of unusual calms or unexpected storms. An unseasonable typhoon can damage the most perfectly built, perfectly prepared vessel.

At times being cook may seem the hardest job afloat. But it can also be the most important and is definitely the most rewarding, especially to an ego-tripper like me. It's a job that requires foresight, planning, then using imagination as you go.

I know of one group of vastly experienced racing sailors —they could almost be called the "elder statesmen" of the fleet—that spent the last three days of a 1,000-mile ocean race completely without fresh water because no one thought to keep track of their consumption. When we were in Antigua in 1976 two young men were towed into harbor. Both were on the verge of starvation and too weak to sail their boat any further. They'd left England with a boat full of food but just ate it all up without realizing they might hit light winds. They assumed that since they were making what was called a tradewind passage, they'd have nothing but tradewinds.

But it's not just the near-disasters that count. Larry has often told me of the otherwise good passage from Honolulu to Newport Beach when he was mate on the eighty-five-foot schooner *Double Eagle.* The cook almost ruined the voyage. He was a paid cook but had a repertoire of two dishes—Teriyaki steak or bacon and eggs.

How often have you heard some one tell the skipper, "Nice job of gybing" or "lovely sail change"? Do you say to the navigator, "Great LOP you have there"? The only compliments the skipper gets may be, "Boat's moving well." The navigator might hear, "Good landfall." Only if all hell breaks loose because some piece of equipment fails and the captain exhibits a feat of seamanship or clever jury-rigging does he really get any appreciation. And even that is tinged with the often unspoken thought, "Maybe that wouldn't have happened if the skipper had kept things maintained better."

But the cook, the holder of the only creative job on board, can win applause three or four times a day. He/she can hear raves for an unexpected batch of cookies, a cup of hot chocolate served at midnight, or a masterpiece of a casserole. If one meal is a bit of a flop, you have three chances a day for the rest of the voyage to override that memory.

On the other hand, I can understand why many lady sailing partners dread the idea of cooking for an extended voyage. I've seen the hassles most sailing wives have when they plan a weekend cruise. Hubby says, "Let's go down to the boat Friday night and sail to the island for the weekend." He throws a few things in the car before they set off and maybe carts the supplies down the dock when they get to the boat. Meanwhile the wife has to spend a day planning meals, shopping for food and supplies, and packing pots, pans, towels, and toiletries for the boat. Once on the boat she has to set up housekeeping and do all the same chores as she does at home without the facilities she's used to. Then come Sunday evening, she has to unpack the boat and clean it out. On Monday, she has to work cleaning up the things that have come back from the boat. Hubby has a weekend off, wife has double the housework load on Friday and Monday and no time off during the weekend. If this situation happens in your family, consider investing in a complete set of pots, pans and cooking ware for your weekender plus a good stock of canned and packaged foods so that nothing has to be brought from home except for fresh fruit and vegetables. Convince your wife to plan extra-simple meals or arrange for some meals out. You offer to take care of some of the cooking; or if you are really a hopeless cook, you take care of the cleaning up after dinner while your wife sits back with the cocktail you prepared for her.

If you are planning a voyage, already living on board, and getting ready to take off on your first ocean passage, remember that you will probably be tired by all of the stocking up, shopping, saying good-bye and storing away. I highly recommend a very short hop as the first leg of any offshore passage. Sail to the next harbor or even just across the bay. Set your anchor, row ashore for a nice dinner or eat the special one you've brought along. Then use the next morning to really put the boat to rights before you sail out to sea. I know we couldn't have had nearly as good a cruise if we'd set off for Mexico direct from Newport Beach where we launched *Seraffyn* and put her through three months of sea trials. We said all our good-byes, put everything we thought we needed on board, and sailed eighty miles to San Diego. There we spent a week being tourists, checking over the boat and storing it properly without the interruptions of friends, family, and friendly onlookers. Even after ten years of voyaging we like to stop away from the hustle and activity of a town where we've stocked up and rest for the night before we set off to sea. That way there are no hangovers from farewell parties. You are well rested, and clearing harbor early in the day means a good chance to get a good offing before nightfall.

During the past year and a half, we've made three times as many long-distance passages as we usually do (14,500 miles in one year one day)—and I've learned that the crew is usually more easily satisfied than the cook is when it comes to food. Just when I am getting tired of the selection of food left on board, Larry will say something like, "That meal sure hit the spot." I guess crew at sea are pleased to have any variety at all. I know most people I have met can tell of one voyage in their life where all they ate was peanut butter and jam sandwiches, or tuna fish casserole and cold cereals. If you can provide any variety at all, occasional treats, and lots of hot soup or hot chocolate during a long passage, plus a few fancy meals at both ends of the trip, you'll be doing great.

Planning for a voyage and buying stores gets easier every time you do it. After ten years of voyaging and delivering boats, I can now feel comfortable about stocking up in almost any U.S. port for a voyage of up to 1,500 miles with 1 1/2 days' warning (unless it's a weekend). Overseas, I am happy if I have three days to shop and prepare.

I am convinced that the galley-slave jokes should be a thing of the past. The days of one-burner stoves and galleys forward of the foremast are gone. Modern galleys can be the most elegant part of a yacht. Good seagoing cooking ware and proper galley equipment is available. But being cook on a voyage will always be a challenge, and the person who accepts the challenge with a good sense of humor will always be welcome on any boat that heads out to sea.

Day 41

noon to noon 121 miles, miles to date 3,640

Sun! Running under full canvas—great!

Lunch—tuna salad
bean salad
mashed potato salad
Dinner—fresh white bread and honey
baked potatoes
sautéed tuna steaks
tartar sauce
1/2 bottle Liebfraumilch
Nana Mascouri sings of love on the tape stereo.

ANOTHER FISH STORY

It must be some kind of coincidence. We've had our fish line overboard for four days, but no go. Then today, just as we were eating lunch—in fact I'd just served the tuna fish salad—whammo, the fish alarm rang and Larry pulled in a fifteen-pound—you guessed it—tuna. But fresh tuna steaks are nothing like canned tuna fish salad.

There were a few moments of comedy pulling that fish on board. Because of the first real sunshine in four weeks, *Seraffyn*'s decks were covered with things drying—the sea anchor, 300 feet of sea-anchor rode, towels, and, of course, 200 feet of fishline, sinkers, and hooks coiling around the cockpit and after-deck. There wasn't one place to put that fish while we beat him on the head and killed him. "Here, Lin, you put a towel around him and hold him over the bucket so his blood doesn't get all over the deck," Larry suggested. He knows I am terrified of touching living, slimy fish; in fact, I hate to touch fish until it is filleted and ready for the pan. This afternoon he learned that that fish was almost as strong as me! Within seconds I was panicked as that fifteen pounds of fish tried to get away. "Larry, Larry, grab him; I can't hold him. He's trying to get loose. I can't stand it. He's dying. I don't want to watch!" I guess I was a ridiculous sight, holding that fish by the tail, rooted in place while his head shook that bucket further and further away from me. Larry was roaring with laughter when he grabbed the fish, whipped a spare sail gasket around its tail, and lashed it to the leeward lifelines where it could bleed in the scuppers. After I got over the convulsive feeling that fish's jerks had sent through my arm, I got the scrub brush and a bucket of salt water and went after the blood and scales scattered around the side deck. I was wondering if catching fish was worth the trouble. Ten minutes later, when Larry handed me a bowlful of beautiful tuna steaks, I changed my mind.

Day 42

noon to noon 132 miles, miles to date 3,772

running before a thirty-five- to forty-knot wind with only the staysail set cold, drizzle, rough sea

barometer falling

afternoon—hove to, gale winds

Lunch—fish steaks
leftover bean salad
leftover potato salad
Dinner—beef stew
bread and butter
hot rum

AGAIN IT'S TOO ROUGH TO DO MUCH FANCY. But I did steam up the last pieces of tuna that Larry caught yesterday. Now they'll be good for tomorrow.

Larry got soaking wet when he went out to take the staysail down and set the mainsail with two reefs so we'd be hove to. His boots have been leaking most of this passage, and he now has a hole in his wet-weather pants. During our past few years of voyaging we've rarely needed the warmth of wet-weather gear that was absolutely watertight. As soon as we get to Canada we are going to look into some new stuff. Meanwhile, Larry came below shivering and blue-lipped. I got him out of his wet clothes, warmed some fresh water so he could wipe down, and got out his dry clothes. But it wasn't until he had some hot, solid food inside that he started to warm up and stop shivering.

Day 43

noon to noon 51 miles, miles to date 3,823

laying a-hull, seas rougher than previous storm, but wind not as strong.

barometer rising

Lunch—stew and bread
Dinner—tuna steak Italian

TUNA STEAK ITALIAN

Simmer 1 can whole tomatoes
10 cloves garlic, chopped
1 large onion, chopped

1 tsp. oregano
1 tsp. worcestershire sauce
1 tbs. sugar
3 tbs. white wine
1 tsp. lemon juice

When onions are soft, pour over precooked fish steaks in a frying pan. Heat 3 minutes more.

DON'T COUNT YOUR CHICKENS

Only yesterday we were figuring if we could continue making 130 miles a day, we could be in within five days. I'd started thinking about what to serve our last night at sea. Shore seemed so close. Then the gale that the reports said was dissipating formed up again right on top of us. So we're hove to, which proves once again that you can't plan the last day of the voyage until the end of the breakwater is past your beam.

The first time this was really brought home to us was when we were delivering the *Vagrant Gypsy,* a fifty-ton ketch from Palma Mallorca to New Orleans, a distance of 5,800 miles. At 1600 Larry and I were discussing our plan of action, since the entrance to the five-mile-long channel into the port of Gulfport was only thirty-five miles ahead of us. We were powering along at almost six knots over a flat sea. That morning it had been at least seventy degrees on deck, but it was cooler now. "We'll keep up full speed for another four hours," Larry suggested. "Then we'll throttle back to two knots so that we don't make the entrance until morning." I agreed wholeheartedly with this idea and decided to really splurge with dinner preparations. I made an angel-food cake using thirteen of our last twenty eggs. I cooked up a ratatoville of the last of our assortment of fresh vegetables from Montego Bay, Jamaica. By midnight we were hove to while a blue norther brought fifty-knot winds, eighteen-degree temperatures (Fahrenheit, that is), twenty-yard visibility, and water spouts. We lay hove to for three days before the wind abated enough so we could set sail. Oh, how I wished I'd had those thirteen eggs and even one of those extra fresh vegetables.

Day 44

noon to noon 27 miles, miles to date 3,850

under way again, winds growing lighter, dead run, foggy

Lunch—scrambled eggs
canned corned beef hash
canned pears
Dinner—I'm sorry, for some reason I didn't write down what we had for dinner.

BAD DAY FOR THE COOK. I found twelve eggs rotten because they had small cracks in them. They were the larger ones in each of the plastic egg holders, so maybe something fell on the egg cartons during one of the storms we've had.

Then I made a pudding—you know the kind, just add cold milk and stir. Well, it flopped. I've had the packaged pudding on board since Malta so that's probably what went wrong.

A survey of the lockers shows loads of food left; the only things I'm cutting it close on are butter, cooking oil, coffee, and eggs. But with luck and fair winds they'll last just until we reach Victoria.

Day 45

noon to noon 120 miles, miles to date 3,970

foggy—running fast under full sail

Lunch—hot dogs (canned)
baked beans dressed up with chopped onions
sweet pickle chips
Dinner—chicken and ginger casserole
creamed corn
fresh whole wheat bread and butter

CHICKEN AND GINGER CASSEROLE

1 1/2 cups cooked rice
1 can roasted chicken without bones

1 chopped onion
8 cloves garlic, sliced
2 tbs. shredded fresh ginger
1/2 cup water
1 tbs. gravy mix

Toss lightly together so chicken doesn't break up too much.
Bake at 350° for 30 minutes

COOK'S COMPLAINT

I must admit I'm running out of imagination. No matter what you add to a can of baked beans, they are still the same old baked beans you've served four times already on the same voyage. And hot dogs are the same; the cans of fruit juice all seem to taste the same. Larry says he's not the least bit bored with our diet and cites examples of families ashore who eat pork chops every Thursday, lamb on Sundays, month in, month out. But I'm tired of looking at the same stock of food. Favorite items are starting to dwindle. I've never felt quite this way before, but then it's a rare voyage that lasts more than twenty-five days; the longest we've ever been at sea before this is thirty-five days. Few passages, races, or deliveries cross 4,500 miles of ocean at one go. Having to buy final stores in Japan also meant we have a lot fewer treats hidden away. I couldn't bring myself to pay three dollars for a four-ounce package of dried apricots or seventy-five cents for a single chocolate bar. We've had about half the number of treats we'd usually carry.

But the real reason for my boredom with cooking is obviously that we are only 500 miles from our goal and I'm getting impatient. There is another gale approaching from the west, but it's 1,200 miles astern of us. With any luck we could outrun it. I sure hope so.

Day 46

noon to noon 127 miles, miles to date 4,097

cloudy, must be almost gale-force winds

running wing and wing with triple reefed main and staysail set on the pole

Lunch—leftover chicken and ginger casserole
creamed corn
Dinner—surprise green beans (freeze-dried)
oven-browned potatoes
fried canned ham slices

WE PICKED UP WEST COAST U.S.A. broadcast stations this afternoon for the first time in 9 1/2 years. So dinner was accompanied by a melange of country music, football scores, women's club meeting notices, and hometown news reports. Nostalgia and the thrill of the approaching landfall spiced our dinner as nothing else could have.

RECOMMENDED READING FOR THE OFFSHORE COOK

I would definitely carry a copy of *Joy of Cooking* by Irma S. Rombauer and Marion Rombauer Becker (Bobbs Merrill). This book not only gives basic recipes but has a good section on canning.

The Cruising Chef by Mike Greenwald (Tab Books) is one of the best cruising recipe books I've come across. It has good fish recipes and an excellent section on bean sprouting plus some light stories that evoke the mood of cooking for onshore cruises.

The Captain is the Cook by Neil Hollander and Harold Mertes (John Murray publishing, London) has some excellent advice and good English-type recipes.

In Search of the Wild Asparagus and *Stalking the Wild-eyed Scallop* by Euell Gibbon (David McKay) are both excellent additions to the cruising sailor's cooking library. They tell about food you can find scavenging for yourself.

Other than that, I would like to find a book that shows fruits and vegetables around the world, what they look like and what to do with them. I have been told such a book exists, but to this day I can't find it.

None of these books will be much help when you are offshore for twenty or thirty days and looking at a selection of canned tuna, sardines, corned beef hash, and chicken meat. But few people make more than one or two voyages that last over ten days during the same year. So plan your cooking library for your time near shore. Your imagination will take care of the voyages.

Day 47 Here we go again, dreaming about steaks and fresh tomatoes.

Day 47

noon to noon 132 miles, miles to date 4,229

beam reach

fresh winds—reefed main and staysail scattered rain showers

Lunch—chopped ham
rice and onion salad
Dinner—spaghetti bolognese

COOK'S REWARD

Here we go again, talking about bowls of ice cream topped with fresh strawberries, thick beefsteaks, fresh tomatoes, crisp cucumbers. But now it's almost reality. If all goes well, in forty-eight or fifty hours we'll make port. It's so close that Larry's planning what he'd like me to wear for the traditional cook's night on the town. Every time we make a passage for more than six days, Larry takes me to a dress-up dinner at the best restaurant in town. Some of these past voyage-ending dinners have been memorable. After a 6,000-mile delivery ending in Biloxi, Mississippi, we shared Chateaubriand, lobster tails with drawn butter, salad with blue cheese dressing, baked Idaho potatoes with sour cream, sherry before, wine with; when it came to dessert we were too full—not only with delicious food but with the thrill of a job well done.

Another voyage-end dinner we both remember well came when we arrived in the Malaysian island group of Langkawi after an eighteen-day passage from Sri Lanka that included a sideswipe from a typhoon. The tiny village had no "good restaurants." But the local Indian restaurant served us curried chicken, strange fried bread cakes, and lemonade with loads of ice. As we walked back toward *Seraffyn* we saw a vendor carrying large live crabs, claws tied together with pink string and a lassolike carrying strap. We bought two that must have weighed a pound and a half each for twenty-eight cents. Dangling them by their little pink ribbon lassos, we strolled the mile back to where *Seraffyn* was anchored and fixed a late snack of steamed crab with lemon butter. Since Larry did the cracking and picking, since we were at anchor in a calm, safe, and beautiful spot, since I had no night watch to worry about, that too was a memorable cook's night on the town.

Day 48

noon to noon 120 miles, miles to date 4,349

blowing near a gale—beam reach with triple-reefed main and staysail

Lunch—leftover spaghetti
Dinner—mushroom soup (canned)
pâté sandwiches
rice salad
red wine

THIS MORNING LARRY WAS TALKING about heaving to at midnight if we didn't get some sights to fix on our position.

It had been six days since we'd last seen enough sun to get more than one Line of Position on the same day. He just didn't want to risk getting within seventy-five miles of the rocky coast of Vancouver Island without knowing our exact position. The currents out here are not always predictable. We could be off by up to fifteen or seventeen miles a day. But with marvelous luck and no little amount of skill and patience on Larry's part, we were able to get a position when the clouds broke up for three hours right at 1100 hours. He shot three sights before noon, a noon sight, and three after noon. So we know almost exactly where we are, right on course for the center of the Straits of Juan de Fuca.

This may be our last night at sea. But there's little chance of a captain's dinner. The motion is too rough to make much more than soup and sandwiches possible. So I'll have to save that blueberry pie and clam chowder for tomorrow, when we hope to be making harbor.

•

SLEEP!

The four men on board their forty-foot aluminum racing cutter had been slogging up the coast of Portugal against wind and current for ten days. Their last resting stop on the windswept lee shore had been Caiscais, just outside Lisbon, where the Atlantic curls around the point and makes the anchorage less than comfortable. Now, three days after that one-night stop, they spotted the cliffs that mark the entrance to the welcoming port of Bayonna, Spain.

It was near dusk, so, motor sailing against the almost ceaseless northwest wind and swell, all four men stayed on deck chatting and planning as voyagers often do when a safe port looms ahead. Current, seas, and underestimation meant the headland was not close on hand until just after midnight. The navigator read off the sequences on the two range lights that keep ships clear of Wolf Rocks, a nasty breaking reef that lies almost a quarter-mile north of the entrance point. All four on board were tired; tired of being at sea, tired of being damp and uncomfortable, tired of going to windward, tired simply from lack of sleep. When the first range light came into view and stayed visible and alone for what seemed ages, the crew made a communal decision—the second range light must be out of order. The helmsman headed onshore. For the first time in days the sheets were eased, and what seemed like only seconds later, a large sea lifted the hull and smashed it against Wolf Rock. A second wave washed over the boat, and one crewman was swept to his death. The next waves sent the boat clear, and the remaining three men were able to nurse the battered hull into Bayonna, where authorities had a search out within an hour. We came into Bayonna three days later. The aluminum hull had dents almost a foot deep along the starboard side. The dead crewman's body had been recovered. Ship captains, fishermen, and other yachtsmen confirmed that both range lights had been working. The crew on the yacht could only comment, "We were tired and wanted to get into port."

Decisions made by tired crew are a frequent cause of groundings, navigation errors, or gear failures. One of our closest calls came after a bad delivery trip out of Miami when we had to leave a crewman in the Bahamas with an infected foot. The two of us stood three on three off watches, constantly hand-steering a motor sailor with defective rigging for seven days, close hauled in the boisterous gulf stream. In the middle of the seventh night we mistook an airfield approach light for the main lighthouse at the entrance to San Juan harbor, Puerto Rico. We too altered course, eased sheets, and spotted our error only one mile off a rocky lee shore when other lights appeared on shore where the harbor entrance should have been. We then had to tack offshore and make up five miles we'd lost because of a tired decision.

Rest is imperative for the sailor. Getting it isn't always easy, but there are important ways to improve your chances.

One rule we've finally learned: start watches promptly at 2000 hours even if you are only on a one-day passage, even if the harbor entrance seems only a short distance away. Time and again, tides, strong currents, adverse winds, or engine failures have delayed what looked like certain just-at-dusk landfalls. Having one watch below decks get some sleep is like insurance. You may not need them, but they don't cost you much. Their well-rested judgment could be the deciding factor in a close situation.

On a short-handed cruising boat it may pay to heave to just before making a landfall so that the whole crew gets some extra rest. Every boat heaves to differently. Test yours in various wind conditions so that when the time comes you can use this sailor's safety valve quickly and easily.* Make sure you have sufficient sea room before you heave to and all go to sleep; a changing wind could set you ashore. If there is any doubt about your position, heave to and wait for dawn. Keep a watch. The more comfortable motion and lack of concern about running full speed onto a reef will help you get the rest necessary for making proper decisions.

Offshore sailors can win or lose races with their sleep habits. The 1974 Round Britain two-man, 2,200-mile race proved this to us. Larry was on board thirty-foot *Chough,* a Sparkman-Stephens half-ton sloop. His partner was Leslie Dyball. After three days of hard racing, the two decided to make it a rule—man off watch stayed in his bunk, day or night, unless the spinnaker had to come down. The on-watch

---

*For further information on how to heave to, read the appendix in *The Venturesome Voyages of Captain Voss,* by Captain J.C. Voss, published by Grey's Publishing Ltd., Sidney, British Columbia.

crew did everything by himself—navigation, sail changes, steering with the help of the windvane. This decision gained them the handicap prize and brought them in thirteenth boat over the line out of sixty-one, even though they were number forty-three on overall length. They beat three Admiral Cup racing yachts boat for boat. The other crews were amazed to see sixty-seven-year-old Leslie eagerly trotting down the roads of Lerwick in the Shetland Islands bound for a famous salmon fishing stream only an hour after tying up after five days of beating around the north end of Scotland.

On racing yachts with a large crew, getting sufficient rest is just as important. Except during all-hands-on-deck emergencies or at the start and finish line, the off-watch crew belongs in the bunk. I was planning on joining a Cal-40 in the 1979 Transpac until a broken leg got in the way. As part of our our preparations for that race I spoke with several successful Transpac sailors, including Don Vaughn, who often crews on seventy-three-foot *Windward Passage* and Doc Holiday with his successful Ericson 35, *Aquarius.* Both agreed off-watch crew belongs in its bunk *at least* one day time watch in addition to the night off watches. Sleep doesn't win races, but good decisions and alert, keen on-watch crew do.

The first two or three days at sea, almost everyone on a small vessel feels tired. The motion, the excitement of a long-planned departure, last-minute preparations, and farewell parties all contribute to this weariness. Tiredness is also the first sign of seasickness, and often the only symptom displayed by those with strong stomachs. Even among voyagers who have only been in port for a week or two, the first few days out create a feeling of lassitude. So plan on arranging for extra sleep until the crew gets its sea legs.

There is only one problem: it is hard to fall asleep at 2000 in a strange bunk with the unusual motion. In far north or south latitudes during summer it may still be light when it's time to start watches. The cook can generally help in this situation.

First, avoid offering any crewman coffee or tea for four hours before watches start. Plan a leisurely but somewhat heavy meal within an hour of 2000 if the crew isn't prone to seasickness. (Seasick crew will usually fall asleep easily.) Finish the meal off with a cup of hot sweetened milk or hot chocolate for the first sleeper, or offer him/her a shot of brandy as he or she gets ready for the bunk.

On board *Seraffyn,* if one of us lies eyes wide open, unable to sleep for more than thirty or forty minutes, we change places and restart watches. Then thirty minutes before the sleepless one's next off watch, one dramamine or marazine tablet assures a sound sleep. We have found these seasickness tablets are the best possible sleeping pill. They leave no side effects and wear off in about two or three hours. I've never felt hung over when I've used them, and if there was a need to get up during my off watch, I didn't feel drugged.

To help the off-watch sleep, make it the on watch's job to quiet down or stop every possible rattle or noise on board, or if that's not possible, at least to investigate and explain the noise. A can rolling around in the locker next to your bunk can wake you each time you almost doze off. But climbing out of the bunk and searching out each noise just doesn't seem worthwhile. So have the on watch do the search as part of his duties. On our last delivery job to Mexico, our crew member Mary Baldwin didn't mention that the noise from the internal halyards inside the empty aluminum mast next to her bunk was driving her crazy. When she finally told us four days out, we were able to find ways of tightening the unused halyards and quieting them a bit. But if one of us had thought to stand next to Mary's bunk and listen while she tried to sleep, we could have helped her get a few more hours of sound, deep, sleep.

If there is any way for the person on watch to leave the helm, be it by leaving steering to the windvane or by tying the helm for a few moments, it pays to take a stroll through the boat past sleeping crew at least every hour. This seems to subconsciously reassure the sleeper that all is well. The watch keeper can also check for wayward pots, pans, and rattles this way.

The captain who doesn't quite trust his crew is rarely going to get enough rest. So take time before any voyage to be sure each person on board knows basic sailing and emergency procedures. Let it be known that calling the captain on deck when something looks amiss is the *right* thing to do. When we delivered a sixty-foot ketch across the Atlantic, I just didn't like the look of some dark clouds forming up astern of us. Though Larry had just crawled into the bunk a half-hour before, I called him up. His second opinion made us decide to drop all sail except for the jib, even though we only had about fifteen knots of wind. Twenty minutes later, the clouds covered us and we roared along in a thirty-knot squall perfectly canvassed. The rest of the crew never woke up. Larry returned to his bunk with these last words, "Call me up any time you have doubts. Sure was easier to shorten down before that one hit." If you can impress your whole crew with the fact that it's easier to handle situations before they're "All hands on deck" affairs, everyone will sleep better.

After two or three days at sea, watch patterns will become a way of life. We usually stick to the same watches all through a passage. We stand three hours on, three hours off, with Larry taking the first watch right after dinner and oil lamp lighting time. With a small crew this works best, since our bodies and minds seem to adjust well to an unchanging schedule. We stand watches at all times at sea with both of us getting two uninterrupted three-hour night sleeping periods plus occasional afternoon naps. Three-hour watches seem to work well with a two-person crew. That gives the sleeper enough time to really rest, yet the watch keeper doesn't seem to get bored. Each crewman gets two full sleeping periods during the twelve-hour night. When we have crew with us on deliveries, we shorten watches to two hours a person.

Nothing helps the person coming off watch fall asleep faster than climbing into a dry, warm sleeping bag. Work to keep it that way. If it has been a wet watch, dry yourself off before you climb into the bunk. Wash any salt water off your hands, face, and feet before you slide between the sheets, or you'll soon have a clammy, salty bunk.

We've all dreamed of nestling down on the foredeck under a starry sky padded by sailbags, lulled to sleep by the low roar of a bow wake in a tradewind sea. Only problem with that is, right after you doze off some crewman will step on your foot when he comes to check the foredeck. A flying fish will land on top of you, or you'll wake up damp and covered with dew. So plan from the first on creating a comfortable below-deck sleeping arrangement. If you can, make sure there is good air circulation into the foot of each bunk that can be increased in tropical conditions. This is an area that many designers, builders, and owners forget. An opening port light at the end of the bunk is one solution. A dorade-type ventilator is better because it can be kept open in wet conditions.

Lee cloths are nicer to sleep against than lee boards. Carry some extra throw pillows. When you are beating to windward, one or two of these spare cushions placed against the hull in the lee bunk will help crewmen settle in more comfortably.

We've found sleeping bags to be the very best solution on board because the bag under you keeps you insulated from chilly bunk cushions. Cotton-lined, two-ounce, fill-washable bags are widely available. Check with the local Boy Scout outfitters for good ones that can zip together to form a double bag. We have made two all-cotton sheets into double sleeping bag sheets which we can change every seven days. In the tropics these sheets become our sleeping bag, with a light blanket available just in case. Cotton is by far the best choice for sheets and pillowcases in very warm or very cold climates. Dacron or nylon may dry faster, but synthetics feel hot and sticky in the tropics, cold and clammy in northern seas.

Washable dacron-filled pillows with cotton ticking are now available. They are a wise choice for sailing. Foam rubber attracts moisture and can contribute to aches such as arthritis or rheumatism. It will also start to pick up odors quickly. Down pillows tend to start leaking after a year of use on board and can't be washed or cleaned easily.

Although fabric-covered bunk cushions are more elegant to look at and nicer to sit on, we've found that vinyl-covered ones are far better for offshore sailing, especially on bunks. If they get wet they can be wiped dry immediately, whereas fabric-covered cushions give you a clammy wet bunk for the rest of the voyage.

Sleeping is just as important to the health of the offshore sailing crew as food. By carefully considering your watch schedule and sleeping arrangements, you can ensure an alert, amiable crew when you need it most.

Day 49

noon to noon 89 miles, miles to date 4,438

becalmed, cloudy, big swell left over

Lunch—potato salad
tuna fish sandwiches
Dinner—pork goulash with canned corn on the cob
fresh whole wheat bread and butter
blueberry pie and double cream
red wine

LANDFALL

Well, here we are only thirty miles from our landfall at Cape Flattery, seventy miles from Victoria. Only twenty hours ago we were worrying about having to heave to in yet another gale. But in a way this calm offers a nice chance to clean up the galley before we get into the hectic greeting I'm sure our family will have waiting for us.

Day 50

noon to noon 40 miles, miles to date 4,478

rain, calms and variable winds, fog patches

Lunch—soup made from cream of mushroom and
leftover goulash
potato salad
corned beef sandwiches with pickle relish and
mayonnaise
Tea—blueberry pie topped with sweetened double cream
Dinner—chicken curry over Chinese noodles
red wine

LAST DAY AT SEA

Spotted the light on Cape Flattery just after midnight.

Just after noon we were able to flag down a sport-fishing boat bound across the straits for some American port. We threw him a plastic-topped peanut can we'd saved. The note inside said, "Yacht *Seraffyn* of Victoria, 49 days out of Yokohama, Japan; all's well. Please telephone Frank and Beryl Pardey, North Pender Island; call collect."

I hope they do telephone and catch someone at home, since Larry's parents live only thirty miles north of Victoria.

As I write this at 2100 we are in the Straits of Juan de Fuca in calm, flat water for the first time in seven weeks. Victoria is only forty miles away. Local forecasts are for winds to freshen from the west. So tomorrow we should be tied up—at home after 9 1/2 years. Looking back over the cook's chronicle of this voyage, I wonder if it was such a good one to choose for this book. Not only was it an exceptionally long passage, but the weather was unusual. According to routing charts and other people's experiences, there should have been less than 2 percent chance of force-seven winds anywhere on our route. Yet we had at least three full gales and one storm. I'm sure if this had been my very first ocean passage, I'd have given up cruising for good.

But, as usual, it's a case of all's well that ends well. We've got lots of food left, probably enough for twenty days more if necessary. There are more than thirty-five gallons of water in our tanks thanks to Larry's rain-catching schemes.

We're looking forward to one of the big joys of cruising—tasting the foods of a new land. The ads we hear on the radio make our mouths water. Fresh Okanagan peaches, turkey breasts, ripe juicy strawberries.

The end of every voyage is a special accomplishment. This one marks the end of an east-about circumnavigation of the world on *Seraffyn.* It may have been a bit rough, but already we're talking about our voyage south to join cruising friends in San Francisco. And I'm thinking about how easy it will be on the cook. I'll only have to buy enough stores for a 700-mile voyage. I'll be shopping in stores where all the labels on the cans are in English.

Day 51

miles from noon yesterday 70, miles to date 4,548

Cool, broken clouds running wing and wing with pole set—full sail

Breakfast—pancakes and maple syrup

THE BREAKWATER FOR VICTORIA HARBOR is less than a mile off. Larry's parents are powering along beside us in the boat they just finished building. My parents have flown up from California and are with the Pardeys. They spotted us just after we rounded Race Rocks at 0800 this morning. As soon as they came alongside, a steady stream of plums, bananas, and apples descended upon us. We've yelled all sorts of greetings back and forth. As soon as we clear customs, they plan on taking us to a wonderful-sounding French restaurant.

We've sailed 4,548 miles in almost exactly forty-nine days, been hove to seven different times for a total of five days (125 hours), so that's not a bad passage time. Larry is most satisfied with the food we've eaten. I can think of a few items I wish I'd bought more of. There is a hot shower waiting, old friends to meet; and even as this voyage is ending, thoughts of future ones come to mind.

Index

THE AUTHOR—LIN PARDEY

THE ARTIST—TADAMI TAKAHASHI

We first met Tadami in Yokohama, Japan, when he came down to visit *Seraffyn* along with several sailing friends. We were shown some of his drawings in the *Kazi* sailing magazine plus the illustrations he did for the Laser association. Our suggestion that Tadami illustrate our projected book was met with instant enthusiasm, and the twenty cartoons are the result. Tadami's work is well known in Japan, where he does illustrations for Yamaha boat company, Performance Sailcraft, and several Japanese men's magazines. He owns and races a *Lazer* and now is outfitting a twenty-one-foot Nora class sloop, which he and his wife plan to race.